Network Learning for Educational Change

Professional Learning

Series Editors: Ivor Goodson and Andy Hargreaves

The work of teachers has changed significantly in recent years and now, more than ever, there is a pressing need for high-quality professional development. This timely new series examines the actual and possible forms of professional learning, professional knowledge, professional development and professional standards that are beginning to emerge and be debated at the beginning of the twenty-first century. The series will be important reading for teachers, teacher educators, staff developers and policy makers throughout the English-speaking world.

Published titles:

Elizabeth Campbell: *The Ethical Teacher*
Martin Coles and Geoff Southworth: *Developing Leadership*
Ivor Goodson: *Professional Knowledge, Professional Lives*
Andy Hargreaves: *Teaching in the Knowledge Society*
Alma Harris and Daniel Muijs: *Improving Schools Through Teacher Leadership*
Garry Hoban: *Teacher Learning for Educational Change*
Bob Lingard, Debra Hayes, Martin Mills and Pam Christie: *Leading Learning*
Judyth Sachs: *The Activist Teaching Profession*

Network Learning for Educational Change

edited by Wiel Veugelers and
Mary John O'Hair

Open University Press

Open University Press
McGraw-Hill Education
McGraw-Hill House
Shoppenhangers Road
Maidenhead
Berkshire
England
SL6 2QL

email: enquiries@openup.co.uk
world wide web: www.openup.co.uk

and Two Penn Plaza, New York, NY 10121–2289, USA

First published 2005

A catalogue record of this book is available from the British Library

ISBN-10: 0 335 21632 3 (pb) 0 335 21633 1 (hb)
ISBN-13: 978 0335 21632 1 (pb) 978 0335 21633 8 (hb)

Library of Congress Cataloguing-in-Publication Data
CIP data applied for

Typeset by YHT Ltd, London
Printed and bound in Poland by Ozgraf S.A.
www.polskabook.pl

Contents

Series editors' preface

Teaching today is increasingly complex work, requiring the highest standards of professional practice to perform it well (Hargreaves and Goodson 1996). It is the core profession, the key agent of change in today's knowledge society. Teachers are the midwives of that knowledge society. Without them, or their competence, the future will be malformed and stillborn. In the United States, George W. Bush's educational slogan has been to leave no child behind. What is clear today in general, and in this book in particular, is that leaving no child behind means leaving no teacher or leader behind either. Yet, teaching too is also in crisis, staring tragedy in the face. There is a demographic exodus occurring in the profession as many teachers in the ageing cohort of the Boomer generation are retiring early because of stress, burnout or disillusionment with the impact of years of mandated reform on their lives and work. After a decade of relentless reform in a climate of shaming and blaming teachers for perpetuating poor standards, the attractiveness of teaching as a profession has faded fast among potential new recruits.

Teaching has to compete much harder against other professions for high caliber candidates than it did in the last period of mass recruitment – when able women were led to feel that only nursing and secretarial work were viable options. Teaching may not yet have reverted to being an occupation for 'unmarriageable women and unsaleable men' as Willard Waller described it in 1932, but many American inner cities now run their school systems on high numbers of uncertified teachers. The teacher recruitment crisis in England has led some schools to move to a four-day week; more and more schools are run on the increasingly casualized labour of temporary teachers from overseas, or endless supply teachers whose quality busy administrators do not always have time to monitor (Townsend 2001). Meanwhile in the Canadian province of Ontario, in 2001, hard-nosed and hard-headed reform strategies led in a single year to a decrease in applications to teacher education programmes in faculties of education by 20–25 per cent, and a drop in a whole grade level of accepted applicants.

Amid all this despair and danger though, there remains great hope and some reasons for optimism about a future of learning that is tied in its vision to an empowering, imaginative and inclusive vision for teaching as well. The educational standards movement is showing visible signs of over-reaching itself as people are starting to complain about teacher shortages in schools, and the loss of creativity and inspiration in classrooms (Hargreaves *et al.* 2001). There is growing international support for the resumption of more humane middle years philosophies in the early years of secondary school that put priority on community and engagement, alongside curriculum content and academic achievement. School districts in the United States are increasingly seeing that high quality professional development for teachers is absolutely indispensable to bringing about deep changes in student achievement (Fullan 2001). In England and Wales, policy documents and White Papers are similarly advocating for more 'earned autonomy', and schools and teachers are performing well (e.g. DfES 2001). Governments almost everywhere are beginning to speak more positively about teachers and teaching – bestowing honour and respect where blame and contempt had prevailed in the recent past.

The time has rarely been more opportune or more pressing to think more deeply about what professional learning, professional knowledge and professional status should look like for the new generation of teachers who will shape the next three decades of public education. Should professional learning accompany increased autonomy for teachers, or should its provision be linked to the evidence of demonstrated improvements in pupil achievement results? Do successful schools do better when the professional learning is self-guided, discretionary and intellectually challenging, while failing schools or schools in trouble benefit from required training in the skills that evidence shows can raise classroom achievement quickly? And does accommodating professional learning to the needs of different schools and their staffs constitute administrative sensitivity and flexibility (Hopkins *et al.* 1997), or a kind of professional development apartheid (Hargreaves, forthcoming)? These are the kinds of questions and issues which this series on professional learning sets out to address.

There is a powerful and growing body of research evidence showing that professional learning and professional knowledge are best acquired by teachers together rather than individually. When teachers work in schools that are true professional learning communities, their access to the knowledge of their colleagues enhances their own learning and improves their students' learning in turn. The same principles apply to professional learning communities in themselves – they grow stronger and become more vibrant when they are connected to other learning communities, rather than when they operate entirely alone. The best way to bring this about is through networks.

In this book, Wiel Veuglers and Mary O'Hair bring together a current and cutting-edge collection of articles on networked learning communities. In their own words, networked learning communities are based on the belief as well as some evidence that "teachers learn best by sharing ideas, planning collaboratively, critiquing each other's ideas and experiences and reducing the isolation encountered in most schools." Networks, they show, increase professional interaction and learning across schools, and for those who participate in them, they generate excitement about teaching and learning.

From America, the United Kingdom, Finland, Catalonia, Hong Kong and elsewhere, Veuglers and O'Hair's authors document and describe the practical power as well as the underlying theory of networks and their educational advantages. Networks take us beyond the mechanical age of standardization, alignment and compliance into complex, diverse yet cohesive communities where teachers learn from their differences in their passionate and engaged pursuit of improving students' learning.

In their own analyses and in the chapters they have collected, Veuglers and O'Hair's book shows how networked learning communities provide opportunities to draw on and develop evidence-informed, research-derived practices; promote innovation and its dissemination across large groups of interested schools; give teachers more of a voice in professional and school-based decision-making; help personalize every school as a learning community, enabling them to adopt emergent solutions to their own needs instead of being subjected to overly prescribed programs; and are flexible and resilient in the face of crises or misdirected system initiatives that turn out to be unsuccessful – allowing new learning and fresh solutions to emerge and fill the gap that false starts and failures have left behind.

If you are considering starting a network or are searching for ways to learn from colleagues elsewhere, this book provides promising directions and compelling examples for how to create and sustain strong networked learning communities. For those who already participate in networks, it elucidates the challenges and complexities that will help you reflect on your practice and push it further forward. And for all those who are dedicated to pupils' learning and their own professional learning, this book provides ways to stretch your knowledge and understanding even further.

List of contributors

Lew Allen is co-director of the University of Georgia's League of Professional Schools.

Linda Atkinson is co-director Phase II, K20 Center for Educational and Community Renewal at the University of Oklahoma.

Tero Autio is a senior lecturer of education at the Department of Teacher Education, University of Tampere, Finland. He coordinates network operations.

Randy Averso is co-director Phase I, K20 Center for Educational and Community Renewal at the University of Oklahoma.

Jean Cate is co-director Phase I, K20 Center for Educational and Community Renewal at the University of Oklahoma.

Dennis W. K. Chan is co-director of the Thinking Qualities Initiative and Associate Professor, Department of Education Studies, Hong Kong Baptist University.

Chris Day is a professor of education and director of the Centre for Research into Teacher and School Development at the School of Education, University of Nottingham.

Victor Forrester promotes International Baccalaureate Organization (IBO) school networks in Asia and is an Assistant Professor at the Department of Education Studies, Hong Kong Baptist University.

Gregg Garn is associate professor of Educational Leadership and Policy Studies at the University of Oklahoma.

Dennis Gentry is principal, Lincoln Elementary, El Reno Public Schools, El Reno, Oklahoma.

Jesse Goodman is a professor of curriculum studies in the School of Education at Indiana University, Bloomington. He is co-director of the Harmony Education Center.

Mark Hadfield is a senior lecturer based in the Centre for Research into Teacher and School Development at the School of Education, University of Nottingham. He is currently seconded to the National College for School Leadership where he is working on the Networked Learning Communities (NLC) Programme.

Barbara Harold is a faculty member at the College of Education at Zayed University, United Arab Emirates.

Frances Hensley is the director of the University of Georgia's Program for School Improvement.

Elaine Jarchow is dean of the College of Education at Zayed University, United Arab Emirates.

Gaetane Jean-Marie is assistant professor of Educational Leadership and Policy Studies at the University of Oklahoma.

Tracey McAskill is a faculty member at the College of Education at Zayed University, United Arab Emirates.

Robin McGrew-Zoubi is a faculty member at the College of Education at Zayed University, United Arab Emirates.

Mary John O'Hair is professor of Educational Leadership and Policy Studies and director of the K20 Center for Educational and Community Renewal at the University of Oklahoma (www.k20center.org). She is director of the International Networks for Democratic Education.

Ulrich C. Reitzug is professor and chair of Educational Leadership and Cultural Studies at the University of North Carolina-Greensboro.

Eero Ropo is a professor of education and vice head at the Department of Teacher Education, University of Tampere.

Joan Rué is a professor of education and head of the Office for Teacher Development in High Education in the Barcelona Autonomous University (UAB).

Wiel Veugelers is a professor of education at the University of Amsterdam and the University for Humanistics. He is the director of the School Network of the University of Amsterdam (www.cna.uva.nl). He is also director of the International Networks for Democratic Education.

Ian Walker is a faculty member at the College of Education at Zayed University, United Arab Emirates.

William Y. Wu promotes thinking school networks in Hong Kong and is co-director of the Thinking Qualities Initiative at Hong Kong Baptist University.

Henk Zijlstra is co-director of the School Network of the University of Amsterdam and principal of the Goois Lyceum, one of the network schools.

one

The case for network learning

Mary John O'Hair and Wiel Veugelers

Introduction

The primary way in which schools have traditionally accessed ideas and knowledge is through formal staff development efforts such as workshops, in-services and conferences. During the past decade, a new way of accessing ideas and knowledge has gained increasing attention globally and involves the participation in school networks (see, for example, Veugelers and Zijlstra 1995, 1996; Lieberman 1996; Lieberman and Grolnick 1996). Essentially, school networks help schools learn from each others' efforts. They consist of educators from a number of schools who come together owing to a shared vision of schooling and who are connected to each other typically via a loose organizational structure that facilitates their interaction across schools. The glue that connects network schools with each other is regular cross-school meetings of teachers, principals and other educators from member schools, monthly meetings of school coordinators, cross-school visitation, attendance at professional development opportunities focused on the network's and participating schools' visions, and a network resource staff which works to facilitate sharing across network schools. The intent of school networks is to accelerate the change process within schools.

School networks are based on the beliefs that you cannot improve student learning without improving teacher learning (Fullan 1993) and that teachers learn best by sharing ideas, planning collaboratively, critiquing each others' ideas and experiences, and reducing the isolation encountered in most schools (O'Hair *et al.* 2000). Networking results in increased professional interaction across schools, which generates excitement and learning. In today's global business and education community, there is no single best approach. Each culture has its own way of building relationships, negotiating and learning. School networks help us learn across cultures to identify, analyse and solve pertinent problems impacting teaching and learning, and just like Socrates, we become citizens of the world, learning and conversing with all.

Emergence of networks

To understand the emergence of networks, scholars from a multitude of disciplines have sought to understand organizational structures. Monge and Contractor (2001: 448) trace structural analysis in the following disciplines: 'In sociology, Herbert Spencer (1982) and Emile Durkheim (1895/1964) are often credited with introducing structural concepts into sociological thinking. In anthropology, Radcliffe-Brown (1952/1959) incorporated structural-functionalist ideas into analysis of cultures. And in linguistics, structural thinking can be traced to the pioneering work of de Saussure (1916/1966).' In education, structural analysis has distinct connections to learning outcomes for students. Educational researchers have found that schools' organizational structures impact student learning (Newmann and Wehlage 1995; Newmann and Associates 1996; Darling-Hammond 1997) with communal structures enhancing student achievement and reducing the achievement gap (Lee and Smith 1994). School networks emerge from our knowledge of communal structures and their impact on learning.

While a number of scholars over the past decades have called for greater clarification of network theory (for example, Rogers 1987; Wellman 1988; Salancik 1995), almost none have provided it (Monge and Contractor 2001: 449). While network theory remains in its infancy, emerging themes suggest that networks and their organizational structures often include aspects of the following traditions: positional, relational, cultural and technological. The positional networking tradition is rooted in the classical work of Max Weber (1947), Talcott Parsons (1951) and George Homans (1958) and is characterized as a pattern of relations among positions leading to the view that positions and roles determine who networks with whom and, consequently, the networking structure within and across the organization. Critics of the positional tradition believe it lacks the ability to consider the importance of 'acts' performed by *any* organizational member rather than formal 'roles' individuals assume in creating and shaping the organization (White *et al.* 1976; Lambert 1998; O'Hair *et al.* 2000). School networks consisting of principals meeting together or science teachers sharing experiences with other science teachers are examples of job-alike or positional networking.

The relational networking tradition focuses primarily on the direct communication among network participants that reduces isolation and establishes trust. The relational tradition examines networking structures that connect different people and groups across organizations irrespective of their formal positions or roles. Rooted in systems theory (Buckley 1967; Bateson 1972; Monge and Contractor 2001), the relational tradition emphasizes: dynamic, constantly changing structures; collegial relationships; and person-to-person communication. In schools, the relational tradition emphasizes networking of teachers across schools and disciplines, and with administrators, parent, and community members.

The cultural networking tradition seeks to understand symbols, meanings and customs transmitted within and across organizations. Understanding culture – what it is, how it is created, how it evolves and how it can be changed to achieve organizational goals are highlighted in this tradition. Researchers who examine organizational culture account for both the creative and constraining aspects of social structure and how it can be changed (Frost *et al.* 1985; Schein 2004). Leading in a culture of change (Fullan 2001) and re-culturing schools for professional learning communities (Louis and Kruse 1995; Hord 1997; Eaker *et al.* 2002) and democracy (for example, Glickman 1993, 1998; Goodlad 1994; Apple and Beane 1995) are examples of the cultural tradition. Democratic, communally-structured schools and networking among such schools rely on cultural as well as relational traditions of networking.

The emerging technological networking tradition has advanced the notion of living in networks rather than in groups, which was implied in previous traditions. Castells (1996) and Wellman (1999) describe these 'networked societies' as having boundaries that are more permeable than groups, interacting with diverse others within multiple networks, and flattening hierarchies. Over the past decade, computer-mediated communication has become embedded in business, education and our everyday lives. Haythornthwaite and Wellman (2002: 34) describe this phenomenon as networked individualism: 'People remain connected, but as individuals rather than being rooted in the home bases of work unit and household. Individuals switch rapidly between their social networks. Each person separately operates his network to obtain information, collaboration, orders, support, sociability, and a sense of belonging.' The technological tradition is profoundly impacting our understanding of networking.

While these are important networking traditions and research has made considerable progress in defining them, we are only beginning to understand what factors and processes account for the stability of network relationships, which factors trigger change, in which particular sequences a change unfolds under specific conditions, and what are the respective outcomes of these change processes for individuals and groups involved and the nature of their relationship (Ebers 1999: 32). This book provides examples and more questions, as all good research and practice should.

Emergence of network learning

School–university networks are becoming an important method to enhance educational renewal and student achievement from pre-kindergarten through to graduate education. Adding university partners to school networks expands the learning continuum and helps reduce tensions of top-down versus bottom-up, pre-service versus in-service, theory versus practice and formal versus informal organizational structures. Although school–university networking is not a well-defined concept, we see several common features involving network development, its obstacles and sustainability, emerging from examples described in this book. We believe the theoretical base of school–university networking stems from networking traditions, as previously described, and educational change theory. In particular, we want to mention work on: educational change processes by Fullan (2001, 2003) and Glickman (1998); empowering of teachers (Hargreaves 1994, 2003); professional development (Day 1999; Goodson 2003); community of practices (Wenger 1998; Wenger *et al.* 2002); the network society (Castells 1996; Wellman 1999); democratic education (Goodman 1992; Glickman 1993; Apple and Beane 1995; O'Hair *et al.* 2000; Veugelers and Oser 2003); and the early educational network writing by Lieberman and McLaughlin (1994), Allen and Lunsford (1995), Huberman (1995) and Veugelers and Zijlstra (1995, 1996).

Based on these concepts and the experiences of chapter authors in working with networks in different parts of the world, we discovered common foundational elements of school–university networks. Emerging from personal to social and institutional levels, each element provides a complementary pathway for exploring how network learning evolves.

Student-centred learning environments

Networks encourage and support student-centred learning environments through the development of high standards for *all* students, smaller and more personalized learning environments, authentic and connected student learning, democratic leadership structures, and the use of data to support continuous improvements.

Reflective practitioner/action research

Teachers and principals are encouraged to reflect on their own educational practice, engage in action research and job-embedded professional development, and serve as critical friends for each other. Through reflective critical study, teachers and principals build their skilfulness as professionals, challenge current school and classroom practices, and begin to develop a shared vision of teaching and learning that impacts every aspect of the school community.

Empowerment of teachers/principals

Teachers and principals are given a voice in networks. Networking participation helps empower them to develop broad-based participation in their own schools by involving students, parents, members from the community and university in the work of the school. Empowerment can also be observed at the local and/or national levels by network participants engaging in political discourse with policy makers, asking critical questions on issues confronting schools and communities, and promoting successful bottom-up strategies and practices supported by school-based educators.

Horizontal learning/peer learning

In networks teachers and principals learn from their colleagues in other schools. They learn by sharing experiences, visiting and hosting school visits, reading and discussing the professional literature, and examining differing views, perspectives and experiences. Learning in networks is a social construction of knowledge.

Deepening educational change theories and practices

Networks focus on understanding, and learning from and leading educational change. Networking enhances its members' abilities to examine and deal with change, learn from it and help students and their communities learn from it, thus deepening educational change theories and practices.

Becoming a member of a broad yet personalized and caring community

By meeting colleagues of other schools, teachers and principals broaden their horizons. Their professionalism is not restricted to their own school. In networks, teachers and administrators experience learning from a broader educational perspective while maintaining a caring and personalized environment or community atmosphere. Traditional educational conferences may broaden an individual's perspective but lack the personalized, caring environment to support individuals beyond the initial awareness stage of development.

Shared ownership and democratic leadership

Networks share ownership and develop democratic leadership by addressing the needs of their participants and by building high levels of skilfulness and participation (Lambert 1998) in their members. Together members formulate goals, methods and programmes. Leadership is embedded in the 'hearts and minds of the many' (Hargreaves 2003) and is represented in leadership 'acts', which include everyone rather than just the formal 'roles' of administrators, directors or university faculty.

Flexible structures

Networks avoid formal structures by responding to the needs of participants and not to the organization itself. Their structures are fluid and follow the interests and challenges of their members.

Partnership between universities and schools

A network is an opportunity for schools and universities to work together as equal partners. In a network, schools and universities assume joint responsibility for developing and sustaining the network. Both types of institutions must have a feeling of ownership and enhanced learning opportunities for their members. Both recognize the benefits and challenges of developing seamless education, from pre-kindergarten through to graduate education, to promote high quality learning environments.

Examining issues of equity and diversity

Networks help expose educators and their students to a wide array of diverse viewpoints, perspectives and experiences. Through networking, participants examine their own practices involving issues of equity and diversity, and collectively develop and promote policies and practices that recognize equity and diversity in accordance with the core values of a democratic and civil society.

Moving from conventional to authentic and democratic practices

Networking opportunities help teachers and administrators share practices, leadership and power. They often move out of the narrowness of 'my classroom is my kingdom' focus and begin to develop a collective vision of schooling within their schools. This collective vision helps develop authentic and democratic practices as evidenced by the sharing of best practices, establishing trust and cooperation, critiquing struggles, sharing power and critical decisions, examining and acting on issues of equity, and serving others (O'Hair *et al.* 2000)

Accelerating and sustaining change

Networking accelerates the change process and fosters learning by providing a safe environment that encourages innovation as well as critical and supportive feedback, designed to help build long-term capacity for improvements.

Learning among networks

Just as schools within a network learn from each other by collaborative interaction, so too networks can learn from each other by interaction across networks. Specifically, the learning of networks is accelerated when networks serve as 'critical friends' for each other. Educational historians and researchers suggest that one of the most powerful reasons that attempts to reform educational practices have been largely unsuccessful is due to the isolation in which teachers operate (see, for example, Hargreaves 1994). The same might be said of school renewal networks. In order to facilitate the movement of school renewal networks to the next level of learning, the networking of networks is needed. This book, in particular Part 3, provides examples of linking networks at the local and national level.

In order to facilitate global school renewal and network learning, the *international* networking of networks is essential. The networks that present their work in this book are members of the International Networks for Democratic Education (INDE). During the past few years INDE has met annually at the American Educational Research Association (AERA) as well as more informally throughout the year when member networks have travelled to observe the daily operations of other member networks.

Learning from networks

The chapters in the book focus on the central issue of how schools move from conventional to authentic and democratic practices. Nested within the discussion of this issue are the following questions:

- What *school-based* processes, practices and dilemmas help facilitate this movement?
- What *educational-policy* processes and initiatives help facilitate networking?
- How do *positional, relational, cultural* and *technological* traditions influence networking?
- What *network-based* processes, practices and dilemmas help facilitate this movement?
- What can each network learn from the experiences of the other networks?

Each network studies its work by gathering data from network participants and external observers (for example, critical friends) via observations, interviews and document collection. Data sources include:

- teachers, principals, students, parents, community members and network staff members (interview data)
- classrooms, schools, network sponsored meetings, school and school district meetings, community meetings and political processes and functions (observation data)
- network- and school-developed documents.

Data are analysed by network participants as well as by external critical friends in an ongoing fashion. The findings and implications are reported in each chapter.

Introduction to the chapters

The book consists of three parts:

Part 1: Theory and practice of networking
Part 2: Developing a network
Part 3: Networking of networks

Part 1: Theory and practice of networking

Part 1 contains chapters of four 'established' networks who have been functioning for several years. These networks describe their accomplishments, challenges and goals, and the theoretical basis of their work. In Chapter 2 we begin with the League of Professional Schools in Georgia, USA. Next, in Chapter 3, we examine the example of the Secondary Schools Network of the University of Amsterdam. Both networks serve as models for other networks in their countries and continents. In the fourth chapter, the University of Nottingham describes how action research stimulates professional development in their network. In Chapter 5 we explore how the Oklahoma network matures from a small network of schools to a state-wide initiative to develop professional learning communities.

Chapter 2

The League of Professional Schools was established in 1989 by Carl Glickman, a professor at the University of Georgia. Over 150 Georgia schools have, at one time, been members of the League with over 40 university faculty members actively involved in League activities. Other networks in Oklahoma (see Chapter 5), Nevada and Washington have been established based on the League's approach to school improvement. Over 25 studies focused on the League's work have been conducted by school practitioners, university researchers, League staff and external evaluators. These studies found, among other things, that high-implementing schools use the League's three-part school renewal framework and services to take thoughtful, data-driven action; lessen teacher isolation; increase the amount of staff involvement in curriculum development, staff development and school-wide planning; and increase the level of trust among all stakeholders. This chapter focuses on lessons learned by the League about how school–university networks can help all stakeholders improve their professional practices in such a way that students benefit.

Chapter 3

Beginning in 1988 and currently with 20 schools working together with the University of Amsterdam, the network described in this chapter focuses on the restructuring of upper secondary education in the Netherlands, which is aimed at more active learning processes and democratic education. The network develops new initiatives in schools and attempts to influence educational policy and is distinguished by the following functions: interpretation of government policies; influencing government policies; learning from other's experiences; using each other's expertise; developing new educational approaches and materials; and creating new initiatives. In particular, the interaction between changing school practice and influencing educational policy will be discussed by looking at the balance between bottom-up and top-down processes and at the different types of citizenship one wants to realize. The chapter focuses on the successes and obstacles of networking. It demonstrates how teachers and school leaders, along with university faculty and students, build together communities of learners and, as a network, develop an educational vision that connects schools in the network.

Chapter 4

Many of the national policies and initiatives over the last 15 years in England, it could be argued, have undermined the traditional autonomy of teachers. As a consequence many teachers feel little ownership of a curriculum that is regularly policed through many national pupil assessments, school inspections and competency frameworks related to role specification; and are consequently insecure in making decisions about pedagogy. It was in this context that the Primary Schools Learning Network was formed through negotiated partnerships between a group of self-selecting schools, the local education authority (district) and the Centre for Research on Teacher and School Development at the University of Nottingham. Its aim was to give ownership for development back to teachers through working collaboratively in creating and sharing knowledge about learning, with a view to improving schools and raising pupil attainment. This chapter draws upon data from an evaluation of a two-year schools networking project. The findings indicate that teacher change is based upon principles of relevance, choice, trust, sustained critical friendship support and active participation in decision making as part of a renewal of professional purposes.

Chapter 5

This chapter describes the strategies and challenges of state-wide school–university networks housed in the K20 Center for Educational and Community Renewal at the University of Oklahoma. These networks are committed to improving student achievement through the development of professional learning communities that integrate technology to enhance teaching and learning. Guided by the democratic education framework (IDEALS – consisting of inquiry, discourse, equity, authentic achievement, leadership and service), these networks engage in change processes and network learning designed to develop authentic pedagogy and professional learning communities. This chapter describes the strategies and challenges of network participants in developing, implementing and sustaining the following practices in their educational settings: a collaboratively developed vision of good teaching and learning; authentic pedagogy; shared decision making; critical inquiry; emphasis on equity issues; service learning; technology integration; and internal and external support networks for educational renewal.

Part 2: Developing a network

In Part 2, three recently developed networks present their 'start-up' experiences and lessons learned. The first example, described in Chapter 6, is from Barcelona. It explains how emerging democracy and autonomy in Catalonia stimulated the networking of schools. Chapter 7 provides a second example from Finland, examining how networking supports teacher education and professional development. In Chapter 8, a third example from the United Arab Emirates demonstrates how networking in a developing educational system can link different partnerships to enhance professional learning.

Chapter 6

In this chapter the University of Barcelona and partner schools' network describes the research and development associated with creating educational networks designed to improve teachers' professional autonomy. Specifically, the chapter addresses the results and implications of six key areas associated with professional autonomy within networks: work intensification versus professional autonomy; moving from assessment to accountability values; promoting learning cultures; networks as shared learning environments; cooperative deliberation in networks; and action research in networks. The chapter also describes the steps taken within the network to foster teachers' professional autonomy.

Chapter 7

This chapter describes a curriculum studies-oriented teacher education programme that was developed and is ongoing at the Department of Teacher Education of the University of Tampere. This programme aims at promoting theoretical ideas on individualization. In the programme networking is viewed as an organizational locus for individualization, in order to provide (according to critical postmodern curriculum theory) informed and enriched options to identify practical problems and to find creatively situated and viable solutions to them.

Chapter 8

Networks that link schools and universities in the Middle East are relatively new. This chapter focuses on Zayed University, the newest United Arab Emirates' government institution established in 1998 for national females, and eight school–university networks. The focus of the networks is quality enhancement of all phases of education to pave the way for renewal, excellence and creativity, and to incorporate modern knowledge and technology into Arab societies. These networks focus on developing a 'shared culture' of teacher development and responding to challenges, as well as issues such as language and communication, sensitivity to cultural expectations, and logistics between schools and universities.

Part 3: Networking of networks

Increasingly efforts are being made to link networks, by developing networking of networks as described earlier. In the first example from Hong Kong we see an overview of different networking initiatives that are loosely coupled. The second example is from the UK where the Networked Learning Communities Programme links networks and examines 'networked learning'. The third example involves the linking of the Harmony Education Center with the National School Reform Faculty in the USA. It is an example of creating a network that connects organizations and schools with similar educational missions, in this case progressive education.

Chapter 9

The goal for the new school curriculum to be implemented in Hong Kong within this decade is to enable students to attain all-round development and life-long learning. The focus of the implementation strategies is to accumulate experiences gradually and to build up partnerships. Different forms of partnership have been identified and implemented. Some important partnerships include university partnership projects; District Teacher Networks formed by professional associations; self-initiated networks of principals and teachers; learning communities in research and development projects organized by the Curriculum Development Institute; Regional Education Offices networks established by the Education Department; curriculum expert groups formed by the government of Hong Kong and mainland China; and international educational networks. This chapter evaluates these partnerships in terms of their designs and implementations from the standpoint of participant and/or independent observer.

Chapter 10

In the UK there is a movement stressing the need to create more formalized networks of schools. At first bringing schools into networks was primarily a means of helping to deliver central and local government initiatives more effectively. Now the agenda is shifting as the power of networks that have come together around local interests is being harnessed as a mechanism for system-wide change. The movement has been from networking, to networks, to what the Networked Learning Communities Programme has termed 'networked learning'. The initial experience of the linking of networks is also discussed in this chapter.

Chapter 11

This chapter presents the work of the Harmony Education Center and its current focus of attention: facilitating the work of the National School Reform Faculty in the USA. Harmony has been kept purposefully small to facilitate a democratic ethos within an 'organization of intimates'. The challenge to create the same ethos and atmosphere within an organization of thousands of people spread across the country has indeed been daunting. Grassroots, decentralized governance and participation are necessary to build a progressive, effective network of educators committed to the authentic intellectual, emotional and communal growth of our children.

Enjoying networking

In summary, we appreciate the patience of all those involved in this international 'networking of networks' project, the many revisions of chapters, and the outstanding group of authors who contributed chapters to the book and with whom it has been a pleasure to work. We also would like to acknowledge the valuable assistance of the series editors, Andy Hargreaves and Ivor Goodson, for their insightful comments and actions regarding networking importance and developing cutting edge, networking theory and practices to improve our learning. We are indebted to Fiona Richman who worked with us in planning and preparing various stages of the book, and to the other professionals at Open University Press who assisted in the publication of the book. Without their encouragement and outstanding guidance, this project would not have reached fruition. We would like to express special appreciation to our spouses and families for their support in our quest to understand network learning in which the intrinsic worth of every individual is valued. We want to thank all the teachers, principals and scholars in the described networks for creating and sustaining their school networks. We hope they keep enjoying networking as much as we do.

References

Allen, L. and Lunsford, B. (1995) *How to Form Networks for School Renewal*. Alexandria, VA: Association for Supervision and Curriculum Development.

Apple, M.W. and Beane, J.A. (1995) *Democratic Schools*. Alexandria, VA: Association for Supervision and Curriculum Development.

Bateson, G. (1972) 'Double bind' in G. Bateson (ed.) (1969) *Steps to an Ecology of Mind*. New York: Ballantine.

Buckley, W. (1967) *Sociology and Modern Systems Theory*. Englewood Cliffs, NJ: Prentice Hall.

Castells, M. (1996) *The Rise of the Network Society*. Oxford: Blackwell Publishers.

Darling-Hammond, L. (1997) *The Right to Learn*. San Francisco: Jossey-Bass.

Day, C. (1999) *Developing Teachers: The Challenges of Lifelong Learning*. London: Falmer Press.

De Saussure, R. (1966) *Course in General Linguistics*. New York: McGraw-Hill. (Original work published 1916.)

Durkheim, E. (1964) *The Rules of Sociological Method*. London: Free Press. (Original work published 1895.)

Eaker, R., DuFour, R. and DuFour, R. (2002) *Getting Started: Re-culturing Schools to Become Professional Learning Communities*. Bloomington, IN: National Educational Service.

Ebers, M. (1999) 'The dynamics of inter-organisational relationships' in S.B. Andrews and D. Knoke (eds) *Networks In and Around Organizations*, 16: 31–56.

Frost, P., Moore, L., Louis, M.R., Lundberg, C. and Martin, J. (1985) *Organisational Culture*. Beverly Hills, CA: Sage.

Fullan, M.G. (1993) *Change Force: Probing the Depths of Educational Change*. New York: Teachers College Press.

Fullan, M.G. (2001) *Leading in a Culture of Change*. San Francisco: Jossey-Bass.

Fullan, M.G. (2003) *Change Forces with a Vengeance*. London: RoutledgeFalmer.

Glickman, C.D. (1993) *Renewing America's Schools*. San Francisco: Jossey-Bass.

Glickman, C.D. (1998) *Revolutionizing America's Schools*. San Francisco: Jossey-Bass.

Goodlad, J.I. (1994) *Educational Renewal: Better Teachers, Better Schools*. San Francisco: Jossey-Bass.

Goodson, I.F. (2003) *Professional Knowledge, Professional Lives*. Buckingham: Open University Press.

Goodman, J. (1992) *Elementary Schooling for Critical Democracy*. New York: SUNY.

Hargreaves, A. (1994) *Changing Teachers, Changing Times: Teachers' Work Culture in the Postmodern Age*. London: Cassell.

Hargreaves, A. (2003) *Teaching in the Knowledge Society*. Buckingham: Open University Press.

Haythornethwaite, C. and Wellman, B. (2002) (eds) *The Internet in Everyday Life*. Oxford: Blackwell Publishers.

Homans, G.C. (1958) 'Social behaviour as exchange' *American Journal of Sociology*, 63: 597–606.

Hord, S. (1997) *Professional Learning Communities: Communities of Continuous Inquiry and Improvement*. Austin, TX: Southwest Educational Development Laboratory.

Huberman, M. (1995) 'Networks that alter teaching: conceptualisations, exchanges and experiments' *Teachers and Teaching: Theory and Practice*, 1 (2): 193–212.

Lambert, L. (1998) *Building Leadership Capacity in Schools*. Alexandria, VA: Association for Supervision and Curriculum Development.

Lee, V.E. and Smith, J.B. (1994) 'High school restructuring and student achievement: A new study finds strong links' *Issues in Restructuring Schools*. Madison, WI: University of Wisconsin Center on Organization and Restructuring of Schools.

Lieberman, A. (1996) 'Creating intentional learning communities' *Educational Leadership*, 53 (2): 51–5.

Lieberman, A. and McLaughlin, M.W. (1994) 'Networks for educational change: Powerful and problematic' *Phi Delta Kappan*, 63: 673–7.

Lieberman, A. and Grolnick, M. (1996) 'Networks and reform in American education' *Teachers College Record*, 98 (1): 7–45.

Louis, K.S. and Kruse, S.D. (1995) *Professionalism and Community: Perspectives on Reforming Urban Schools*. Thousand Oaks, CA: Corwin Press.

Monge, P.R. and Contractor, N.S. (2001) 'Emergence of communication networks' in F.M. Jablin and L.L. Putnam (eds) *The New Handbook of Organisational Communication*. Thousand Oaks, CA: Sage.

Newmann, F.M. and Associates (1996) *Authentic Achievement*. San Francisco: Jossey-Bass.

Newmann, F.M. and Wehlage, G.G. (1995) *Successful School Restructuring: A Report to the Public and Educators*. Madison, WI: University of Wisconsin System.

O'Hair, M.J., McLaughlin, H.J. and Reitzug, U.C. (2000) *Foundations of Democratic Education*. Fort Worth, TX: Harcourt Brace.

Parsons, T. (1951) *The Social System*. New York: Free Press.

Radcliffe-Brown, A.R. (1959) *Structure and Function in Primitive Society*. New York: Free Press. (Original work published 1952.)

Rogers, E.M. (1987) 'Progress, problems, and prospects for network research' *Social Networks*, 9: 285–310.

Salancik, G.R. (1995) 'Wanted: a good network theory of organisation' *Administrative Science Quarterly*, 40: 345–9.

Schein, E.H. (2004) *Organisational Culture and Leadership* (3rd edn). San Francisco: Jossey-Bass.

Spencer, H. (1982) *Principles of Sociology*. New York: Appleton-Century-Crofts.

Veugelers, W. and Zijlstra, H. (1995) 'Learning together: in-service education in networks of schools' *British Journal of In-Service Education*, 27 (1): 37–48.

Veugelers, W. and Zijlstra, H. (1996) 'Networks for modernizing secondary schools' *Educational Leadership*, 54 (3): 76–9.

Veugelers, W. and Oser, F.K. (eds) (2003) *Teaching in Moral and Democratic Education*. Bern/New York: Peter Lang.

Weber, M. (1947) *The Theory of Social and Economic Organisation*. Glencoe, IL: Free Press.

Wellman, B. (1999) *Networks in the Global Village: Life in Contemporary Communities*. Oxford, UK: Westview Press.

Wellman, B. (1988) 'Structural analysis: from method and metaphor to theory and substance' in B. Wellman and S.D. Berkowitz (eds) *Social Structures: A Network Approach*. Cambridge, UK: Cambridge University Press.

Wenger, E. (1998) *Communities of Practice: Learning, Meaning and Identity*. New York: Cambridge University Press.

Wenger, E., McDermott, R. and Snyder, W.M. (2002) *Cultivating Communities of Practice: A Guide to Managing Knowledge*. Boston, MA: Harvard Business School Press.

White, H.C., Boorman, S.A. and Breiger, R.L. (1976) 'Social structure from multiple networks: blocks-models of roles and positions' *American Journal of Sociology*, 81: 730–80.

Part 1

Theory and practice of networking

School–university networks that improve student learning: lessons from the League of Professional Schools

Lew Allen and Frances Hensley

School–university networks, properly carried out, are powerful ways for educators to form collaborations that can result in improved practice and results for students. Carl Glickman wrote in the introduction to Allen and Lunsford's (1995: 1) book *How to Form Networks for School Renewal*: 'Every willing school ... deserves to have the chance and the support to work with other schools striving to provide a good education for all students. Such a challenge demands the proliferation of networks to provide access to these schools.

However, it can be difficult for university colleges of education and public schools to form partnerships partly because, in most parts of the world, it's not customary for them to work together. Schools normally work within the parameters of a local administrative unit and universities generally serve individual educators. Still, we believe there are compelling reasons why these two sides of the same educational coin should and can work together to create networks that are available to all interested schools and universities. We hope that telling the story of the League, and sharing the collective lessons learned, will be helpful to others interested in educational networks.

Our story begins over 30 years ago when Carl Glickman took his first principalship and soon realized that the students assigned to his care would greatly benefit from their teachers having a strong voice in the school's instructional practices and curricular choices. It was then that he began to advocate that the key to improving student achievement was schools becoming democratic learning communities, where teachers participated in the planning and implementation of ongoing, collegial, professional development experiences and were treated as professionals who have a voice in the life of their school beyond their classrooms. Years later, he created a three-part school renewal framework that could be used for creating these learning communities: (1) a covenant of teaching and learning that is brought to life using (2) shared governance and (3) action research (Glickman 1993). This framework became the guiding premise of the League's work.

In 1983, as part of one of his personal projects, Glickman, then a faculty member of the University of Georgia's College of Education, began working with several local schools. By 1988 these collaborations had produced dramatic, positive results. His ideas about democratic school governance and the expertise of school-based educators combined to form a powerful alliance that resulted in good things happening for teachers, students and administrators. Then, in an unusual move, he and the dean of the College of Education worked out an arrangement whereby the College provided support in the form of a secretary, office space and the release of Carl from his traditional professorial duties (teaching, advising students, serving on various committees) to work with schools full time. In 1989, in partnership with school and university educators, including the two of us, he founded the League, a school–university network.

Since it was established over 150 Georgia schools have, at one time, been members of the League and over 40 university faculty members have been actively involved in League activities. Other networks in Oklahoma, Nevada and Washington have been established based on the League's approach to school improvement. Over 25 studies focused on the League's work have been conducted by school practitioners, university researchers, League staff and external evaluators. These studies found, among other things, that high-implementing schools use the League's three-part school renewal framework and services to: take thoughtful, data-driven action; lessen teacher isolation; increase the amount of staff involvement in curriculum development, staff development and school-wide planning; and increase the level of trust among all stakeholders. Member schools have improved student learning as evidenced by improved grades, higher standardized test scores, fewer disciplinary referrals and suspensions, improved attitudes towards learning, increased participation in higher-level courses and better grade point averages among graduates who attend college (Allen *et al.* 1999b). Because of these achievements, the League and its member schools have caused quite a stir in Georgia and beyond. As we have detailed elsewhere:

> League schools have won state and national recognition for their restructuring efforts: Georgia and National Schools of Excellence, newspaper and television features and invitations to present their work throughout the continental United States, Hawaii, and Canada.

The League has been formally validated by the U.S. Department of Education's National Diffusion Network and recognized as an organization that is making a positive contribution to students and schools by the National Alliance of Business and Higher Education, the Merrow Report, and the National Center for Restructuring Schools and Teaching. The U.S. Department of Education recently included the League in a publication entitled *Promising practices: New ways to improve teacher quality* (U.S. Department of Education, 1998). Similarly, the American Institutes of Research included the League in a publication entitled *Judging Schoolwide Reform: A teacher and administrator guide to 26 noteworthy approaches* (American Institutes for Research, 1998).

(Allen *et al.* 1999b: 165–6)

The success that League schools have experienced is, first and foremost, a result of the hard work and expertise of their teachers, administrators, students and parents. But the League services and activities, which have constantly evolved as part of our ongoing learning, have also played a critical role in this success. What follows are the lessons we've learned about how university–school networks can help all stakeholders improve their professional practices in such a way that students benefit.

Practitioner-driven networks

One of the first decisions we made in forming the League was whether school districts, schools or individual educators would join the network. We were concerned that if districts were the membership unit, people in schools would be required by their central office to participate, and we wanted participation in the League to be completely voluntary. We were also concerned that if we allowed individual educators to join, we would perpetuate the very tradition of isolation that we were trying to change. As we were strongly committed to school-wide collaboration, reflection and commitment, we decided that the membership unit would be the school and that schools would decide democratically, by secret ballot with a positive response of at least 80 percent of those voting, whether or not to join. Further, because the main purpose of our network was to renew the work of the educators in the member schools, we agreed that these educators must have a central role in planning and carrying out the operations and services of the network. League colleagues coined the phrase 'practitioner-driven network' (PDN) to describe this type of collaboration.

Practitioner-driven reflects the idea that such networks are not organizations that schools simply join and then passively follow existing operating procedures. In these networks, the practitioners decide what services they want. They constantly monitor network activities, modify them to meet changing needs, and play key roles in the network leadership.

(Allen and Lunsford 1995: 1)

When school-based people are involved in planning and evaluating network services and activities, then those services will reflect more accurately the needs of their schools. We have found that any time we drift away from involving people in schools in the life of the League, excitement, commitment and participation drop off. A high level of practitioner involvement not only benefits the network and its members' schools, but it also provides individuals in schools with professional experiences that can expand and deepen their professional confidence, knowledge and expertise. The benefit is realized at every level – network, school and individual – and creates an ongoing cycle of improvement.

However, it isn't always possible for school-based educators to be as involved in the life of a network as everyone would prefer. There are several factors that work against this active engagement. While people often develop strong loyalties to networks, their top priority remains with their schools. Paying for teachers' supplies and travel can stretch limited budgets. There is a great deal of pressure for educators and students to meet various external standards and time spent away from classrooms and schools is considered by many as lost time no matter how it enhances teachers' and principals' work.

So what's to be done? We offer the following suggestions and examples from our work:

1. If your network covers a large geographic area, limit the amount of time and expense involved in travelling for any group of schools by moving meeting locations around, or holding multiple sessions of the same meeting in different locations so that the same people don't always have to travel long distances, and the costs of travel are spread equally among schools. Equalizing meeting locations and travel also helps to ensure that all members feel equally valued. In our network, with schools located across the large geographic area of Georgia, holding meetings in the same location is likely to convey to those who are at a distance from the meeting site that their participation is not valued. When League membership was over 130 schools, our three annual meetings were held in different locations across the state. Our Fall Institute took place in the eastern part of the state. The winter meeting was held in two locations, one convenient to schools in the south and south-central part of the state and the other for schools in the

populous greater metropolitan Atlanta region. Our spring meeting was traditionally held in Athens, the home of the University of Georgia and the League, in the north-eastern part of Georgia. Member schools believed this was a reasonable and equitable way to deal with the fact that we were spread across a state that is the largest east of the Mississippi.

2. Networks-within-a-network can offer people small learning communities that are close to home. However, competing with this idea is the fact that people don't want to be regulated to networking only with those in their immediate geographical area. In most cases a balance needs to be struck between gatherings of the subunits and the whole network. We have tried regional subunits in several different ways. At one time we had three different Leagues: one for metro Atlanta schools, one for schools in the northern part of the state, and one for schools in the southern part. Each League had its own set of meetings and governance structure. Eventually, however, after several years, this organization was reconsidered and abandoned for a number of reasons. For our schools dividing into subgroups had the unintended consequence of exacerbating existing feelings of isolation among our rural, urban and suburban schools. We also started to question the efficiency of providing three different sets of identical services. When asked, our members initially elected to have a common meeting in the autumn involving all of the subgroups so they could each learn from a diverse set of schools, and to continue their individual meetings for the remainder of the year. We did this for several years, but eventually the three Leagues were combined. Some members found they liked the larger network. Others missed the more intimate involvement and interactions and focused networking opportunities that the smaller networks provided. This issue can be an ongoing conundrum for networks spread over a large geographical expanse.

3. Make good use of technology for communication purposes. Email, listservs, teleconferences, interactive websites, conference calls can all help in bringing people together. These types of communication cannot replace face-to-face meetings but they can complement them. As mentioned elsewhere in this chapter, the League's congress has one face-to-face meeting and one meeting in several sites using two-way communication audio and video connections. Each site has its own facilitator and participants divide their time between discussing issues across all sites and within their own face-to-face group. We have also set up listservs that enable individual teachers to share ideas and concerns across schools. So far participation has been low. We think it will pick up as we manage and promote the use of technology more aggressively, as described in a later section.

4.   Agree on the level of participation that will be required of members. Some networks have policies that make participation optional. They offer a menu of services and schools chose their own level of involvement. Others have required amounts of participation. When the League was founded we did not have a participation policy. There was such an aura of excitement around the ideas of the League and a network that put educators at the centre of its work that we took high levels of participation for granted. As the League grew in size, and as the reality of the many outside pressures on schools increased in intensity, levels of participation emerged as an issue. After two years of conversations among stakeholders, we reached the agreement that making the significant changes promoted by the League required full commitment by all members. We have learned that anything less will not produce the kind of results we have all agreed we want. People in networks must decide carefully for themselves what level of participation is appropriate for what they want to accomplish.

Governance and leadership

Currently, the League has one part-time and two full-time co-directors and an office support staff member. The co-directors, who are faculty members in the College of Education, provide leadership in carrying out the League's services and research efforts, and in setting policy. Practitioner-driven networks obviously involve participants in their governance structures. As mentioned earlier, the League has a congress, made up of a representative from each school and a representative from the League staff, that meets twice a year, once as a part of our annual autumn Institute and once in the spring, using several sites around the state that have two-way audio and video capabilities. Congress makes general decisions about League services and membership. It is also a place for League staff and representatives to discuss common issues and concerns, and to reflect on our collective work. These discussions help build understanding and momentum to push collaboratively the work of the network and of individual schools to new levels.

The League's Principal Consortium is another group that plays an important role in the governance of the League. All principals in League schools are members of this consortium that meets several times a year and serves as a forum for principals to learn about and reflect on their role in leading a democratic school and as a communication conduit between League staff and principals. Before League staff members take actions that have the potential to impact member schools or make recommendations to the League's congress, we consult the Principal's Consortium. While the League's by-laws do not call for this consortium to be a part of our formal decision-making process, we have learned that it is imperative to seek their advice and support on a regular basis.

Another important group of people that play an important part in the League's governance is our university associates. The College of Education has an official representative on our congress, but beyond that, University of Georgia (UGA) faculty members play a vital role in our decision-making process by acting as ongoing partners and advisors to League staff. As the League develops more formalized roles and structures for the involvement of university associates, we imagine that their role in League governance will also evolve. We will explain more about this later.

Expecting to improve student learning

It is critical that all participants in a network agree upon what is to be gained by their collaboration and to set up ways to monitor their progress. It is easy for people to confuse structures, procedures and activities with desired results. School-based educators typically work in isolation with few opportunities to work with colleagues from down the hall let alone from miles away. Participating in a practitioner-driven network where people are treated with professional respect is a very stimulating and fulfilling experience for everyone. Certainly, this may be a legitimate reason to create a network, but it is our experience that the benefits gained by individuals as a result of their participation is not sufficient to sustain a network or to realize the school improvement goals it aspires to achieve. It is important, therefore, that networks state their expectations for what will be accomplished and then make sure that their actions are linked to these specific desired results.

Each year the League holds an autumn Institute. Its purpose is to provide professional development opportunities that will lead ultimately to improved student learning. The expectation is that school teams will:

1) come to the institute with some particular instructional issue or concern in mind,
2) strategically plan how they will use the Institute to help address their instructional questions,
3) share their learning with their colleagues back home, and
4) collaboratively plan how they might use their new learning to improve student achievement in their school.

Indeed, this does happen with some schools. Other schools, however, send individuals to the conference simply because it is their turn to go with no plans to incorporate what they learn into the life of the school. The hope is that those attending will be rejuvenated and feel rewarded, which is important, but, if the learning stops there, then it has fallen short of our expectation of improving the teaching and learning of everyone within the school. It is imperative that we constantly remind ourselves of our agreement that our collaborative work is student-oriented and focused on improving teaching and learning for all.

Another expectation is that schools open their doors and practices to each other so that they can learn from each other. Certainly schools can decline when asked to present at League meetings or when a school asks to send visitors but, in general, being a member of the League means being open to collaboration.

These expectations also guide the action research that we conduct to monitor our work. League work involves the creation of structures and processes that are used to support the school as a democratic learning community and its attempts to focus our enquiry on these structures. There are many complex and fascinating issues that influence how schools go about empowering teachers, administrators, parents and students to collaborate in democratic ways. Developing a deeper understanding about these issues is vital but, again, it is not sufficient. We must also include studies of our most important expectation: improved student learning.

Beliefs

We have learned that there are several key beliefs that participants in a network should agree upon and make explicit. If these agreements are not reached, or are only alluded to in general ways, it will leave the collaboration vulnerable to decisions based on expediency and circumstance rather than on thoughtful and agreed upon expectations. There are several areas that we recommend people reach agreement on up front, with the understanding that as the organization evolves so will these decisions.

1. Size of the network is the first to consider. How many schools can the network serve? The optimal size of membership is related most directly to the type of relationships you hope to foster among members, the type and level of services you expect to provide, and the financial and organizational capacity of the network. Initially, we limited membership, but as interest and demand grew, we lifted the cap and over the next two years doubled our membership. This sudden growth spurt had significant programmatic and financial consequences. On the basis of our experiences, we encourage others just forming a network to consider carefully the issue of size. It influences the type and scope of the interactions among members and between members and staff, and obviously influences the level and costs of services.

For example, if you believe that school renewal work is most effective when those involved can form close, ongoing, professional relationships, then the size of the network should be small. A smaller membership more easily lends itself to developing intimate, helping relationships among the participants. If, on the other hand, you hold the belief that school renewal efforts of individual schools can be best spurred on through the diverse and dynamic exchanges found among large numbers, then the size of membership would reflect this belief.

2. By-laws for network governance are best written before there are issues to be addressed. It can be very difficult to make decisions while creating a decision-making process. Also, there are practical dilemmas surrounding governance that need to be settled. For example, we learned it is not enough for people to agree that network participants and its staff should have an equal voice in a network's governance. It is one thing to have such by-laws written down, and it is quite another for them to actually be played out. Typically, university-based staff members have more flexible schedules than their school-based counterparts. This may lead to the staff exercising a larger voice in the life of a network than school people without anyone intending for this to happen. Networks must carefully and strategically think through when and where leadership teams, committees and task forces will meet. If this is not done, some people may not be able to participate as fully as others.

3. How will the network be supported financially? If a network is established initially using funds from a grant or other temporary types of financial support, how will the work be sustained? Will you charge a membership fee? If so, a fee structure and policies to support it need to be in place. Among the issues we considered in our deliberations were: 1) Will all schools pay a membership fee? 2) Will all schools pay the same fee? 3) Should large schools pay more than small schools? 4) What about a sliding scale depending on schools' resources? 5) Who will decide when fees are to be raised or lowered? From the beginning, the League held the belief that no school that wanted to become engaged in our work should be denied access because of the inability to pay membership fees. Working through our congress, membership fees were established and a scholarship fund was authorized. A task force of League principals and teachers established scholarship guidelines and an application process, which they then administered. League staff raised funds from external sources to fund the scholarships.

In the heady first days of establishing a network when excitement is high and the coffers are full, issues of financial sustainability are easily set aside. It is imperative that a network establishes a plan and process to make financial decisions.

Services

The heart and soul of a network is the services it offers to its members. When the League was being formed, the university-based and the school-based founders made several key decisions about services. For financial and philosophical reasons, we agreed that the League would not offer extensive services to its members. We wanted to keep membership fees low enough that all schools could afford to pay them without relying on outside funds. It had been our experience that activities which require resources beyond a school's normal financial budget are often seen as temporary and tangential to a school's primary work. We wanted people to perceive this collaboration as fundamentally changing the way they did business. Membership in the League, therefore, was something members would pursue as long as they felt it was of use, not until their source of income expired.

Philosophically, we believed that the expertise and skills found in the network itself would be sufficient to support member schools. Allen and Glickman (1998) described this philosophy and the League's services:

> The League operates under the assumption that a key source of expertise that needs to be tapped to facilitate schools' efforts is found in the schools themselves (Allen and Lunsford 1995). League services therefore seek to provide schools with ways to network among themselves so that they can learn from each other. While League staff and university colleagues do play an active part in many League services, League school practitioners are at the centre of most League activities. League services include
>
> 1) Four days of meetings (two-day autumn Institute, one-day winter and spring meetings) provided annually for teams of six participants from each school. All activities at these meetings (keynote addresses, concurrent sessions, structured and informal dialogues) are related to the League's framework. League practitioners conduct more than 70% of all sessions.
> 2) A bi-annual newsletter and an annual school directory are disseminated. The newsletter is written by staff and features articles by League practitioners about their work, reflections on the League's premises, and items noting outstanding achievement of the schools and their staffs. Schools wanting more information on any of the information and work described in the newsletter are encouraged to contact the contributing school. The school directory provides a profile of each school including instructional initiatives. Schools pursuing similar goals can stay in contact. The League website and associated list servs have supplemented the newsletter and directory in recent years.

3) Member schools have access to an information retrieval system which responds to requests for information about issues, concerns, and practices related to the League's framework. In response to a request, a school receives an information packet that may include research and applied articles on the issues of interest, sample products such as curricular materials, and contact information for other schools who have similar instructional interests or concerns.

4) An annual site visit is made to each member school by a League staff member, university associate, or League practitioner. Initially, the visits were focused on examining the implementation of the framework. A protocol was followed and stakeholders were interviewed, documents examined, and meetings observed. These data were analysed and a written report summarizing the results along with suggestions for next steps was provided to the school. As the network evolved, the visits were broadened so that each school determined the structure and focus of their visits. League staff also received copies of all site visit reports and used these reports to monitor progress and effectiveness of services and to guide network decisions.

5) Special topic institutes provide member schools with extended time to address issues of interest and concern. Examples of past summer institutes include team building, governance development, data collection and analysis, analysing and interpreting test data, conflict resolution, and grant writing.

6) League staff members also respond to questions, inquiries, and requests from schools via telephone, fax, and electronic mail communication.

(Allen and Glickman 1998: 508)

Within the past two years, collaborative research and reflective conversations among League participants and staff have led to changes in the focus of League services. We have deepened our work from using democratic principles as guidelines for school governance to producing guidelines for instructional practices in classrooms across member schools, what we call 'democratic learning' (Glickman 1998). We have also changed how schools participate in network services.

As described earlier, in the past, some member schools were particularly adept at establishing an instructional focus and using League services to help move their particular focus forward. Other schools were not so focused and for them, League services became a series of one-time professional development experiences that did not lead to any substantial changes in practice. Now the autumn, winter and spring meetings are planned as a year-long professional development experience focused on 'democratic learning'. To make sure these meetings have the desired impact, we ask schools to select an administrator and four to five teachers who are willing to make a commitment to implementing democratic learning in their classrooms and to attend all meetings. We originally asked participants to make a one-year commitment, but teachers reported that they believe they needed two years to gain the depth of understanding that will allow them to provide leadership to their peers, so the period has been changed to two years. In studying the impact of League services, we have documented that many participants have made substantial gains in their levels of understanding of the guiding principles of democratic learning and are beginning to implement appropriate instructional strategies and activities. At the end of two years, these original team members will rotate out of active participation in the professional development cycle and new teams will be chosen. We anticipate that original team members and new team members will work closely together at their school sites. We expect that they will not only interact with one another, but they will also engage other faculty members so that this work will eventually be a school-wide effort.

We will continue other network services including the Principals' Consortium, site visits, information retrieval system, newsletter, school directory and technology-based networking through a website and listservs. These services will shift, as needed, to ensure that they support democratic classroom learning. We anticipate that our concentrated focus will allow us to be more proactive in providing participants with assistance. We also anticipate that this shared focus on democratic learning will enhance individuals' networking across schools because it will allow people to share specific ideas, lesson and unit plans, resources, challenges and successes.

University participation

University–school networks vary greatly in the role that university faculty play. Some networks are housed in the university but there is little participation by affiliated faculty members. Other networks involve university people in every aspect of their work. In the early years of the League, there was a core of university faculty involved in the League's work, primarily as consultants to schools, professional development providers and advisors to League staff. Involvement was limited to the interest of individual faculty members and there was little interaction between the work of the League and its schools in the teacher preparation programmes. Several years ago we began to make changes in the level of participation in the League of UGA's College of Education faculty, students and graduates. We wanted to make sure that the lessons we were learning from our school-based colleagues were being put to use in the university and that the expertise found in the college was being put to good use in the work of the League.

With this in mind, we have established roles for university faculty members and created the role of League Fellows for undergraduate students. We invite university faculty members (League Faculty) who are applying the League's democratic learning principles in their classrooms to participate in planning and implementing League activities and services. League staff have formed a Critical Friends Group (developed by the National School Reform Faculty, www.nsrfharmony.org). Critical Friends Group is a collaborative learning community that will allow us to interact closely with other College of Education faculty members. League Fellows are College of Education students who have participated in specific courses, taught by League Faculty, that are aligned with the League's principles of democratic learning. Many League Fellows attend our meetings and, in some cases, have done service learning projects that have benefited League schools. League Fellows, if they so choose, may become League Teachers upon graduation. Those that take jobs in League schools will enter into a community of learners with a commitment to democratic learning. These new teachers will join more experienced colleagues as they all continue to grow in their understanding and practice of democratic learning. Those that take jobs in non-League schools will have the opportunity to continue to use League services as part of their own individual professional development.

Inviting individual teachers to join the League marks a departure from our original philosophy of only allowing whole-school membership in our work. This change has come about as a result of honing our focus to democratic learning and practices and the subsequent realization that there are individual educators who can greatly enhance our understanding of democratic learning. While we still believe that school-wide renewal is the most powerful way to improve student learning and plan to continue advocating and learning about it, we see the need to unite individuals to our collective efforts.

Creating a learning cycle

Facilitating school renewal through school–university networks is a complex endeavour that requires its own learning cycle to ensure reflection and improvement. Like their school members, networks must find ways to gather, analyse and interpret information about their actions to monitor their success and make necessary adjustments. In the League we use twice-a-year retreats as an opportunity to gather representatives from schools, university and League staff to reflect on the data from on-site visits, research studies, evaluation efforts and observations. We reflect on the progress we are making in bringing our covenant to life. Sometimes, depending on the issue, we make decisions. Other times, we develop recommendations to take to the League Congress and/or Principals' Consortium. We also use 'think tank' meetings to build awareness of the League among our university colleagues and to ensure that we take advantage of their perspectives as we struggle with issues or concerns. We invite College of Education colleagues to participate in a meeting where we lay out an issue that we are considering. Following a structured agenda, our colleagues explore the issue and make recommendations. We benefit from the experience and knowledge of these 'outside' thinkers and, in turn, they have a chance to take on interesting and complex ideas and keep up with the League and its work.

The League has never repeated the same year twice. Each year we make adjustments based on a combination of data, observations and informed intuition. This cycle of learning has been vital to our success and helped us stay focused on student learning. School–university networks must be learning organizations to succeed. When they are, they create unique opportunities that can't be duplicated in any other format. The League has enjoyed 15 successful years and we look forward to many more to come.

References

Allen, L., Glickman, C.D., and Hensley, F. (1999a) 'The League of Professional Schools: A decade of school-based renewal' in J. Block, S.T. Everson and T.R. Guskey (eds) *Comprehensive School Improvement: A Program Perspective*. Dubuque, IO: Kendall Hunt.

Allen L., Glickman, C.D. and Hensley, F. (1999b). 'A search for accountability: The League of Professional Schools'. Paper presented to the American Educational Research Association Annual Meeting, San Diego, 13–17 April.

Allen, L. and Glickman, C.D. (1998) 'Capturing the power of democracy for school renewal' in A. Hargreaves, A. Lieberman, M. Fullan and D. Hopkins (eds) *International Handbook of Educational Change*. Hingham, MA: Kluwer Academic Publishers.

Allen, L. and Lunsford, B. (1995) *How to form networks for school renewal*. Alexandria, VA: Association for Supervision and Curriculum Development.

Glickman, C.D. (1993) *Renewing America's Schools: A Guide for School-Based Action*. San Francisco: Jossey-Bass.

Glickman, C.D. (1998) *Revolutionizing America's Schools*. San Francisco: Jossey-Bass.

three

Keeping school networks fluid: networks in dialogue with educational change

Wiel Veugelers and Henk Zijlstra

In modern Western society, the traditional structures and organizations from the 'first modernity', with its hierarchical models and well-structured and distinct components, are today confronted by the individualization trends of the 'second modernity' (Beck *et al.* 1994; Castells 1996; Beck and Beck-Gernsheim 2002). The 'second modernity' stresses the growing autonomy of individuals and individual organizations. Governments are being forced to find new ways of bringing these relatively autonomous subjects and institutions together, and to change their own structures of leadership and control. This need for new structures is particularly apparent in present-day education. Education in the 'second modernity' is still regarded as a vital agency for identity construction and a significant component of a national cultural policy.

School networks are seen as important new structures for bringing about change in education. In order to change upper secondary education in the Netherlands, we stimulate bringing schools together in networks. Schools learn from each other, analyse each other's practices and develop various joint initiatives. In this chapter we present our experiences and analyse critical elements in creating and sustaining networks.

The political, cultural and educational climate in Dutch education

Networks always function in a political, cultural and educational context. They are at the same time a product of these influences and they also influence this context. For analysing the relationship between educational change and identity development, we use the concept of citizenship (Giroux

1989; Van Gunsteren 1992; Turner 1993). We distinguish three main types of citizenship: the adapting citizen, the individualistic citizen and the critical-democratic citizen (Veugelers 2000). In the vision of the adapting citizen, a person has to accommodate to society and the traditional values it tries to maintain. Changes in society are, at best, incorporated into traditional ways of life. The local community is celebrated, and in education the emphasis is on the traditional curriculum and on character education.

In the vision of the individualistic citizen, society is a liberal market in which each idea and every person has to find their own way. The individual has their own responsibilities and is accountable for their own competences. It is a technical rationality based in liberal philosophy. In education it emphasizes choice, individualization, self-regulation and accountability.

The vision of the critical-democratic citizen attempts to combine individual and social development. A person is seen as a social being that actively participates in society and is critically engaged in the transformation of the community, by working with cultural differences. A balance has to be found here between personal development and social commitment and emancipation. The educational foundation for critical-democratic citizenship is critical pedagogy or critical theory and certain forms of cooperative learning and moral education.

Educational policy

In the concrete educational policies of governments, schools and teachers, one will not recognize these three types of citizenship in their pure forms. One will always find a specific articulation. We believe that at present in the philosophy of the policy makers, the individualistic citizen is the dominant form in the western world, but elements of the adapting citizen and the critical-democratic citizen are also part of that educational policy. We would like to describe this educational philosophy as it has been worked out in educational policy for senior secondary education in the Netherlands.

From the vision of individualistic citizenship (the dominant element in contemporary citizenship education policy) it borrows:

- stimulation of self-regulation of the students' learning processes
- support for individual learning routes and flexibility
- focus on learning skills
- stimulation of the use of information technology
- measuring student development in line with 'objective' assessment.

From the educational view of the adapting citizen it retains:

- the emphasis on traditional subjects

- traditional methods of assessment
- disciplinary practices
- keeping control over schools, educational goals and the learning process of students
- conformity to local community.

From the critical-democratic view, it incorporates to a certain extent ideas of:

- authentic learning with space for personal signification processes and extra-curricular activities
- critical thinking, but often in a formal, value-neutral way, not in a transformative way
- cooperative learning as a way of learning to work together
- attention to cultural differences.

Schools in the Netherlands have the freedom, within certain boundaries, to develop their own interpretation of national educational policy. They can, for example, focus more on the adaptive perspective, or they may place the emphasis on the critical-democratic perspective.

Managing educational change

Top-down and bottom-up

Western states today advocate greater autonomy for students, teachers and managers in educational institutions, while at the same time they pursue new structures for coordinating and controlling these trends towards autonomy. Greater autonomy is a bottom-up approach for empowering students, teachers and schools. National educational policy is in a position to support these bottom-up developments by giving students, teachers and schools the space to develop their own education. However, policy may also apply a top-down approach in order to control and regulate the process of autonomy.

According to Darling-Hammond (1992: 72), two different theories about educational policy and school reform currently work in parallel and they sometimes conflict. One theory focuses on tightening control: more courses, more tests, more mandatory curricula, more standards encouraged by more rewards and enforced by more sanctions. This is a top-down approach. The second theory devotes more attention to teachers' qualifications and capacities and to developing schools through changes in teacher education, licensing, certification processes, professional development and efforts to decentralize school decision-making processes, while infusing knowledge, changing local assessment practices, and developing school and teacher networks. This is a bottom-up approach.

Top-down approaches in school reform are fairly ineffective (Fullan 1991). The implementation of true reform requires support from teachers (Sikes 1992). Reform should therefore also be directed at developing capacity, in particular in schools themselves (Hargreaves and Fullan 1998). In actual school reform, these top-down and bottom-up processes work in parallel and often interact. Analysing changes in education requires attention to be given to the interplay of these top-down and bottom-up policies, or, in other words, to the interplay of control and extended autonomy (Hargreaves 1994; Hartley 1997; Datnow and Castellano 2000; Veugelers 2004).

Top-down and bottom-up processes at different levels of the educational system

In education, educational policy sets out a cultural project in which it steers the development of certain educational practices. But this policy allows schools room to develop their own interpretation of that policy: for formulating their own educational views; for making choices in the operationalization of the curriculum; and for organizing the learning process. To a certain extent, it is a top-down operation: top-down first from the Ministry of Education to the schools, then from the principal to the teacher, and from the teacher to the learner.

However, modern social ideas as presented in the first part of this chapter demand an active learning process in which the learner co-constructs his or her own education. Therefore, at the micro-level there is not only a top-down movement at play, but also a bottom-up movement from the learner to the curriculum and to the school. The concrete process at the micro-level of the learning process is a combination of top-down and bottom-up.

Similar processes can be seen to play at the level between the principal and the teachers (Hargreaves 1994). Together the teachers co-construct the curriculum, the culture and the organization of the school. Also on this meso-level, there is a combination of top-down from principal to teachers and bottom-up from teachers to principal. Together they create the learning organization in which school development and professional development coincide. The same processes can be seen at work between the government and schools (Hartley 1997).

Changing secondary education in the Netherlands

When analysing networks of schools for secondary education it is important to show the curriculum policy. In the Netherlands, the curriculum and assessments are centralized and well-controlled by government. Only 30 per cent of secondary schools are public schools. The 70 per cent 'private' schools consist of 25 per cent Catholic, 25 per cent Protestant and 20 per cent with some special pedagogical approach such as Montessori or Dalton. These 'private' schools receive public funding and have to follow the national curriculum and assessments, but they do have some room for religious or humanistic education. All schools, both public and private, may appoint their own teachers and have some room for their own pedagogical vision on education.

In 1988, the Dutch Ministry of Education started a restructuring process for senior secondary education. In senior secondary education, students aged 15 to 18 prepare for further study either at a university or a poly-technic. There is a pre-university variant (VWO) and one for the poly-technics (HAVO). About 40 per cent of the youngsters of that age group are in senior secondary education in the Netherlands. The other 60 per cent are in vocational education.

The problems in senior secondary education at the end of the 1980s and in the early 1990s could be formulated as follows:

- a lack of motivation among many students
- traditional teaching methods
- insufficient flexibility in the school organization and teachers' tasks
- insufficient academic level
- too much subject choice for students.

There was much discussion during the first half of the 1990s about these problems and a search for suitable 'solutions'. These solutions can be summarized as follows:

- reduction in choice by introducing four learning 'profiles': culture, economics, health and technology
- new curricula with higher standards and with more learning skills defined
- more centralized assessments
- introduction of new forms of teaching methods for more active learning
- more opportunities for schools to organize their own way of teaching.

Before the new curricula were formally introduced in 1998, a few schools experimented with the introduction of more learning skills in the curricula, new forms of teaching and different ways of organizing their education (more flexibility in the timetable and in grouping students). Central notions were self-efficacy (Bandura 1995) and restructuring (Newmann 1993; Lieberman 1995). In 1998, all schools started with the new curricula, the profiles and the new exams. In this process of educational change we can roughly distinguish four periods, but there is of course some overlap:

1988–1992 Analysis
1992–1995 Formulating possibilities
1995–1998 Experiments in schools, developing the national curriculum and
        exams
1998–2004 Implementation of the new curriculum and exams

This is the educational context in which our network started and created a
practice of change.

Forming our network

We believe that networks are strong instruments for linking professional
development and school development, and for bringing about educational
change. Networks can be seen as communities of practices (Wenger 1998),
they can connect personal stories with historical and political discourses
(Goodson 2003), and they can stimulate new transformative professionalism (Sachs 2003). We will go on to demonstrate these ambitions by
describing the developments, changes and continuity in our network.

We started our network in 1988. We invited schools we had worked with
in earlier projects and schools that were partners in the teacher education
programme at the University of Amsterdam to participate. We started by
discussing the first text published by the Ministry of Education on the
restructuring of secondary education. This text was entitled 'Modulariza-
tion of Secondary Education' and was, in fact, a technical approach to
education which was so popular in the late 1980s. The vision it incorporated was that of a calculating or individualistic citizen, but without any
explicit moral or pedagogical ideas.

In monthly meetings we analysed this text and formulated a critique that
we later discussed with several officials from the Ministry of Education. In
this analysis and in the discussions, schools also took time to examine their
own school. They tried to find out which problem was being articulated in
'their' school and what kind of solutions 'they' wanted to work on. From
the very beginning, we wanted to create a learning culture in which there
could be a reflexive practice in which all could participate; in which we
could dream about possibilities, in which we could find commonalities in
experiences and in which we could support each other.

At that time, we referred to our group as a 'working group'; in the early
1990s when our group became 'institutionalized' we referred to ourselves
as a 'network'. We believe that a network has to be constructed; you cannot
just announce the existence of a network. People have to experience for
themselves that they have something in common and that they can contribute to each others' school development and professional development.

After a few years' work, we were able to formulate a number of different functions that our network had for its participants.

Functions of the network

Our network can be characterized by the following functions (see Veugelers and Zijlstra 1995a, 1996a, 1998a):

1. *Interpretation of government policies*
   Discussions among teachers from different schools can provide greater insight into the consequences of and the various opportunities for restructuring education and implementing policy.
2. *Influencing government policies*
   A network of schools can also try to influence government policies by giving feedback as a group.
3. *Learning from the experience of others*
   In our view, learning from one another is the most important difference between professional development in networks and other forms of professional development.
4. *Using each other's expertise*
   A participating school may invite expertise from another school or from the Centre for Professional Development.
5. *Developing new educational approaches and materials*
   Participants create products other schools can use, for example guides or curriculum timetables, bringing some coherence to the teaching of skills, or changing the moral climate in the school.
6. *Creating new initiatives*
   In a true partnership, both schools and university can benefit from the collaboration and develop new initiatives together.

When we compare the functions of our network with the characteristics of networks in the USA as described by Lieberman and Grolnick (1996) and Pennell and Firestone (1996), our network is focused more on policy: on analysing policy, but also on trying to influence policy.

Organization and practice of the network

At present, 20 schools participate in the network. Two people from each school (usually one of them a vice-principal) participate in the regular network meetings. These meetings are held once a month. The meetings focus on the educational vision of the schools, the schools' organization, teaching methods, learning activities and the educational change process. In addition, we also have thematic working groups. First, in the period of experimentation, we had groups for career education, self-regulated learning, and moral and democratic education. In the current implementation period, we have four working groups that are subject based: humanities, social studies and economics, health and technology, and career education. The former topics have now been integrated into these groups. Eight teachers from different schools participate in each group. In addition to the secondary school teachers, teachers from the University of Amsterdam are also members of these working groups. These groups focus on the content of the curriculum, pedagogical-didactical teaching methods and learning experiences. These groups meet six times a year. Furthermore, we also hold two conferences each year. One of these conferences is a meeting between student panels from the schools. Approximately 120 teachers from 20 schools have participated in the network over the past two years.

These groups are chaired by staff members from the Centre for Professional Development in Education at the University of Amsterdam. Some members, like the second author of this chapter, work in one of the schools participating in the network but are hired in by the University to chair groups in the network. The chair and three teachers from the schools prepare the sessions. The network enables these teachers to do this work. All the meetings are held on Thursday afternoons; half the meetings are at the university, and the other half are at different schools. These school-based site visits are prepared together with the school.

There is a specific topic for each meeting. Someone gives a presentation on that particular topic, and we then reflect together on that practice and everybody contributes their own ideas and relates their own personal experience. The presentations may be about plans, ongoing projects or project evaluation. This is a kind of action research for the teachers. We prefer to monitor such developments in the network or the working group.

About every other year we compile a book that gives examples of 'good practice' or descriptions of failures. There are about 20 different contributions in each book. Teachers and principals write about their own practice and their own action research projects. The four books published so far have in fact sold quite well and have been important sources for other schools (Veugelers and Zijlstra 1995b, 1996b, 1998b, 2001). In 1996, the network was awarded a prize for its first book as the best project in secondary education in the Netherlands.

Networks in the Netherlands

Our network has been used as a model for starting up more networks. The principal from one of our schools was assigned by the government to stimulate the start of networks nationwide. The government has been awarding grants for the start up of networks. By the mid-1990s, there were some 30 networks for secondary education in the country. The emergence of more networks enabled schools to make a choice between networks. Most of the more traditional Protestant and Catholic schools in our region are members of an alternative network from the Protestant University in Amsterdam.

The emerging network

What do participants appreciate about the network?

How do the participants assess the functions of the network? We asked our participants to indicate how the network provides the different functions for themselves (Veugelers and Zijlstra 2001, 2002). According to the participants, the network mainly provides the functions of 'learning from other's experiences' and 'using each other's expertise'. Most respondents stress the importance of a joint interpretation of government policies, yet the chances of influencing government policies are considered minimal. Despite many meetings with members of the government network, participants are not optimistic about their impact, however, they keep trying to influence policy.

Working together in the network can lead directly to the joint development of new initiatives. It is, though, a stimulus for new initiatives in one's own school and one's own practice. In reply to a question regarding the differences between meetings of the network and traditional methods of teacher education, many respondents indicated the importance of an exchange of experiences and learning from someone else's practice. The meetings were characterized by 'equality amongst participants who discuss experiences from a practical perspective and with an emphasis on finding solutions'. The exchange of experiences was in no way limited to the Thursday afternoon meetings at the university. Most of the participants indicate that they also consult each other, phone or visit each other outside the meetings to ask for and give information. The network is mainly associated with active participation and continuity of activities, as 'giving and taking'. Traditional teacher education, on the other hand, is often 'passive' and oriented towards 'taking'.

Attracting schools to the network: shaping a network identity

Another important parameter for evaluating the network is the level of school participation. In 1989 there were 20 schools in the network, and now there are 20 schools again, most of the schools being the same ones. In the intervening period, a total of 42 schools participated in the network for some period of time. Two groups of schools joined the network but left again. The first group comprised six schools from the north of Amsterdam, a rural and a more traditional area. They were mixed with some other new schools in a new sub network. After a few years they left the network partly because they had to travel too far to get to Amsterdam, but also because of their educational philosophy. They focused more on adaptive ideas and much less on the critical-democracy ideas that were the dominant pre-occupation of the network.

The second group comprised six grammar schools, which were interested in forming a sub network of independent grammar schools. We agreed to this as an experiment for a one-year period and we hoped that they would later want to integrate more with the larger network and our working groups. However, they also considered the educational vision of the network to be too critical-democratic and they found that schools that have different types (levels) of education from their schools tended to dominate the network. Some of these schools also provide vocational training and there are even some comprehensive schools. For us, as directors of the network and for the old network schools, their departure was not a big problem. Schools that want to join our network are always welcome, but we do have our own educational vision. Of course there is space for other educational visions but within some common foundation. This foundation is not always well articulated but it does form the 'local colour' of the network; it provides the boundaries of the educational vision. We are even proud that people recognize our vision and from a democratic and pluralist perspective it is good that they opt for their own vision. So the network creates an identity that attracts some schools and dispenses with others.

However, some schools left because the participants found that their school had blocked their development and they felt that they could no longer contribute to the network. They felt that they were only taking and no longer giving. We tried to support these people by accepting their passive participation for a while but they generally left one or two years later, in the hope of coming back in better times.

Some schools left because they wanted to concentrate on their own school development and they believed that they were not learning enough. However, some of these schools did return a few years later; they missed being part of a community of learners. They lacked new ideas and they said that the network helped to keep them sharp.

The network in its educational environment

Bottom-up flow in formulating opportunities and conducting experiments

Networks are powerful tools in circumstances where schools have the opportunity to shape their own education; when they can think and work together in finding out how education might be organized. In the second half of the 1990s, we had that opportunity in upper secondary education in the Netherlands. Schools could experiment with their pedagogical and methodological approach. Students, and sometimes parents, were involved in thinking about desirable changes and evaluated ongoing experiments. Despite a lot of criticism, the involvement on the part of quite a lot of students did improve. Occasionally, student panels from different schools met as a network. Many teachers also became involved in their school and in the network activities. People gained a feeling of empowerment.

The type of citizenship teachers could officially work on was the individualistic person, but a more humanist version with the emphasis on self-responsibility, creativity and personal development. There were also opportunities for a critical-democratic citizenship in cooperative learning and in students' own research projects inside and outside school.

Top-down restriction on implementation

The final formal national curriculum, with its high standards and centralized assessments, that started in 1998 restricted the opportunities for restructuring secondary education (Veugelers 2004). The content is stringently controlled by a system of central assessment and the curriculum is overloaded. Teachers have to really concentrate on 'time-on-task'. They do not have much time for more experimental learning and they have to monitor intensively students' progress. Traditional subjects and traditional content in subjects maintained their position in the curriculum. All the new learning skills, the research activities for students and the more social-oriented themes came in addition to the traditional curriculum instead of being substitutions for parts of the old curriculum. When the Ministry of Education was forced to do something about the overload in the curriculum, it further reduced the new content.

Another restriction for a possible bottom-up process was the changes in assessment. More subjects are now being assessed nationally (for most of the students, more than seven subjects). Even the school-based assessment is more strictly regulated. Schools themselves also feel monitored because the role of the school inspectorate has intensified. Teachers have the feeling that their work level has intensified considerably. And this is not only a subjective feeling.

The type of citizenship that is aimed for now in education is still that of the individualistic person, but now a more adaptive one as a result of the traditional curriculum content and the intensive monitoring of students. The opportunities for a more critical-democratic citizenship are still there, but marginalized.

It is interesting to see that for the common Dutch secondary school there is, compared with the previous era, more room for personal, humanistic and also more critical-democratic education. For the majority of Dutch schools, education has changed for the better. But the opportunities for the more innovative schools, like the ones we have in our network, to shape their own education in more critical and democratic ways of learning, are even fewer than they were before under the old system.

Consequences for the network

As far as the network is concerned, all this means that the era of experimentation is over and, now that the time has come for implementing the new curriculum, that schools have to defend their achievements. The discussions in the network are often about how a more critical and democratic education can still be achieved, with opportunities for students to conduct their own research projects and to choose their own learning activities.

The intensification of teachers' work levels, and that of principals, means that they have less time to attend network meetings. The schools in the network want the network to continue, but possibly with fewer meetings a year. They still appreciate working together and they want to benefit from the mutual trust and expertise available in the network.

We needed this contextualization of the network in the educational landscape because making and sustaining a network is not context-neutral. We have seen that a bottom-up movement in a period of exploring possibilities and experimentation provides better conditions for a network than a top-down movement during implementation. Schools must also have the opportunities, the conditions and the subjective feeling that they can articulate their own educational vision, organization and pedagogical-didactical method. Networks can benefit from an educational and political climate in which schools can formulate their own interpretation of the national policy and the official curriculum. Where they can learn from differences and similarities.

This might be phrased in a different way. Networks can flourish in an era when people can have their educational dreams, when they can conduct their own projects, in which they can function together as a collaborative group. In periods of a strong top-down movement, the strategy of a network is more defensive: defensive in its educational goals but also in its chances of survival. We still try to learn from each other, now more from the small steps each school takes. We also try to give participants in the network new opportunities to experience and learn from educational practices in other countries, in different political and cultural contexts. In 1996, we went to Lund in Sweden. In 2001, 20 teachers and principals travelled to Finland to meet the networks at the universities of Helsinki and Tampere. And in March 2003, we met with the network of the Autonoma University in Barcelona. The networks of Tampere and Barcelona are similar to our network members. The contacts between networks at the level of teachers and principals are a strong component in the developing international network: The International Network of School Networks for Democratic Education.

And of course we work hard to get more room for a bottom-up approach in learning from students, in professional development and in school development. Maybe the more 'objective' and the more ideological developments in society force this bottom-up approach. The type of citizenship a modern pluralist society needs cannot only be an individualistic one, society has to organize its moral and democratic support, and the type of citizenship that is needed must be more critical-democratic (Veugelers and Vedder 2003; Veugelers and Oser 2003).

Developments in the network

The development of the network depends not only on educational policy. Internal factors are also important. In this last part of the paper we will analyse these factors.

Shared ownership of the network

Schools and universities must both have a feeling of ownership in the network. Networks cannot be organized from the top down. In our network, we try to combine the influence of schools and the university on all levels. We have two directors (the two authors), one from one of our network schools and one from the university. Some of the groups are chaired by teachers or principals from the school. When we receive grants, a large part of the money goes to the schools so they can encourage teachers to participate in the network and to do action research. The agenda for the year programme and for each meeting is formulated by all the participants.

Most networks for secondary schools in the Netherlands that started in the 1990s, in the period of experimentation, stopped their work. They often did not succeed in sharing power in the network. And unfortunately some universities and Institutes for Professional Development of Teachers never intended to empower the participants or share grants. They were more interested in the short-term benefits of money and research opportunities, or they even continued to believe in top-down implementation strategies.

Important factors for sustainable networks are:

• shared ownership and a sense of belonging among all participants
• an established tradition, so that breaking with tradition is a difficult decision to take
• continuation of participants
• being productive so participants receive concrete products and they themselves can show their own products
• constantly finding new challenges.

Network participation and the other teachers in the school

We believe that networks are powerful tools in the restructuring of education. But in the way we organized our network only a few of the workers in the school participate actively in the network. One might even say that we focus mainly on school management and that we support those change-agents in their work. Although promoting democratic education, a network like the one we have supports the most powerful people in the school in particular. Other methods of school development and professional development have to be added to networking.

Extended professionalism

A final remark can be made about the professionalism that networks bring. Working closely together with colleagues from other schools can broaden teachers' perspectives. Teachers experience that they are part of a larger educational community. It helps to see the particular and the common in your own educational experience. You have to reflect on your educational practice together with colleagues that become 'critical friends'. It gives you information about other practices. You know better what to do or what not to do in your classes and in your schools. You become a critical-reflective practitioner. And in the dominant educational philosophy of the network we try to become, to some extent, a critical-democratic practitioner (Liston and Zeichner 1991; Beyer 1996). The network gives teachers a collective voice. Of course we realize that the network cannot achieve all its intentions and neither can it explain all the changes in teachers' practice.

For university teachers and researchers working together with schools, a network forces them to make their theoretical notions more concrete. For them, participating in networks is also a kind of action research. It gives them practical knowledge. The working relations between university-based staff and school staff in networks is more equal than in traditional research or restructuring projects. Schools and universities can both benefit from this kind of partnership. For us, and by that we mean all network participants, the challenge now is to continue in a less stimulating educational climate.

The paradox of flexibility in sustaining a network

We started the chapter by showing that modern society needs more flexible structures like networks. But the paradox of our network is that now the participants want to continue the network because of the structure we have built together. Giving up the network now implies that you lose the foundations of collegial support that the network gives to its participants. The network, despite its flexibility in arrangements and activities, became a structure in its own. Some other network directors that failed in sustaining their network even blamed us for continuing the network.

Flexibility, balancing top-down and bottom-up, and adjusting to the needs of all participants should keep the network as lively and as fluid as possible. Finding new challenges and new ways of learning and professional and school development should steer the network.

Finding new challenges in daily practice

In the first part of this chapter we described how networking became popular in the Netherlands during the mid-1990s. Networking was an important tool for involving schools in the change processes addressed by the government. In networks, schools could help each other to find their own way while implementing the required changes and to use the growing autonomy that these changes implied. We have shown how our network originates from the political debate about the aims of the restructuring process and how the network developed as an important factor for the schools that where involved during the process of experimentation. During that creative period, schools helped each other with far-reaching changes in structure, methods and learning processes. During the period of official implementation of the new national curriculum for upper secondary education, the central exams, and the intensification of control by the educational inspectorate, the network supported schools in defending their own way of teaching and learning, and in using the space in the official policy for their own benefit. These different periods all demanded different types of activities and network organization.

We now find ourselves in a period where the educational policy for upper secondary education is quite calm and is aiming at consolidation. In the network, the interests of schools are now aimed less at adapting to educational policy and more towards working again on their own concerns and interests; schools are perceiving new challenges in their daily practice. In general, the same questions about teaching and learning and the organization are being raised. However, these questions are no longer the ideals of schools or of educational policy that have to be met, but they tend to be concerns that shape teachers' and students' normal school life and that are articulated in their own discourses.

This change to daily practice brings with it a new energy and new impulses to the network participants; their own concerns are now at stake. As network directors we stimulate the exchange of experience, visit each other's schools and create small thematic groups that cover certain topics. These groups organize their own meetings and together they prepare and execute workshops for the whole network. The themes include active participation by students in schools, the mentoring of younger students by older students, social-constructivist learning, authentic assessment, bridging the gap between technology in school and in a student's personal life, motivating less academically oriented students, working with more intensive blocks, mentoring students, community building in schools, interdisciplinary work, and democratic methods of leadership and quality control.

The themes and the work of thematic groups are now what drives the network, they set the agenda, they structure the formal meetings of the whole network and participants have regular contact about these issues. During each network meeting, one of the themes is focused on and the other groups have the opportunity to put forward issues and questions about these themes. A national conference took place in November 2004. At this conference all these groups held a workshop with members of the network schools and other interested teachers, principals and policy makers.

The network is rejuvenated by using the old network structure, making new adaptations to current needs and addressing the issues that the schools themselves are now concerned with. The trips we made to our colleague networks in Finland and Barcelona gave new impulses, broadened the horizon and contributed to the network feeling. The network is a lively and fluid organization.

Network rules

Finally, we would like to summarize our experiences by formulating a few rules for 'good networkship'. This advice is an expression of the way we have worked over the past 15 years. We believe that these rules have helped turn us into a creative, lively and powerful network.

1. Set the agenda together.

2. Find a balance between the formal and the informal in meetings.
3. Have one or two special topics during each meeting and a lot of space for ongoing points and concerns.
4. Have a calendar of dates for the whole year so participants can plan their work.
5. Plan the content of the year both with structure and with flexibility.
6. Celebrate differences in ideas, experiences and concerns.
7. Make sure that everyone is given the opportunity to voice his or her own ideas and experience.
8. Do not have a newsletter for the members of the network, but communicate as far as possible by email, regular mail and in meetings. A newsletter is too formal for the network itself.
9. The network should enhance each individual's educational practice.
10. Personal professional development and school development have to go together as far as possible.
11. Network participants should communicate a lot with other people in the school. Show them ideas and experiences coming from the network, and bring their questions to the network, and sometimes bring these people themselves.
12. Communicate with the participants in an informal but well-structured manner.
13. Ensure that there is a balance between theory and practice, between inside the network and the outer world, between reality and idealistic ideas.
14. Communicate with the world outside the network by showing the 'good practice' from the schools and the network itself (by publishing books and articles, giving workshops, and participating in public educational debate).
15. Try to develop an educational vision as a network, but within this broad vision there must be opportunity to express different ideas.
16. Try to use the flow of educational change in a period of bottom-up processes for starting a network. Or try to use the fight against top-down processes to create spaces for opposing practices.
17. Be flexible in the organization and activities of the network. Adjust the network to new challenges without becoming an organization for its own sake.

References

Bandura, A. (ed.) (1995) *Self-efficacy in Changing Societies*. Cambridge: Cambridge University Press.

Beck, U. and Beck-Gernsheim, E. (2002) *Individualization*. London: Sage Publications.

Beck, U., Giddens, A. and Lash, S. (1994) *Reflexive Modernization: Politics, Tradition and Aesthetics in the Modern Social Order*. Cambridge: Polity.

Beyer, L.E. (1996) *Creating Democratic Classrooms*. New York: Teachers College Press.

Castells, M. (1996) *The Rise of the Network Society*. Oxford: Blackwell Publishers.

Darling-Hammond, L. (1992) 'Reframing the school reform agenda' *The School Administrator*, November: 22–7.

Datnow, A. and Castellano, M. (2000) 'Teachers' responses to Success for All: How beliefs, experiences, and adaptations shape implementation' *American Educational Research Journal*, 37 (3): 775–99.

Fullan, M. (1991) *The New Meaning of Educational Change*. New York: Teachers College Press.

Giroux, H.A. (1989) *Schooling for Democracy: Critical Pedagogy in the Modern Age*. London: Routledge.

Goodson, I.F. (2003) *Professional Knowledge, Professional Lives*. Buckingham: Open University Press.

Hargreaves, A. (1994) *Changing Teachers, Changing Times*. London: Cassell.

Hargreaves, A. and Fullan, M. (1998) *What's Worth Fighting for Out There*. New York: Teachers College Press.

Hartley, D. (1997) *Re-schooling society*. London: Falmer Press.

Lieberman, A. (ed.) (1995) *The Work of Restructuring Schools*. New York: Teachers College Press.

Lieberman, A. (1996) 'Creating Intentional Learning Communities' *Educational Leadership*, 54 (3), 51–5.

Lieberman, A. and Grolnick, M. (1996) 'Networks and Reform in American Education' *Teachers College Record*, 98 (1): 7–45.

Liston, D.P. and Zeichner, K.M. (1991) *Teacher Education and the Social Conditions of Schooling*. New York: Routledge.

Newmann, F.M. (1993) 'Beyond Common Sense in Educational Restructuring. The Issues of Content and Linkage' *Educational Researcher*, 22 (2): 4–13.

Pennell, J.R. and Firestone, W.A. (1996) 'Changing Classroom Practices through Teacher. Networks: Matching Program Features with Teacher Characteristics and Circumstances' *Teachers College Record*, 98 (1): 41–76.

Sachs, J. (2003) *The Activist Teaching Profession*. Buckingham: Open University Press.

Sikes, P.J. (1992) 'Imposed Changes and the Experienced Teacher' in M. Fullan and A. Hargreaves (eds) *Teacher development and educational change*, pp. 36–55. London: Falmer Press.

Turner, B.S. (1993) *Citizenship and Social Theory*. London: Sage.

Van Gunsteren, H.R. (1992) *Eigentijds Burgerschap (Contemporary Citizenship)*. Gravenhage: SDU.

Veugelers, W. (2000) 'Different Ways of Teaching Values' *Educational Review* 50 (1): 37–46.

Veugelers, W. (2004) 'Between Control and Autonomy. Restructuring Secondary Education in the Netherlands' *Journal of Educational Change*, 5 (2): 141–60.

Veugelers, W. and Oser, F.K. (eds) (2003) *Teaching in Moral and Democratic Education*. Bern/New York: Peter Lang.

Veugelers, W. and Vedder, P. (2003) 'Values in Teaching' *Teachers and Teaching: theory and practice.* 9 (4): 377–89.

Veugelers, W. and Zijlstra, H. (1995a) 'Learning Together: In-service Education in Networks of Schools' *British Journal of In-Service Education*, 21 (1): 37–48.

Veugelers, W. and Zijlstra, H. (eds) (1995b) *Netwerken aan de Bovenbouw van HAVO en VWO* (Networking in Upper Secondary Education). Leuven/Apeldoorn: Garant.

Veugelers, W. and Zijlstra, H. (1996a) 'Networks for Modernizing Secondary Schools' *Educational Leadership*, 54 (3): 76–9.

Veugelers, W. and Zijlstra, H. (eds) (1996b) *Praktijken uit het Studiehuis* (Good Practice from the Study House). Leuven/Apeldoorn: Garant.

Veugelers, W. and Zijlstra, H. (1998a) 'Learning in Networks of Schools and University' *International Journal of Leadership in Education*, 1 (2): 169–80.

Veugelers, W. and Zijlstra, H. (1998b) *Lesgeven in het Studiehuis* (Teaching in the Study House). Leuven/Apeldoorn: Garant.

Veugelers, W. and Zijlstra, H. (2001) *Leren in het Studiehuis* (Learning in the Study House). Leuven/Apeldoorn: Garant.

Veugelers, W. and Zijlstra, H. (2002) 'What Goes on in a Network? Some Dutch experiences' *International Journal of Leadership in Education*, 5 (2): 163–74.

Wenger, E. (1998) *Communities of Practice*. Cambridge: Cambridge University Press.

four

Harnessing action research: the power of network learning

Christopher Day and Mark Hadfield

Contexts clearly matter for teachers' work and for how that work is experienced. One's teaching, and what one believes is possible and desirable in one's teaching all vary according to the context in which the teaching is done.

(McLaughlin and Talbert 1993)

In England schoolteachers and head teachers are faced with a myriad of challenges in coping with the pressures of managing the dynamic and diverse institution which is their school within an imposed, centralized, standards driven change agenda, which has been characterized by increased workloads, intensification, diversification and surveillance. It could be argued that many of the national policies and initiatives over the last 15 years have directly or indirectly, consciously or unconsciously, undermined the traditional autonomy of teachers. Alongside this, morale has declined among many, and recruitment and retention have become key issues for schools. As part of governments' drive to ensure the effective and efficient implementation of new school and classroom focused initiatives, they have been inundated also with demands to attend professional development courses, which focus on the implementation of imposed initiatives, but have little time or energy for reflection on their practice and reflection on the impact that imposed change is making on pupils' motivation, learning and achievement.

The Primary Schools Learning Network

It was in this context that the Primary Schools Learning Network (PSLN) was formed through negotiated partnerships between a group of self-selecting schools, the local education authority (district) and the Centre for Research on Teacher and School Development at the University of Nottingham. Its aim was to give ownership for development back to teachers through sustained collaboration in enquiry based creation and sharing of knowledge about teaching and learning, with a view to improving schools through enhanced efficacy, motivation and commitment of teachers, and, through this, raising pupil achievement.

In English schools, the climate of 'performativity' or 'audit' (Power 1994) is pervasive through the national curriculum: standard attainment tests for all at ages 7, 11 and 14 and examinations at 16, 17 and 18; published league tables of schools' achievements in relation to these; external school inspections with all teaching graded; judgements on the quality of school management and leadership; and annual performance management reviews (which include pupil progress) of all teachers by the schools' senior management. All these have led to an increased bureaucratic burden. Associated also with the performativity context is the introduction by government of a 'contract culture' in which teachers' minimum annual work time has been defined (at 1265 hours). Within a burgeoning managerialist climate in schools, a raft of 'subject leadership' and other management roles have been developed, particularly in primary (elementary) schools; 'threshold' pay allowances have been introduced on a competitive basis; and 'Advanced Skills Teachers' have been established. It is true to say that schools in England are now 'managed' from within and audited from without more intensively than in almost any other country.

The origins of the PSLN project lie in a professional relationship built over time between an advisor from Milton Keynes and two tutors from the University who themselves had established, again over time, a close working relationship. The 'connections' between the three were, significantly, based also upon shared values. We all believed, for example, in the notion of schools as learning communities for all. In relation to this, the need to provide opportunities that would enable teachers, who were already hard pressed in the existing accountability/performativity context, which appears to limit teacher development to those activities that promote the agenda of 'the system', to rediscover the power of choice upon motivation, commitment and new learning challenges alongside others within and without the school.

It has been important, at the beginning of this chapter on the power of network learning, to describe the broader reform context for three reasons: first, because the nature and extent of the imposed changes are unusual in the international context. No other government has populated teachers and schools in its country with so many root and branch ideological reforms over such a sustained period; second, because there are a number of well documented consequences. For example, teacher recruitment and retention problems have grown and teacher morale has declined; and third, because parallel to (though not necessarily associated with) these reforms have been changes in the external environment. In many schools, especially those in cities, lack of parental support, problems of pupil motivation, behaviour and attendance have grown to the extent that there is national recognition of the negative effects not only upon their learning but on the learning of others who share the same classroom. In England, then, schools are now in a position where short-term measurable achievement results appear to have improved. However, this improvement seems unlikely to be sustained as teachers' own motivation, energy and commitment declines.

Some of the local issues in Milton Keynes add to the 'mix' of stressors on schools and individual teachers already cited. Milton Keynes is a new and vibrant town with a mobile school population that has a diverse range of needs. Its uniqueness as a local education authority (LEA) is recognized by Ofsted (the national schools inspection service managed by the Office for Standards in Education, a government body) as having no close statistical neighbours. Some of the key contextual factors that affect the schools are:

- high pupil mobility, 87 per cent of middle and combined schools have levels of mobility higher than the national median figure
- a significant turnover of head teachers (37 per cent of schools) and deputy head teachers (33 per cent of schools) in the last three years
- significant difficulties in the recruitment of teachers, with many teachers leaving after three to five years in teaching
- standards of attainment as demonstrated by end of Key Stage SATs are lower than the national averages
- lack of overall improvement in standards in English and Mathematics since 1999.

High pupil mobility combined with high teacher turnover, which is in some schools combined with change of leadership, has put considerable 'stress' on the school system. This problem was identified by Milton Keynes LEA and by some local primary schools alongside a recognition that many schools and teachers had become dependent on 'outside' intervention to solve their problems. It was felt, therefore, that there was a need to develop the expertise of teachers in reflection and enquiry in order to create new knowledge about teaching and learning, which addressed the needs of schools and pupils in the local context.

Work in all the schools has continued despite a number of setbacks or imposed processes and initiatives. Two schools have experienced Ofsted inspections and two have become partners in the Milton Keynes 'Excellence' Cluster, others have had significant staff turnover. However, despite the issues and difficulties facing them all, schools have remained committed firmly to the project. This in itself is a significant factor as many schools in the past have buckled under these types of pressures and improvement initiatives have ground to a halt.

Growing evidence from research points towards the development of learning networks of schools as a vehicle for addressing issues of professionalism and professional development. Such networks not only create new knowledge within individual schools but also enable teachers to work with others outside their school.

> Knowledge networks will enable staff inside schools to become plugged in to the world of ideas outside their professional contexts, as well as offering them the chance to explore their work with the help of others situated outside their schools. These networks will be highly interactive thereby making them not only instruments for information dissemination but also learning networks. Through interaction people will create new knowledge for themselves which is relevant to their professional situations and needs.
>
> (Southworth 2000: 287)

The PSLN is founded upon ten professional learning and capacity building precepts:

- successful schools are learning communities for adults as well as children
- teachers learn best when they participate actively in decisions about the content, processes and outcomes of their learning
- successful learning requires time for reflection of different kinds, in, on and about action
- learning alone through one's own experience will ultimately limit progress
- successful learning requires collaboration with others from inside and outside the workplace
- teacher learning and development should contribute to school improvement
- school leaders play a significant influencing role in teacher learning and in the development of a school's capacity to improve and cope with change
- at its best, learning will have personal and professional significance for teachers
- supported, sustained learning over time is likely to be more beneficial to the individual and organization than short-term learning

- if schools are to operate effectively in devolved systems, much reliance has to be placed on trust in professional judgement at school level.

These precepts have been drawn from the plethora of research into the professional education and development of teachers. Central to this is the notion that successful schools are learning communities for adults as well as children. There is also a recognized need to build the school's capacity to support teachers' learning and development in order to achieve improvement at the school level. The PSLN works to achieve this by replacing the notion of the individual teacher working in isolation with the utilization of a range of social and intellectual capital available within the school and beyond. Teachers and schools are supported and encouraged to engage in sustained learning experiences to which enquiry is central, where they are able to research their own and other's practices.

The PSLN also builds on the notion of choice, and individual and collective responsibility, by stressing the role of risk taking. Drucker, in writing about teachers as knowledge workers in a knowledge society, points out that as well as talking about 'empowerment' and 'entitlement', we should also talk about 'contribution' and 'responsibility'.

> What we should ask, is not, 'What should you be entitled to?' but, 'What should you be responsible for?' The job of management in a knowledge-based organisation is not to make everybody a boss. The task is to make everybody a contributor.
>
> (Drucker 1994: 99 cited in Day 1999)

How the PSLN operates

The PSLN encourages everybody – teachers, TAs (teaching assistants), school leaders, LEA advisors and university staff – to become contributors to the creation, utilization and dissemination of new knowledge. Collaboration and partnership are key components to the work of the PSLN. The schools and staff involved in the project also have real responsibility in designing the project, carrying out research, evaluating the results and disseminating the findings.

Another essential element is the recognition of the part played by emotion in teaching and learning, and the reliance of trust in the professional judgements and competence at school level. Teachers have found that negative feelings of anxiety, insecurity and distrust are replaced by openness, honesty and the confidence to take risks in order to learn about learning and school improvement.

Lieberman and Grolnick (1997) observed five descriptive organizational themes and tensions present 'woven into the fabric' of 17 networks in America. These themes were:

1   creating purposes and directions
2   building collaborations, consensus and commitment
3   creating activities and relationships as building blocks
4   providing leadership through cross cultural brokering, facilitating and keeping the values visible
5   dealing with the funding problem (p. 196).

Tensions were:

1   negotiating between the purpose of the network and the day-to-day activities that communicate network 'work'
2   dealing with the balance between 'inside' knowledge and 'outside' knowledge
3   creating a structure to resolve contradictions between centralization and decentralization
4   moving from informality and flexibility to more formal and rigid forms as networks grow
5   making decisions about how inclusive or exclusive membership policy should be (p. 203).

Implicit in these themes and tensions is the necessity of active participation based upon principles of choice and diversity, ownership, sustained critical friendships, capacity building, sustained interactivity and mutual trust. For example, each school in PSLN instigated its own 'School Improvement Group' (SIG) formed by any number of teachers and teaching assistants (TA) and led by a SIG coordinator who was any member of staff other than the head teacher. This was to ensure that dispersed or distributed leadership was practised from the outset. Members of the SIG were all volunteers. In some of the smaller schools, the whole staff elected to be part of the SIG. The practices within schools to involve staff who were not in the SIG varied greatly. This was due in part to the size of the school and in part to the culture and ethos within individual schools. The smallest school in the project had six teachers and a small number of TAs all of whom formed the SIG. At the other end of the scale were schools of 25 teachers and a number of TAs. The SIGs were often a small, core group of staff who ran the project and who were responsible for disseminating results. Dissemination strategies included participation in the research by questionnaires or peer observation, staff workshops and INSET and through informal staffroom 'chat'. Some schools were proactive in setting up more 'formal' communication channels by having an internal PSLN newsletter or setting up a PSLN notice board in the staffroom. Many schools involved school governors by giving regular updates on the project. Pupils were directly involved through questionnaires, interviews and, in some cases, through the school council.

At the start of the project, schools were given guidance on the precepts underlying the project and training in developing and carrying out research. Through a process of a school analysis and self-evaluation schools decided on an area for research. This was followed by dialogue with other schools, the LEA and the university. Underlying all the projects was the desire to find out more about teaching and learning styles, how to raise pupil self-esteem, and an excitement in learning. Individual schools selected foci that were particularly relevant to their own context. These included areas of the curriculum such as assessment for learning or developing thinking skills and also the needs of particular groups of pupils. All schools expressed the view that being able to identify their own focus was a major motivator and a strength of the project.

A structure of regular, monthly meetings for SIG coordinators, led by LEA and university staff, was developed and agreed. Alongside this were termly strategy group meetings. This strategy group was representative of head teachers, SIG coordinators, LEA and university staff. Two residential 24-hour 'Milestone' conferences were held each year. These acted as a means of checking, sharing and celebrating the progress of individual projects, and included keynote speakers and training sessions to develop knowledge and skills. At the beginning of the project, SIG coordinators also attended a one-day conference on 'inquiry in action'. The LEA's role was to support schools to develop their projects alongside the national and local initiatives. The university acted in a consultancy role, particularly in leading seminars, providing regular support to individual SIG coordinators and in ensuring there was sustained, focused support for the school-based research process. The LEA and university also had important roles in offering moral support and, through their presence, giving security and legitimacy to participants for experimentation and risk taking. While this structure offered support and help to participants, it left teachers unequivocally responsible for undertaking the enquiries.

The head teachers' roles within the project were key to success. They ensured that staff were given time and opportunities to develop the skills in communication and collaborative working that were essential for working within and across schools. Thus head teachers facilitated leadership of staff by ensuring an emphasis on collaboration, consultation and participation. By encouraging and supporting the leadership development of others, and by engaging in their own learning project, head teachers were, in effect, lead learners of capacity building for school improvement. Through developing collegial approaches to school improvement, schools developed the capacity to continue with initiatives and research projects even when key personnel moved on.

All participants in the project had opportunities to participate in professional development to develop their knowledge, understanding and leadership skills. The first PSLN milestone conference gave schools the opportunity to share their knowledge and gave SIG coordinators the first taste of presenting their work to others. University-led workshops at this event dealt with leading collaborative action inquiry projects, data collection and analysis, interviewing adults and pupils, and analysing pupils' writing. In addition, SIG coordinators continued to meet on a regular basis. Throughout the first two years teachers developed greater confidence in their ability to use their skills and SIG coordinators gained great experience in leading a group of fellow professionals. Other staff, including TAs, were given new opportunities. In one school a TA was trained by the university to identify different learning styles. She became able to work across the school supporting teachers in recognizing the learning styles of their pupils. As individual projects developed, schools entered into joint working. They shared ideas, materials, resources and acted as critical friends. In some schools the early results of their research resulted in a refocusing of their project as their first untested assumptions and hypotheses were challenged by their inquiries into practice. One SIG coordinator described how a teacher's assumptions and beliefs had changed as a result of their work into the effects of marking on pupil self-esteem. Initially, the teacher has been adamant that there was no correlation between the two.

School-to-school networking

In the PSLN there were two equally important levels of cross-school networking: formal and informal networks. The formal, network-wide strategy group and monthly SIG coordinators' meetings relied upon a number of structures and practices that had been put in place. However, the informal networking that took place relied on the development of close working relationships. While the formal networking arrangements brought people together and facilitated the means by which relationships could develop and grow, it was through the development of cultures of trust, honesty and openness, that relationships developed within groups of teachers from across a number of schools.

In order to ensure school-to-school networking a number of structures were put in place. These included regular monthly meetings for SIG coordinators, training events, two 'Milestone' conferences and the production of a PSLN newsletter, which gave schools the opportunity to disseminate their work across the LEA and beyond. The SIG coordinators were an essential part of the school-to-school networking process. Their monthly meetings became a forum for addressing issues arising from the projects, for training and for passing on information about individual projects. They were also a source of mutual peer support. The meetings started with just the SIG coordinator from each school attending, but increasingly they were attended by at least one other member of the SIG. This helped to develop the notion of co-leadership and helped with succession planning. The schools involved in the project came from across the LEA and would not in other circumstances have worked together. As the year progressed relationships formed, particularly where schools had a similar research focus. These individuals maintained contact outside the meetings through telephone calls, emails and occasional visits to each other's schools. The 'Milestone' conferences brought together all partners and staff involved in the projects, and played a key role in developing collective purpose and camaraderie. As well as sharing information about their own projects, the participants were exposed to other work and research going on outside the network.

The relationship between systemic and individual change

Unlike some other networks (Veugelers and Zijlstra 1995), the PSLN was not concerned with interpreting or implementing government policy. On the contrary, our experience had taught us the importance in learning not only of choice but of ownership, active participation in decision making and collaborative interdependence rather than independence in learning. The network learning partnership therefore aimed to:

1   provide synergy of the knowledge which university-, school- and LEA-based educators possess
2   encourage an explicit personal and professional connection among the 50 participants in the participating schools to their own learning by giving value and shape to their ideas through setting up appropriate organizational structures in response
3   promote action research as the central (though not exclusive) mode of inquiry into practice as a means of improvement
4   build broad-based leadership through individual school coordinators, whose roles extend to those of teacher, scholar, proposal writer and facilitator of meetings
5   acknowledge the need for head teacher (principal) support through the formation of a network strategy group on which they and the coordinators sit
6   engage head teachers themselves, as a cohort, in network learning
7   ensure collaboration at all levels among the network members
8   provide opportunities for the regular formal celebration of achievement through 'milestone' meetings of the network twice each year, and dissemination among all schools in the district of any news of work in

progress and plans for further developments through a newsletter and website

9   ensure end products in the form of classroom and school improvements
10 create and support a continuing learning community by building and sustaining trust through mutual knowledge sharing.

In a very real sense, then, the PSLN aimed to provide a sustained learning experience in which choice and individual and collective responsibilities played key roles, and to which practical collaborative inquiry was central. It was based upon a view of teacher professionalism in which teachers are not only recipients of policy change initiated from outside their schools and classrooms but are also themselves *initiators of change*, who have educative purposes that go beyond these policy changes. In other words, teachers have an essentially moral commitment 'to serve the interests of students by reflecting on their well-being and their progress and deciding how best it can be fostered or promoted' (Eraut 1995: 232). The core set of guiding principles is different, also, from those of networks in England that ally their work directly to that of current reform agendas and which claim systemic change as their aim (Hopkins *et al.* 2000). One of the dangers of the growth in 'Network Learning', which involves partnerships between schools, LEAs and universities is that this important means of learning, development and achievement will become associated exclusively with the implementation of centrally-initiated reform. In other words, it will become another means by which teachers are seen as conduits or technicians rather than as activist professionals (Sachs 2001) whose responsibilities encompass a wider, more profound educative change agenda and whose purposes are moral (focusing upon the betterment of the whole person) and not simply instrumental (with the focus upon increasing the expertise of the individual in a limited number of areas of the curriculum designated by the government of the day as being of particular importance).

Much has been written of the importance of combining 'internal' with 'external' pressures for change (Earl and Lee 1998) in order to achieve 'systemic change' (Hopkins 2001). Less research has been conducted into the relationship between 'systemic' (organizationally controlled) and 'individual' (personally empowered) change. It seems to have been assumed that the peer pressure exerted explicitly or implicitly by those directly involved in active participation through what are often called 'School Improvement Groups' or 'Cadres' will somehow move the school further in the desired change direction. This is a key issue, which needs to be addressed if the effectiveness of network learning upon the system in which the work of individuals who are already committed to its success (and thus likely to benefit) is to be evaluated.

Trust, risk and the activist professional

> If schools are to operate effectively in devolved systems ... there needs
> to be a broad community understanding ... that much reliance has to
> be placed on trust in professional judgement at school level.
> (National Schools Project Report 1993: 13)

Over the last 20 years in England, the notion of a teacher as a person whose
purpose is to shape and influence what people become through the exercise
of discretionary judgements has been challenged. Teachers' 'room to
manoeuvre' has been reduced. Continuing external imperatives for change,
adverse media coverage and increasing bureaucratic burdens have been
among the most important negative influences, which have caused many to
question their professional identity, the substantive self which is the principal 'driver' of their motivation and commitment to their work. In her
recent work, Judyth Sachs (2001) suggests the need for a 'revised professional identity (which) requires a new form of professionalism and
engagement' (Sachs 2001: 12). Such a new identity, however, requires
particular conditions which include:

- 'The open flow of ideas ... that enables people to be as fully informed as
  possible.
- Faith in the collective capacity of people to create possibilities for
  resolving problems.
- The use of critical reflection and analysis to evaluate ideas, problems and
  policies.
- Concern for the welfare of others and "the common good".
- Concern for the dignity and rights of individuals and minorities.
- An understanding that democracy is not so much our "ideal" to be
  pursued as an "idealized" set of values that we must have and that must
  guide our life as people.
- The organization of social institutions to promote and extend the
  democratic way of life' (Beane and Apple 1995: 6–7).

In a multidisciplinary review of the theoretical and empirical literature on
trust spanning four decades, Tschannen-Moran and Hoy (2000) highlight
the need to pay attention to trust, particularly in terms of change. They find
that trust is:

- a means of reducing uncertainty in situations of independence
- necessary for effective cooperation and communication
- the foundation for cohesive and productive relationships
- a 'lubricant' greasing the way for efficient operations when people have
  confidence in other people's work and deeds
- a means of reducing the complexities of transactions and exchanges

more quickly and economically than other means of managing organizational life.

Conversely, distrust 'provokes feelings of anxiety and insecurity ... self protection ... minimising (of) vulnerability ... withholding information and ... pretence of even deception to protect their interests' (Tschannen-Moran and Hoy 2000: 550).

While much has been written about the nature of inquiry collaboration; partnership and emotion in teacher and school development and network learning, the conditions necessary for the successful sharing, exchange and respect for others' expertise, the willingness to 'inhabit each others' castles' (Somekh 1994) have received less attention. While working with others involves 'one to induce or suppress feelings, in order to sustain the outward countenance that produces the proper state of mind in others', what Hochschild calls 'emotional labour' (Hochschild 1983: 7), even this is not enough. If the partnership is to be successful, trust is essential.

There is a sense, then, in which successful networks embody the three primary ingredients of democracy: 'i) social trust, ii) norms of reciprocity and iii) networks of civic engagement' (Putnam 1993: 180). Trust, then, is important in network learning because if the network is to achieve success, its members will need to be willing to take risks (i.e. risk vulnerability), rely upon each other to gain in self efficacy (a sense of increased competence), exercise honesty and openness, and be emotionally confident in their relationships with each other so that they can work towards knowledge-based trust. These components of network learning apply equally to relationships between organizations that support network learning and they suggest sustained attention by leaders in the building of collective intra- and inter-organizational trust.

The PSLN, then, is a new social learning framework that connects with those in which all participants spend most of their work time. Because it operates according to the conditions described above, at its best it provides a sustained experience of a democratic institution. Central to all its activities are four pillars:

1 *Enquiry* – in which the 'activist' participants are supported as researchers of their own and others practices.
2 *Collaboration and partnership* – in which there is a reciprocal commitment of all to contribute their diverse but complementary academic, professional and practitioner knowledge to the challenges of learning, change and improvement: the sharing of power.
3 *Emotional investment* – in which the recognition of the part played by emotion in teaching and learning is central to the management of the network.
4 *Trust and risk taking* – in which all those in the network rely on others'

competence and their willingness to take risks within relationships and an atmosphere of mutual trust (Baier 1986, cited in Tschannen-Moran and Hoy 2000).

Capacity building: the facilitators' roles

In order to achieve this, the facilitators of the PSLN network had to do two jobs simultaneously: to build the internal capacity of the schools and to build the capacity of the network as a whole to deal with change, carry out investigations and develop leadership across different levels. These two strands of activities were conceived from the beginning as linked and interdependent. We did not want to adopt a strategy of concentrating on the internal capacity of individual schools and then proceed to use this to help build the network. This was because we felt this approach to network development had two problems.

First, it failed to recognize that primary schools are relatively fragile places in terms of developing and sustaining their internal capacity. This is because they have the potential to be both very dynamic, in that they are able to switch resources quickly to an area and away from it, and volatile, in that they can lose and gain capacity quickly. For example, the loss of a single teacher can have a dramatic impact on levels of internal capacity. Similarly, an Ofsted inspection can have a dramatic impact on any school's improvement activities. For smaller schools it can represent an administrative and leadership burden which virtually halts all other developments. If we had tried to work 'out' from school we could have been faced with many schools never actually getting involved in network activities as they struggled to deal with issues outside their school. The project then would have fallen into the trap of the network facilitators, essentially supporting schools 'to get involved', being drawn into the organizational and personal issues which would have prevented them from being an active learning node within a network. The second reason for adopting a strategy of working to build the capacity of both schools and the network simultaneously was that we needed to create more external capacity for schools to draw on than we as network facilitators could provide. Very quickly we had to reach a point where the network itself became a source of external capacity for schools to draw on, rather than being a drain on their internal resources. Even schools that had overall low levels of organizational capacity had individuals who themselves were able to act as support for other schools, who would help out as critical friends and provide access to other professional networks.

How then did we go about building capacity? First, we developed the capacity model of Mitchell and Sackney (2000), which stops at the boundaries of the school, and therefore makes a distinction between internal and external capacity and which does not apply to a network. Conceptually we needed to break away from thinking of capacity being bounded by the limits of schools and to reconceptualize the relationships between different levels of capacity – personal, interpersonal and organizational – so that they fitted better within the notion of a network of schools.

Our starting point was the initial recruitment of head teachers and coordinators of the School Improvement Groups (SIGs). Here it was important for us to establish effective network norms and forms of shared leadership that we wished to see develop across the whole network and individual schools. In terms of key norms, probably the most important was that the network would run at a pace and on foci determined by the schools themselves. In a context of so many externally imposed changes this was a difficult process. No matter how much we discussed the principles that underpinned our work, it generally ended up with us having to define and reinforce the ethos underpinning the network. No, the network was not limited by any local authority concerns or by central government policies. No, the facilitators would not decide what the focus of the network would be (although we stressed that it would be easier and possibly more effective if schools could choose areas that were linked). No, there was no set dates by which their school-based inquires would have to be completed or changes made. We began to ask ourselves whether the difficulties we were experiencing were evidence of what has been glibly described as a 'culture of dependency' among head teachers and schools in the UK.

The appointment of the SIG coordinators was the first visible sign of our commitment to shared leadership. Their role was to provide the initial leadership to the SIGs inside their own school. The head teachers were 'advised' not to be members of these SIGs. Rather, their role was to create the structural arrangements within the school to enable the SIGs to operate and the coordinator to lead. This was also the first point at which the issue of trust became explicit as the head teachers were being asked to trust the coordinators to develop the school-based inquiries. We in our turn had to trust them to allow this to happen.

The group of SIG coordinators that we brought together became the focus of our initial work on building capacity at the interpersonal level, as they spanned the whole network and were the key to involving every school. The coordinators needed to be built into a team and, in their turn, create teams within each school. We set about developing an affective climate within this group marked by openness and reflection upon the task at hand. They all had to cope with the varied leadership styles of their head teachers, and their school cultures differed considerably, as did the contexts they worked in and the issues their schools faced. Dealing with these differences in context and needs required us to hold a series of open discussions both within the coordinators' group and subsequently within schools. Running in parallel with these discussions, we set about modelling different approaches to team building, provided examples of how to structure their SIGs, brought in fellow teachers who had run similar groups in other schools and provided expert inputs on managing change, dealing with difficult colleagues and running small-scale research projects.

The SIG coordinators provided the focus for capacity building efforts at the interpersonal level within the network. They, in turn, were charged with developing this level of capacity in their schools. Their efforts, though, would still be dependent upon their head teachers providing sufficient time and resources for this to happen. Our approach to ensuring this would happen was to work directly with the head teachers as a group and to generate discussion among them about what had worked and what had not in terms of supporting their SIGs and coordinators. We also pushed for them to put the network at the centre of their school development plans, so that its work was not seen as tangential or peripheral to their school improvement work. As network facilitators we also set out to try and create additional resources for these coordinators by helping them apply for external funding, which they would personally control.

The SIG coordinators also provided leadership at the network level. They determined the content of the events at which we brought together all the SIG members, and were the first individuals to present at these events as the network moved away from relying on the facilitators or external experts. They also were the group that started to develop the physical networking between schools as they visited each other's classrooms and went out on study visits to other schools and networks.

At the individual level of capacity, we initially concentrated upon teachers producing their own knowledge and reflecting on practice by launching inquires within each school. A series of workshops were provided to all members of the SIGs on different aspects of school-based research and these were further supported by facilitators who not only offered advice but also practical support in the design of tools and the analysis of data. The coordinators also played a key role in this as they took a lead in trying out new ideas within their classrooms and mentoring others in the SIG.

The task facing facilitators at this stage increasingly was to hand over the task of strategically planning for capacity building to the members of the network. This process had already started within the Network Strategy Group, involving the external facilitators, head teachers and local authority representatives and was further developed by the appointment of a network facilitator from within the network itself. At this point, the network moved into a new phase of development as it generated sufficient capacity to manage its own development.

Renewal, reform and the roles of universities

PSLN is emerging as an example of school and individual teacher renewal, rather than reform:

> Renewal is self-initiated, involves learning from experience, and is a higher-order educational endeavour of replacing or adding to behaviour or circumstances that the individual or collections of individuals perceives as inadequate and less than satisfying. It rarely is self renewal because renewing organisms and ecosystems tend to seek out relevant support from others. Responsibility, in contrast to accountability, is built in, not imposed. There are lessons learned and lessons to pass on to others challenged by the prospects of renewal.
>
> (Goodlad 1999: xviii)

Writing from his own experience of school–university partnerships, Osguthorpe (1999) suggests a model for individual and organizational renewal, premised upon sustained collaborative reflection as a prerequisite for success, which is mirrored in the PSLN experience.

Wagner (1997) analysed three different forms of direct cooperation, which are manifested in exchanges, transactions and agreements negotiated directly between individual educational researchers and schoolteachers or administrators: data extraction agreements, clinical partnerships and co-learning agreements. Each of these reflects different conceptions of the researchers' and practitioners' roles. In data extraction, the two are bifurcated, with the researcher holding the technical expertise. In clinical partnerships, there is an understanding that practitioners and researchers can add to knowledge about educational practice by working together, so the two roles are established through negotiation, and boundaries are blurred. However, the practitioner remains an object of inquiry (Wagner 1997: 16). In terms of capacity building and change, it is this last form of cooperation which is most likely to lead to lasting change – provided that it takes place over time through 'sustained interactivity' (Huberman 1995).

This form of cooperation in network learning involves the academy in researcher-consultancy roles in which its traditional role as creator and transmitter of generalizable knowledge is extended to that of 'enhancing the knowledge creation capacities of individuals and professional communities' (Eraut 1994: 57).

While there appears to be an a priori 'open and shut' case for this, there are both difficulties and tensions in trying to join two cultures whose life-worlds are essentially different in terms of tempo, focus, reward and power (Stevens 1999: 292); and whose competences to 'cross borders, cultures and dialects, the learning and translation of multiple languages (the political, the everyday, the academic) and the courage to transgress when faced with social injustices' (Walker 1996) cannot be guaranteed.

The disenabling effect of the two task cultures of school and university upon their ability to form long-term relationships should not be underestimated. To achieve success requires not only a different mind set but also:

1   equitable relationships between researcher and 'researched'
2   the possession of human relating, negotiation and technical skills and an ability to engage in collaboration which is not always comfortable, to work together sometimes under stressful and distressful conditions
3   an understanding of change processes
4   a willingness to reflect upon own and other's values and to acknowledge difference
5   a willingness to serve teachers' agendas before those of the academy
6   a belief that authentic settings are best researched by those practitioners experiencing them direct, but that outsider perspectives and knowledge may enrich understandings
7   an acknowledgement that those most affected by new understandings have the primary responsibility for deciding upon courses of action which seem to them most likely to lead to improvement – the difference between system control and individual empowerment.

The PSLN combines the opportunities for self direction by schools with sustained, planned and responsive external intervention from universities in particular phases. The specific and temporary intervention roles make use of the special professional research, content knowledge and skills held by those in the academy. While many networks exist, it is as yet rare to come across those which are self-sustaining.

Conclusion

Successful models of learning networks between universities, school districts, schools and others must assert connections between thinking, learning, planning and practice through *self-generated*, supported reflective work at a number of levels, work that is perceived as relevant, is appropriate to individuals' developmental needs, as well as those of the organization, and which is shared and enhanced through appropriate intervention which challenges and supports. Researcher-developers from higher education have a key role to play here in building individual and collective capacity as do collaborative school cultures, which build and develop strategies for challenge and support within the notion of teachers as activist professionals. Both recognize the need for teachers, within clearly defined frameworks of external accountability, to retain also a high degree of control over the direction of their work and the confidentiality surrounding their contributions, while at the same time having access to appropriate critical support.

There remains in the minds of politicians and teachers a perceived theory-practice, theoretician-practitioner problem: a separateness between those who work in schools and those who work in higher education, between those who are said to practise and those who are said to theorize. This exists partly because of history and partly because of function – after all, few schoolteachers have time built into their work, which allows them to reflect, theorize, research and write. It also exists within higher education, we suspect partly out of habit. Teachers who become teacher educators have for years wrapped around themselves the cloak of busy practicality, which has served to comfort and insulate them against change. The separation thus exists because many have implicitly encouraged or colluded in this. There is a consciously calculated protective 'mystique' surrounding 'theory' and 'research'. How, then, are these two groups of relative and alienated strangers going to connect? Certainly there will need to be a change in attitude and relationships. Legislative changes in the UK, the Netherlands, Sweden and elsewhere in Europe, Australia and North America have provided opportunities for new relationships to be formed between higher education, schools and other. Our own view is that there will always be a creative tension in the alliance between teachers, administrators and academics who are committed to developing partnership roles across schools and higher education. Thus, notions of emancipation and empowerment of teachers (Stenhouse 1979), the recognition of a need to develop a new language for communication between teachers and academics (Nias 1991), and the establishment of self-critical, self-reflecting communities (Handal 1991), while attractive, depend for their fulfilment upon the willingness, social skills and abilities of participants to create and negotiate contracts, either collectively or individually, which are based on forms of critical friendship and the exercise of trust.

In network learning the work does not belong to any one individual or interest group. The voices of all are listened to and heeded. Teachers and significant others are actively involved in negotiating processes and outcomes; and the power relationships of co-optation rather than collaboration are avoided (Erickson and Christman 1996: 150). The key role of the academy is to promote and sustain an environment that provides challenge and support through research and which is embedded in development. Teacher educators are, in a sense, interventionists who aim to seek questions, which are perceived by the teachers as relevant to their needs, to investigate answers to these questions collaboratively and to place the onus for action on the teachers themselves.

The creation of networked learning communities of the kind described in this chapter takes time and is not always easy. There will always be individuals and groups whose individual or collective vested self-interest may not be served by this. In the process, new knowledge and skills will need to be developed and tentative steps to change supported. This will not always be easy and it may make new demands on busy professionals. But it is within this shared landscape that the future investment of schools and universities in their own lifelong development can be seen as making sense and being fit for purpose. It is within this landscape that universities can play their part in the challenge of supporting the lifelong learning of teachers and, through this, the raising of standards in schools.

References

Beane, J. and Apple, M. (1995) 'The Case for Democratic Schools' in M. Apple and J. Beane *Democratic Schools*. VA, ASCD.

Day, C. (1999) *Developing Teachers: The Challenges of Lifelong Learning*. London: Falmer Press.

Drucker (1994) cited in Day, C. (1999) *Developing Teachers: The Challenges of Lifelong Learning*. London: Falmer Press.

Earl, L. and Lee, L. (1998) *Evaluation of the Manitoba School Improvement Programme*. Winnipeg: Manitoba School Improvement Programme.

Eraut, M. (1994) 'Developing Professional Knowledge within a Client-centred Orientation' in T.R. Guskey and M. Huberman (eds) (1995) *Professional Development in Education: New Paradigms and Practices*. Columbia University: Teachers College Press.

Eraut, M. (1995) *Developing Professional Knowledge and Competence*. London: The Falmer Press.

Erickson, F. and Christman, J.B. (1996) 'Taking stock/making change: stories of collaboration in local school reform' *Theory in Practice*, 35: 149–57.

Goodlad, J.I. (1999) 'Introduction' in W.F. Smith and G.D. Fenstermacher (eds) *Leadership for Educational Renewal*. San Francisco: Jossey-Bass.

Handal, G. (1991) 'Promoting the articulation of tacit knowledge through the counselling of practitioners' in H.K. Letiche, J.C. van der Wolf and F.X. Plooij (eds) *The Practitioner's Power of Choice in Staff Development and In-service Training*. Amsterdam/Lisse: Swetz & Zeitlinger.

Hochschild, A. (1983) *The Managed Heart*. Berkeley: University of California Press.

Hopkins, D. (2001) *School Improvement for Real*. London: Routledge Falmer.

Hopkins, D., Harris, A., Singleton, C. and Watts, R. (2000) *Creating the Conditions for Teaching and Learning*. London: David Fulton Publishers.

Huberman, M. (1995) 'Networks that alter teaching: conceptualisations, exchanges and experiments' *Teachers and Teaching: Theory and Practice* (2): 193–212.

Lieberman, A. and Grolnick, M. (1997) 'Networks, Reform and the Professional Development of Teachers' in A. Hargreaves (ed.) *Rethinking Educational Change*

With Heart and Mind. Association for Supervision and Curriculum Development, Alexandria, VA.

McLaughlin, M. and Talbert, J. (1993) *Contexts That Matter for Teaching and Learning*, Stanford: Center for Research on the Context of Secondary School Teaching, Stanford University.

Mitchell, C. and Sackney, L. (2000) *Profound Improvement: Building Capacity for a Learning Community.* Lisse: Swets & Zeitlinger.

National Schools Project Report of the National External Review Panel (1993) in J. Sachs (1997) 'Reclaiming Teacher Professionalism: An Australian Perspective'. Paper presented at the 6th Norwegian National Conference on Educational Research, University of Oslo, May 1997.

Nias, J. (1991) 'How practitioners are silenced, how practitioners are empowered' in H.K. Letiche, J.C. van der Wolf and F.X. Plooij (eds) *The Practitioner's Power of Choice in Staff Development and In-service Training.* Amsterdam/Lisse: Swetz & Zeitlinger.

Osguthorpe, R. (1999) 'The Role of Collaborative Reflection in Developing a Culture of Inquiry in a School-University Partnership: A US Perspective'. Paper presented at the annual meeting of the American Educational Research Association, Montreal, Quebec, 20 April 1999.

Power, M. (1994) *The Audit Explosion.* London: Demos.

Putnam, R.D. (1993) *Making Democracy Work: Civic Traditions in Modern Italy.* Princeton, NJ: Princeton University Press.

Sachs, J. (2001) *Learning to be a teacher: Teacher Education and the Development of Professional Identity.* Keynote address, ISATT Conference, Faro, Portugal, 21–25 September 2001.

Somekh, B. (1994) 'Inhabiting Each Other's Castles: towards knowledge and mutual growth through collaboration' *Educational Action Research*, 2 (3): 357–81.

Southworth, G. (2000) 'How Primary Schools Learn' *Research Papers in Education*, 15 (3): 275–91.

Stenhouse, L.A. (1979) 'Research as a basis for teaching' in L.A. Stenhouse (1983) *Authority, Education and Emancipation.* London: Heinemann Educational Books.

Stevens, D.D. (1999) 'The ideal, real and surreal in school-university partnerships; reflections of a boundary spanner' *Teaching and Teacher Education*, 15: 287–99.

Tschannen-Moran, M. and Hoy, W.K. (2000) 'A Multidisciplinary Analysis of the Nature, Meaning, and Measurement of Trust' *Review of Educational Research*, Winter 2000, 70 (4): 547–93.

Veugelers, W. and Zijlstra, H. (1995) 'Learning Together: in-service education in networks of schools' *British Journal of In-Service Education*, 21 (1): 37–48.

Wagner, J. (1997) 'The Unavoidable Intervention of Educational Research: A Framework for Reconsidering Researcher-Practitioner Co-operation' *Educational Researcher*, 26 (37): 13–22.

Walker, M. (1996) ' "Subaltern" professionals: acting in pursuit of social justice' *Educational Action Research*, 4: 407–25.

five

Networking for professional learning communities: school–university–community partnerships enhance student achievement

Mary John O'Hair, Ulrich C. Reitzug, Jean M. Cate, Randy Averso, Linda Atkinson, Dennis Gentry, Gregg Garn and Gaetane Jean-Marie

Teachers, more than anyone, are expected to build learning communities, create the knowledge society and develop the capacities for innovation, flexibility and commitment to change that are essential to economic prosperity. At the same time, teachers are also expected to mitigate and counteract many of the immense problems that knowledge societies create, such as excessive consumerism, loss of community and widening gaps between rich and poor. Somehow, teachers must try to achieve these seemingly contradictory goals simultaneously. This is their professional paradox.

(Hargreaves 2003: 1)

We believe the best way to address the 'professional paradox' is through networking partnerships designed to support and strengthen participants' individual and collective efforts to improve learning while addressing problems created through knowledge societies. The K20 Center for Educational and Community Renewal at the University of Oklahoma is one such effort. The K20 Center is a consortium of school–university–community partnerships committed to improving student learning from kindergarten through graduate education (K20) through the development of professional learning communities. These professional learning communities share a common focus based on the promotion of democratic principles including inquiry, discourse, equity, authenticity, leadership and service (IDEALS), and are grounded in research-based instructional and organizational practices, essentially a constructivist and democratic approach that leads to increased student achievement (O'Hair *et al.* 2000). All work at the K20 Center is based around the IDEALS framework:

I. INQUIRY is the critical study of our practice by gathering and considering data, new knowledge and others' perspectives. The primary purpose of inquiry is the improvement of our individual practice and our school's practice.

D. DISCOURSE refers to conversations, discussions and debates focused on teaching and learning issues. Discourse nurtures professional growth, builds relationships, results in more informed practice and improves student achievement.

E. EQUITY refers to seeking fair and just practices both within the school and outside the school.

A. AUTHENTICITY refers to authentic learning that is genuine and connected rather than fake and fragmented. Teachers who practise authenticity help students connect learning to life.

L. LEADERSHIP (SHARED) in schools is the development of shared understandings that lead to a common focus and improve the school experience for all members of the school community.

S. SERVICE refers to the belief that making a difference in the lives of children and families requires serving the needs of the community as well as the school (O'Hair *et al.* 2000).

The K20 Center for Educational and Community Renewal began in 1995 as a small network of schools with the support of the Annenberg Institute for School Reform; League of Professional Schools (described in Chapter 2); Danforth Foundation; and the University of Oklahoma. Over the years, the K20 Center has maintained its common focus and brought Oklahoma stakeholders together to share ideas, observe best practices, identify and analyse problems, and develop strategies for the improvement of teaching, learning and community life. The stakeholders involved were students, parents, teachers, administrators, school board and community members, business and government leaders, and university faculty and students. Against this background, the chapter will highlight these practices and problems, including continuing issues raised by the K20 Center's critical friends.

Professional learning communities: practices

The K20 Center seeks to improve student achievement by developing, implementing and sustaining ten practices of high achieving schools. A description and example of each practice follows.

Practice 1: shared value system

Schools functioning as professional learning communities develop shared values about students, learning and schooling, which lead to a collaboratively developed set of core learning principles that guide the curriculum, instruction and instructionally related operations of the school (Glickman 1993; Bernhardt 2002). For example, a school might embrace learning principles which hold that students learn best when they

1   are required to personally construct knowledge about the topics being addressed
2   engage in disciplined inquiry to gather more information and data about the topic
3   work on tasks that have some value beyond the lesson and the assignment (Newmann and Associates 1996).

A teacher from a partner elementary school describes the process of developing shared values as follows:

> We invited educators, parents, students and business partners to join with us in discussing what we believed about teaching and learning. Our PTA meetings were focused on meaningful learning and we looked for themes and commonalities from the parent responses. We did this as a group, discussing and sharing as we looked through the information. From our work together we were able to construct a shared vision and common learning principles for our school. The vision and common learning principles would give us directions and purpose as we faced difficult decisions, hired new staff members and chose new textbooks.

This school's core learning principles include: academic excellence; a safe and comfortable environment; nurturing the needs of all learners; achievement through varied learning strategies; tolerance and respect by all and for all; celebrating diversity; providing success for all learners; and connecting learning to real life experiences (Cate *et al.* 2002).

Practice 2: authentic teaching, learning and assessment

Rather than teaching in a didactic manner that focuses primarily on the memorization of factual information, authentic teaching requires that teachers design and facilitate learning experiences that:

- engage students in the personal construction of new knowledge
- result in their conducting a disciplined inquiry about the topic at hand
- have value beyond the school (Newmann and Wehlage 1995; see also Sizer 1992; Wood 1992, 1999; Newmann and Associates 1996; Darling-Hammond 1997).

Researchers found that when teachers taught authentically, their students consistently outperformed those taught in more conventional ways (Newmann and Wehlage 1995). When teaching is focused on the development of understanding and meaning, and on connecting lessons to students' interests and experiences, rather than on memorization, students did better on assessments of advanced skills as well as on standardized tests. These findings suggest that students who think carefully about subjects, study them in-depth and connect them to their personal experiences are also more likely to remember the facts and definitions called for on standardized tests (O'Hair *et al.* 2000). A principal in a partner school describes how the curriculum is being restructured as follows:

> Emphasizing hands-on learning, teachers have given students opportunities to examine concepts and problems directly and provide their own interpretations and solutions, rather than just listening to or reading about ideas. Taking an integrated, thematic approach to the major ideas in curriculum, we got a jump start at summer institute, where many hours were spent mapping our curriculum and finding those areas where connections could easily be made. We have placed a renewed emphasis on writing, believing, as Stephen King says, that 'Writing is thinking through the end of a pen.' We have increased our proficiency at authentic assessments with varied strategies. Teachers have successfully used student-led conferences and have developed rubrics to assess a wide variety of projects and products. We keep a writing portfolio for every student, with specified writing samples required for each grade.

Practice 3: shared leadership

The K20 Center focuses on creating broadly distributed leadership by developing a culture of collegiality and, in doing so, reducing hierarchical decision-making practices. Hierarchical decision-making practices close down the conversation about the school's beliefs, values, learning principles and purpose, and the multiple ways in which these can be put into practice. Shared decision making permits the articulation and exploration, via inquiry and discourse, of the diverse perspectives of the school community's stakeholders. It permits members of the learning community to decide collectively which decisions are consistent with the school's purpose, core values and learning principles, and how best to promote these purposes, values and principles. Allen *et al.* (1999) encourage schools to design shared leadership documents (i.e. decision-making charters) to formalize shared decision making and governance in their schools. As a result, leadership 'acts' stem from constructivist forms of leadership and can come from anyone, anytime and anywhere in the school community (Lambert 1995: 50). An example of shared leadership is provided in the writing of a principal in a partner school:

> This final activity in the school year gave me the opportunity for sharing my idea of implementing a 'Shared Leadership Team' for the next school year. [My belief is that] 'Participation becomes a true value only when we believe that participation produces a collective wisdom that surpasses an individual's knowledge of an issue' (Patterson 1993). In order to establish that collective wisdom, each grade level would elect a representative to serve on a team. There were also representatives elected from special services, special team (PE, Music, Media) and support staff. This would create a team of eleven members with each representative responsible for gathering input and reporting back to four to six people. 'Leaders acknowledge that different types of expertise exist at different levels of the school' (National Association of Elementary School Principals 2001). The staff warmly accepted this proposal. The 'Shared Leadership Team' members were elected at the first staff meeting of the [following] school year. It was decided that parent representatives would also be asked to serve on our 'Shared Leadership Team'. The first staff meeting of the school year afforded us the opportunity to brainstorm and share our values and beliefs regarding this question: What are the curriculum, instruction, assessment and environment factors that support effective learning for all students? Due to time constraints, I compiled the answers to this question and created an online survey using SurveySuite to administer to the staff. The staff receives their regular staff announcements on the principal's staff web page. They check their email daily and when the web page has been updated, they receive an email with the link. When the survey was ready for the staff in late August, there was a link on the principal's staff web page for the teachers to complete the survey. Within 24 hours, 90 percent of the staff had responded to the survey. Within 48 hours, all staff members had responded. I assessed the

results via the SurveySuite website (http://intercom.virginia.edu/cgi~bin/cgiwrap/intercom/SurveySuite/ss_wizard.pl). Results were available immediately and progress could be checked at any time after posting the survey. The staff has responded to numerous online surveys in my one and a half years as principal and we all agree that they are efficient and effective ways for gaining input from all staff. Although we are only into the second full month of school, our Shared Leadership Team is meeting twice a month to discuss issues of importance to the whole school.

Practice 4: small, personalized schools

Over the past few decades, large schools have become a way of life across the United States and the number continues to increase. Wasley (2002) found that large schools lessen the educational quality for disadvantaged students and indicates that small schools and small classes increase the success for students. Allen (2002) describes successful strategies for establishing smaller, more personalized connections for students within the context of a large high school by establishing 'home bases' for a small group of 15 students, developing project-based learning strategies, communicating the vision of treating each child with nurturing and caring, developing small academies for special interest curricula within the school, and renovating the school creating clusters for these academies.

'Smallness is a prerequisite for the climate and culture that we need to develop the habits of heart and mind essential to a democracy,' states Deborah Meier (1996) founder of Central Park East Secondary School in East Harlem. She cites the following seven reasons for small schools:

1   governance through a small involved group
2   respect based on knowing each other
3   simplicity of organizational structures
4   safety with reduced anonymity
5   parental involvement through personal relationships with parents
6   accountability through creating a responsible community
7   a sense of belonging for students resulting from interactions with adults with whom they have a relationship.

A K20 Center partner high school has visited schools across the country and shared their findings on how schools create a sense of community. These findings include: developing authentic assessments and service learning projects; providing adult advocates and student voice opportunities; restructuring into advisories, houses or academies and being flexible; providing academic support and ways to keep students on campus; and establishing professional development time.

Practice 5: teacher collaboration

When teachers have the opportunity to engage in regular professional discussion with their peers and receive honest but supportive feedback, not only does their own practice benefit, but student achievement also improves (Cushman 1998). Conversations, discussions and debates focused on teaching and learning issues nurture professional growth, build relationships and result in more informed practice and improved student achievement. Printy (2004) identified communities of practice (Wenger 1998: 23) as 'critical to the ability of a faculty to capitalize on members' knowledge, and to improve, adapt, their instructional practices'. Working together towards a shared vision for student learning, teachers discuss with colleagues difficult questions such as: How can we talk about and share our practices? How can we engage in critical study of our practice? How much do we trust each other? Is our teaching authentic? How do we know what students know? How do our practices match our beliefs about teaching and learning?

Change theorist Michael Fullan (1995) believes that 'in order for students to be learning, teachers must be learning'. Job-embedded staff development activities, such as book studies, peer coaching and studying student work focus teacher learning on student learning. Communicating via email, coaching each other in technology and developing an authentic technology-rich curriculum, are ways that teachers can use technology to learn together. A K20 Center partner school describes their plans for ongoing collaboration that includes parents and teachers:

> PTA meetings focus on our site goals. The monthly parent and community newsletter contains articles related to site goals and our progress in attaining them. Classroom visits are made by the principal to observe examples of how site goals are connected to daily teaching and learning. Our faculty meetings, grade-level team meetings and vertical team meetings focus on sharing effective lesson plans, best practices and how to address problems and issues we face. Faculty meetings are hosted by teachers who open their rooms and share personal successes and struggles. We strive to collectively accept responsibility for all students learning in our school.

Practice 6: inquiry and discourse

Inquiry is the study of our practice by considering relevant perspectives, data and knowledge. It refers to the way we reflect on, gather information and analyse the effectiveness of what we are doing in our classrooms and our schools. Inquiry and discourse involves educators coming together and questioning and discussing factors related to student learning, and the relationship of school policies and practices to learning. Decisions about instructional practices are not based upon how well teachers 'like it' or 'don't like it' but upon how instructional practices affect student learning. Teachers working collaboratively to analyse student data and seeking out the best teaching and learning practices are the fundamental work of inquiry and discourse.

In addition to standardized test scores and other forms of statistical data, student, teacher, administrator and parent perspectives are forms of data to be discussed and analysed. Key questions associated with inquiry and discourse are the following:

- What do we want our students to learn?
- How will we know whether they are learning what we want them to learn?
- What can we do when students are not learning?
- Are we getting the results we want in student achievement? If not, why not? What will we do about it?
- On what basis are we doing what we are doing? What evidence or support do we have to justify our practices? How do we know whether what we are doing is effective?
- What information, data, knowledge and perspectives can we gather to assist us in studying our practice?
- How does what we are doing fit with our values and beliefs as a school?
- How does what we are doing serve the needs of the diverse individuals and groups who make up our community? Whose interests do our practices serve? Whose interests do they not serve? (Sirotnik 1989; O'Hair *et al.* 2000; Eaker and DuFour 2002).

Without engaging in inquiry we have no basis for determining whether what we are doing works and how it fits with what we believe in (O'Hair and Reitzug 1997). Inquiry should guide classroom and school-wide practice and decision making. It should inform instructional practices as well as the development of school policies, curriculum and programmes (O'Hair *et al.* 2000). The professional discourse associated with inquiry helps teachers to examine and modify their beliefs about student learning and enables them to make changes in their instructional practices.

A partner school provides an example of inquiry:

> Over the course of the school year, teachers worked collaboratively to focus on reading skills development, student by student. This was achieved by scheduling time for teachers to analyse data collected from the computer lab (*Success Maker* and *Waterford Early Reading* software), various assessments (Yopp-Singer/phonemic awareness, *Lightspan Achieve Now* placement tests, Gates-MacGinite Reading Test,

the Reading Renaissance *Star Reading* assessment), classroom work products and numerous assessments given to individual students who demonstrated the need for more information. The data collected was reviewed collectively by the classroom teacher, the administrator, Title I Reading Specialists, parents and, when necessary, special education personnel. Interventions designed and implemented included after-school tutoring, additional access to technology-based curricula, Family Literacy participation, take-home literature and instructional strategies.

Practice 7: supportive leaders

Superintendent and principal involvement in a school's or district's efforts to become a professional learning community can range from being actively resistant to actively supportive of democratic efforts. Resistant leaders can deliberately place obstacles in the way of teachers attempting to become more democratic (for example, withholding financial or material support; refusing to engage in certain practices, such as shared decision making). Actively supportive superintendents/principals publicly and privately communicate support for democratic efforts, personally participate in such efforts, and provide time for discussing the school's movement towards professional learning communities (Reitzug and O'Hair 2002).

Nearly one-third of newly qualified teachers leave the field within five years (Starr, 2002). A study of teacher supply and demand in North Carolina found that almost two-thirds of teachers who quit teaching said that a lack of administrative support was a determining factor. A similar survey of teachers in the Cleveland area found that those teachers who reported receiving little support from their principals were almost three times as likely to say that they were considering leaving teaching as those who said they did receive such support (Starr, 2002). Kouzes and Posner (1999, 2003) emphasize the importance of encouraging the hearts of the school community by recommending seven essentials to developing supportive relationships. These essentials include:

1   setting clear standards
2   expecting the best
3   paying attention
4   personalizing recognition
5   storytelling
6   celebrating together
7   setting the example.

Goffee and Jones (2000) ask the question, 'Why should anyone be led by you?' They note that those who lead should inspire and support by managing with tough empathy (caring intensely about employees and about the work they do). A partner school principal describes what he believes about supportive leadership:

> Good professional and personal relationships exist, but we cannot overlook the trust and mutual respect for the talents and competencies each person brings to the process. Without this foundation built on the establishment of a complete relationship between individuals through the development of shared commitment to ideas, issues, goals and management processes, school-based shared decision making will be positioned for failure or, at the very best, ill-prepared to meet the demands of the future.

Practice 8: community connections

Professional learning communities are connected to their parents and community through various ways. The broader community impacts who and what the children and school are and can be. On one level, schools should involve families and communities in the work of the school, developing means for parent input and guidance, and educating students in civic participation. On a second level, the school should involve itself in the work of the family and community, seeking connections and healthy environments for children within the community (O'Hair *et al.* 2000). In addition, schools and teachers should attempt to create more family-like schools (Epstein 1995), viewing families and communities as partners in the educational process and having common and shared interests and goals in educating their children. The obligation of schools goes beyond just school–home communication, but extends to developing connections through which families and communities can collaborate throughout the educational process. A partner school shares an example of how they work with students and parents:

> We have recently rewritten our Mission Statement. Our students have written a new pledge that is displayed through PowerPoint and recited by students. Our Student Council is meeting with the leadership team to discuss school concerns. The PTA is focused on parental growth and is seeking to understand and share our vision with the larger community.

Practice 9: concern for equity

Equity refers to seeking fair and just practices both within the school and outside the school. Equity results in asking and acting upon questions such as: How do our practices meet the needs of individual students? Do our practices work for all students, or for only some students? Do the practices serve to keep students under control, or do they enhance intellectual growth? Is there a difference?

Professional learning communities have a positive effect on the success of all students. Not only is overall student achievement higher in professional learning communities, but achievement gains are also distributed more equitably. That is, the achievement gap between students of lower socio-economic status (SES) and students of higher SES is narrower in professional learning communities (Lee and Smith 1994).

An example provided by a principal in a partner school describes how the school plans to use technology in the process of addressing equity concerns:

> Technology enables us to organize and view graphically a large amount of data. Through inquiry and discourse, these data can inform our practice and help us to gain new insights. The Internet has many resources that include research-based solutions that we can employ to address inequities in the educational system.

Practice 10: access to external expertise

Teachers and other members cannot presume that all worthwhile knowledge can be developed within the school itself. Fullan (1993) makes note that the isolation of a teacher within the classroom limits insights to the experiences of that individual. Similarly, this isolation can happen at the school level. In schools that are professional learning communities, teachers and others are regularly exposed to ideas and knowledge from sources external to the school. These schools are constantly participating in individual or collective staff development issues (O'Hair *et al.* 2000). Research is reviewed, critical friends are invited to observe and the community is invited to provide feedback. Inviting critical friends to review practices within the school can shed light on 'hidden curriculum and practices'. Ideas and knowledge brought in from external sources are not simply 'adopted' and put into practice, but rather discussed, debated and subjected to inquiry and discourse. One partner principal described how he observed his school using external expertise:

> In order for any innovation to be sustained it must become a part of the culture of the site or district. For professional development to continue, it must rise out of individual teachers and site needs. These must, in turn, be nurtured and supported by site, district, state and federal resources. With this in place, mechanisms can then be developed for continuous examination and adjustment of practices. We will utilize action research, site plan and action teams, networking with other support groups, to develop a culture of learning that includes those

directly impacted in the decision-making process (...) to support the renewal process.

Professional learning communities: problems

The K20 Center has encountered numerous problems while engaged in professional learning community development. We believe, as Fullan (1993) notes, that 'problems are our friends'. Problems give us a chance to deepen our understanding and accelerate professional growth organizationally and as individuals. In this section, we describe key problems encountered, strategies designed to address these problems and critical friends' comments relevant to the problems.

Problem 1: in-depth learning

This problem might be fully articulated as: How does the K20 Center establish in-depth learning while addressing state-wide needs and expectations? As a result of extensive state-wide networking and capacity building over the past ten years, the K20 Center has developed structures to initiate professional learning community partnerships in all 77 Oklahoma counties. These structures evolve around three interrelated phases:

- **Leaders (Phase I)** developing principals and superintendents to lead systemic change and technology integration in their schools and districts.
- **Schools (Phase II)** supporting leaders in creating professional learning communities that use technology to enhance student achievement.
- **Learning (Phase III)** creating in-depth authentic learning across all disciplines.

Each phase develops initiatives designed to deepen the focus of the IDEALS framework and ten Practices of High Achieving Schools. The phases occur concurrently and support and strengthen each other. After the initial Leaders phase (involving 1100 Oklahoma principals and superintendents as well as pre-service administrators), Phase II deepens the focus to include the entire school community in 'whole school/district' change to emphasize professional learning communities. Phase III helps strengthen the previous phases by concentrating on authentic teaching and classroom change involving in-depth, connected and meaningful student learning. We believe that all phases must be present to establish in-depth learning. Each phase is described in subsequent sections.

Leaders (Phase I) – In 2001, the K20 Center received a state leadership grant from the Bill and Melinda Gates Foundation to create the Oklahoma

Achievement through Collaboration and Technology Support (OK-ACTS) programme. OK-ACTS uses the IDEALS Systemic Change Framework and ten Practices of High Achieving Schools to help develop educational leaders who can lead systemic reform initiatives to develop professional learning communities in their schools and districts.

The OK-ACTS programme seeks to develop strong leaders who share a common set of characteristics that include: developing and maintaining a clear, shared vision; facilitating the design of the curriculum that is aligned with this vision; as well as integrating technology to enhance professional learning community and student learning. In addition, OK-ACTS seeks to develop principals as instructional leaders and teacher coaches, provide job-related learning experiences and time for teachers to work together, as well as developing learning partnerships with businesses, community groups and institutions of higher education.

In Phase I, principals and superintendents receive a laptop computer and attend a 2-day leadership seminar designed to introduce the IDEALS framework and ten Practices of High Achieving Schools. Throughout the year, administrators learn leadership strategies to develop, implement and sustain the following practices in their schools: a collaboratively developed vision of good teaching and learning; authentic teaching, learning and assessment strategies; data-driven, shared decision making; critical study based on action research; equity analysis; service learning; and internal and external support networks for school renewal. Participants experience hands-on activities to provide them with an understanding of how technology can be used as a tool for school leaders and for student learning. Technology use is modelled during the leadership seminar and throughout Phase I. Additional professional development opportunities are offered for Phase I participants through OK-ACTS and partner organizations, including cluster networking sessions, distance learning using video conferencing, and online learning opportunities. Upon completion of Phase I, participants submit an action plan designed to implement fully one of the ten Practices of High Achieving Schools and receive feedback from OK-ACTS staff. In addition, regional networking and online collaboration opportunities are provided to all members of OK-ACTS as they continue to deepen the IDEALS and ten Practices in their schools and districts. The regional networks meet quarterly and are designed for superintendents and principals to share actively best practices as well as to address common issues and problems.

In addition to principal and superintendent leadership development, the K20 Center has developed a Master of Arts in Educational and Community Renewal (ECR) designed to prepare community members (specifically school board members) and educators to restructure schools and communities as professional learning communities, to better meet the needs of children and families. The ECR Masters programme places educational and community renewal in the context of economic, social and cultural issues. The programme is collaboratively developed and team taught by university and school faculty as well as by nationally recognized educators serving as critical friends of the K20 Center. The ECR Masters consists of 36 hours of required coursework, delivered in an integrated format around the IDEALS model, a Centerpiece renewal project and an internship. (See http://k20center.org/http://k20center.org.)

Schools (Phase II) – In order to develop professional learning communities, administrators must build capacity for systemic change by encouraging the voices of teachers, students, parents and community members in networking processes. Phase II was established to provide school and district leaders with one year of professional development designed to develop leaders as described above and to promote continuous learning in subsequent years through regional networking and web-based learning opportunities.

Research on change indicates that systemic change takes much longer than one year (Fullan 1993, 2001). As a commitment to long-term, state-wide educational reform and improved student achievement, the Oklahoma Educational Technology Trust (OETT), a $30 million trust fund designed to enhance student learning through technology integration, established a partnership with the K20 Center titled 'Phase II OETT Grants-to-Schools' to assist Phase I administrators in developing professional learning communities in their schools and districts. During Phase II, OETT provides individual school site and/or district competitive grants to 21 schools per year. Each grant consists of $50,000 in technology equipment, $25,000 in professional development through the K20 Center's OK-ACTS programme, and $4000 in staff release time to participate in professional development. The grants are available only to schools/districts whose superintendents and/or principals have completed OK-ACTS Phase I.

A key component of professional learning communities in high schools involves developing small learning communities with no more than 100 students per grade level. Many high schools have become large and impersonal institutions in which young people do not feel connected, involved, special or safe. Large high schools participating in Phase II seek to create small learning communities that engage the intellectual and emotional lives of students.

Learning (Phase III) – Researchers have found that when teachers teach authentically, their students consistently outperform those that are taught in more conventional ways (Newmann and Associates 1996). That is, when teaching focuses on making connections for students and deepening the learning to create meaning, rather than relying solely on memorization, students do better both on assessments of advanced skills as well as on standardized tests. These findings suggest that students who think carefully about subjects, study them in-depth and connect them to their personal experiences also are more likely to remember the facts and definitions called for on standardized tests (Lee and Smith 1994; O'Hair *et al.* 2000).

Phase III is designed to deepen Phase II's emphasis on professional learning community and 'whole school change' by focusing on authentic teaching and learning in every classroom. To enhance authentic learning, the K20 Center is at various stages of developing four K20 interdisciplinary institutes:

1   science, technology, engineering and mathematics (STEM) institute
2   literacy institute
3   arts institute
4   health and readiness institute.

The K20 Institutes are supported by national and local foundations (i.e. the National Science Foundation; Howard Hughes Medical Institute; Noble Foundation) and focus on interdisciplinary themes that attract researchers and practitioners from across disciplines, educational levels and institutions, with the purpose of developing 'communities of scholars' devoted to authentic teaching and learning. For example, the STEM Institute is designed to improve significantly authentic teaching and learning of science, technology, engineering and mathematics. In 2001, the K20 Center received a GK-12 grant from the National Science Foundation to develop the Authentic Teaching Alliance (ATA). ATA connects engineers and scientists and their undergraduate and graduate students with middle and high school teachers in order to develop integrated and authentic curriculum and instruction. These curricular units focus on the Oklahoma PASS Objectives for math and science (the state-wide curriculum and testing initiative) and seek to redesign STEM classrooms through team-building, interdisciplinary connections and in-depth, performance-based learning to enhance student interest and career options.

The K20 Center through its partnerships with schools, state agencies, professional organizations and foundations seeks to improve student achievement through the intertwined phases. Based on research and practice, it is our belief that all phases must be present to establish in-depth learning while addressing state-wide needs and expectations. What follows are several issues proposed by the K20 Center's critical friends.

The K20 Center's critical friends have asked whether, for future efforts, the three-phase format is the best way of developing in-depth learning. Given the likely limited impact of a single 2-day seminar and a few related cluster networking meetings and activities of the 800 plus administrators who participate in Phase I only, aren't a significant amount of K20 Center resources being consumed by providing a limited set of professional development activities for these individuals? What is the reason for the large number of participants?

Our response to this is that we are reducing the numbers of administrators we serve in the next cycle as well as reducing the size of each seminar. The reduction in numbers and size will afford us additional opportunities to make connections with individual administrators. One finding has been that the administrators who had not originally believed that the seminar, follow-up sessions and action plan would impact their practice, report that they are implementing the IDEALS and ten Practices in their work. Results from the 2004 National Staff Development Council (NSDC) study of each of the 50 states' school leadership programmes funded by the Bill and Melinda Gates Foundation, found that the K20 Center's statewide programme was ranked third out of 50 in developing K12 leaders that make systemic, substantive changes to improve student learning (Killion *et al.* 2004: 83).

Problem 2: building capacity

Problem two can be fully articulated as: How does the K20 Center build school, university and community readiness and capacity for change? That is, how can the K20 Center help schools build knowledge and skills in developing, implementing and sustaining professional learning communities?

Developing knowledge and skills is not simply about acquiring existing skills and knowledge, but also about teachers and administrators reflecting critically on their practice and fashioning new knowledge and beliefs about content, pedagogy and learners (Darling-Hammond and McLaughlin 1995). The K20 Center strives to accomplish this through professional development programmes for teachers and administrators that develop processes and activities which enhance the professional knowledge, skills and attitudes of educators and connect them to teaching practice and student achievement.

The K20 Center emphasizes a balance among direct instruction, job 'embedded' learning, coaching and networking. Direct instruction involves skill demonstration, modelling and simulated skill practice. Embedded professional development includes processes such as inquiry, discussion, evaluation, consultation, collaboration and problem solving, and is stimulated by new roles for teachers (for example, teacher leader, peer coach, teacher researcher) or new structures (for example, problem-solving groups, decision-making teams, common planning periods, self-contained teams) and new tasks (for example, leading an in-house workshop, journal writing, collaborative case analysis, grant writing, curriculum writing, school improvement team membership).

Coaching and mentoring opportunities are a third form of professional development (Joyce and Showers 2002). Planning and working together are ways to develop mutual support between coach and learner. In addition, Joyce and Showers (2002) suggest that coaches need time to reflect and share together what they are learning and how to best facilitate growth of participants that leads to higher student achievement. Coaching and mentoring are provided during Phase I by 'cluster coaches' who work in follow-up activities with a small group of participants during the months following the leadership development seminars.

Networks are a fourth, recently emerging form of professional development. Networks are collections of educators from different schools that interact regularly to discuss and share practices around a particular focus or philosophy of schooling (for example, new technology standards, authentic instruction). They are held together by a typically loose organizational structure that facilitates their interaction across schools. They interact via such means as in-person sharing meetings, cross-school or cross-classroom visitations, professional institutes, critical friends groups and electronic forms of communication. Pennell and Firestone (1996) found that networks were effective in helping teachers get students more actively involved in learning, and Lieberman and Grolnick (1996) and Yee (1997) found networks to have a number of positive effects on the professional development of teachers and administrators as well as to accelerate whole-school change and student achievement.

The K20 Center embeds the four forms of professional development by using the following strategies to build knowledge and skills:

- **Leadership seminars.** Principals and superintendents attend a two-day leadership seminar in which they are introduced to the IDEALS framework and ten Practices of High Achieving Schools. Leadership, professional learning community and technology strategies are interwoven throughout the seminar. As described earlier, each participating administrator receives a laptop computer and is assigned to a cluster of 10–20 administrators. Led by an acting administrator serving as coach, the cluster networks together for one year.
- **Learning coaches and teaming.** School-based learning coaches work regularly at Phase II partner schools to help principals and teachers enhance systemic change based on the IDEALS and ten Practices of High Achieving Schools. Each participating OK-ACTS Phase II school receives a learning coach, on a part-time basis, to work with school and community and to serve as a liaison with the K20 Center. The learning coach assists the principal in developing school-based learning teams representing students, teachers, parents and community and business partners to help design and implement the IDEALS and high achieving schools practices.

- **Team leaders.** Each school-based team selects a team leader who works with the learning coach and principal in coordinating school and cluster activities. The team leader is responsible for scheduling monthly meetings of the team and assisting the learning coach in addressing the team's needs in developing strategies and structures to enhance professional learning community in the school.
- **Book study sessions.** These sessions bring together teachers and others from a school to discuss best practices and professional literature that they have agreed to study and that is relevant to improving their professional practice. Some topics examined to date include advisory/ advocate systems, authentic assessment, flexible scheduling and pacing, development of blocks of time for ongoing and embedded professional development and coaching, data-driven decision making and building partnerships. These sessions are a way of bringing in new ideas, research and practices into the school and connecting them to the school's values, beliefs and context.
- **Work sessions.** The focus of work sessions is to develop communities of practice that develop broad understandings of the ten Practices of High Achieving Schools and to target specific practices for additional in-depth work. Two federal partners, National Science Foundation (NSF) and Southwest Educational Development Lab (SEDL) as well as the K20 Center's state partners assist with these work sessions. These small and large group sessions help participants (including students and community members) learn how to study critically current practices and how to ensure that future practices are congruent with high achievement. Through the critical study of practices, communities of practice are created that allow teachers to share their learning, build leadership capacity and better address students' needs. Work sessions occur in summer, autumn and winter, as well as during professional development days throughout the year.
- **Lesson study.** Lesson study originated in Japan and has been credited with bringing about Japan's evolution of effective mathematics and science teaching (Lewis and Tsuchida 1997; Lewis 2002; National Research Council 2002). Lesson study differs from 'lesson planning' because it focuses on what teachers want students to learn rather than on what teachers plan to teach. In lesson study, a group of K20 teachers develops a lesson together and ultimately one of them teaches the lesson while the others observe the student learning. The group comes together to debrief the lesson and often revises and re-teaches the lesson to incorporate what has been learned.
- **Winter institute.** The institute differs from the work sessions in that the institute features teachers, students, parents, administrators and business and community partners from participating schools who share best

practices for developing professional learning communities via a variety of breakout sessions.

- **Site visits.** Each participating Phase II school regularly hosts a site visit in which groups of teachers, principals, students, parents and community members from other Phase II schools visit the school. During a site visit, the school showcases its best practices and also allows visitors to observe everyday practices. The purpose of site visits is to learn from the best practices of other Phase II schools and to serve as critical friends for each other in accelerating the change process.
- **Peer coaching.** Peer coaching complements the other forms of professional development by supporting principals and teachers as they implement new professional learning community strategies. Teachers, administrators, parents and community/business partners participate in job-alike peer coaching teams.
- **Administrator regional networking.** Principals and superintendents of participating schools meet a minimum of three times a year to share progress and obstacles. Superintendents and school board members of participating districts also meet annually at the jointly sponsored meeting between the Cooperative Council for Oklahoma School Administration (CCOSA) and the Oklahoma State Schools Boards Association (OSSBA).
- **Connection with external critical friends and successful systemic change efforts.** These connections occur through site, virtual and network visits, email and conference calls, Winter institute and serving as external feedback providers for each other. Current partnerships exist with individuals as well as with organizations including the National Science Foundation, United States Department of Education's Southwest Educational Development Lab, League of Professional Schools, and members of the International Networks for Democratic Education (consisting of ten international school–university networks with a common focus on student achievement and democratic citizenship).
- **Technology professional development.** The K20 Center's technology professional development goal is to provide school administrators and teachers the opportunity to learn about technology integration that is appropriate, timely and meaningful. To help accomplish this goal, OK-ACTS Phase II provides six days of professional development for teachers to gain knowledge about the ten Practices of High Achieving Schools and technology integration. Combining technology equipment with professional development opportunities in a timely manner ensures the technology purchased is not under-utilized. It is pointless to offer training to educators before they have the technology available. More importantly, if the technology is available but educators are not technologically proficient, it is unlikely the technology will benefit the

teaching and learning experiences. Meaningful technology professional development consists of learning a minimum set of technology skills embedded within curriculum activities. While teachers are learning 'just enough' technology to produce a product, instructional practices are also being modelled and experienced, for example, cooperative learning activities, learning-centred approaches, and authentic teaching and learning experiences. Curriculum activities embedded within technology learning provide a framework for teachers to construct their own relevant student learning experiences appropriate for the grade level or subject they teach. To ensure the sustainability of technology usage, teachers will be also supported with an in-house mentor who is recognized as a technologically competent colleague.

While the K20 Center's professional development structures identified above help us build readiness and capacity for change and assist in the implementation, we continue to struggle with sustainability. What follows are some issues posed by the K20 Center's critical friends.

The K20 Center's critical friends raised the following issues about capacity building. While the K20 Center is to be commended for developing an extensive professional development plan that encompasses and integrates various forms of professional development, several key issues remain. Specifically, beyond the initial leadership seminar and subsequent contracted activities, Phase I schools may choose not to engage in some of the other professional development components (for example, school-based teams, regional networks). These may be precisely the components that add depth to the initial learning experience and bring new knowledge, skills and dispositions to life within the school.

A second issue concerns whether the schools who do wish to fully pursue opportunities provided by the K20 Center are able to receive sufficient facilitation services (for example, from their learning coach who, currently, works with two to three schools) to get to the stage where their primary professional development occurs due to embedded forms of professional development. It is the latter (i.e. embedded professional development) that is the true key to building capacity and, thus, fostering in-depth learning.

A third issue revolves around the K20 Center's ability to find an adequate number of qualified personnel. Will the K20 Center be able to find sufficient numbers of people with systemic change/professional learning community experiences who wish to serve as directors, coordinators and coaches, especially if this means giving up their current employment as teachers and principals or significantly curtailing the amount of time they devote to these primary responsibilities? Without additional qualified people will the K20 Center be able to grow and meet the needs of the state? This issue is particularly problematic in areas outlying some distance from the K20

Center's geographic location, where the educators are less well-known by the K20 Center's leadership, and in the rural regions of the state. The issue of sufficient qualified personnel will become crucial in Phase II where the K20 Center will need to have learning coaches who work daily in schools.

Our response is that: these issues cited by our critical friends are very real concerns for the K20 Center. With limited resources we are unable to continue to work in-depth with all Phase I and II schools, however, through intentional networking and job-embedded professional development we seek to enhance the school's capacity to continue its renewal work. We have established network meetings in each region to facilitate the process for ongoing school renewal and networking for the administrators and teachers who choose to stay involved. We continue to work with our local, state and national partners to extend and create new opportunities for our network schools, and to search for strategies to support administrators and teachers who wish to stay involved with K20 Center initiatives. The issue of resources is an ongoing struggle but well worth the fight. After ten years of seeking and obtaining resources, we have discovered that funding and resources are linked inextricably to one's ability to identify, analyse and significantly address educational issues at the local and state community levels. If successful, adequate resources are usually available.

Problem 3: sustaining the work

Can be fully stated as: How do we sustain the work? How do we develop structures that are flexible enough for innovation and growth while supporting connections to existing, often traditional, structures to ensure sustainability?

Initially, we struggled as a network of schools as to where we belonged in the university structure. Our work transcended traditional university programme areas, departments and colleges. After two years of networking, our university president provided start-up costs to develop a university-wide Center designed to connect the schools network with the university faculty and students across all colleges within the university. His goal was to provide every university student with the opportunity to work meaningfully in K-12 education while at the university, with the goal that university graduates develop an understanding of how to make a difference in their local schools and communities. As a result, the K20 Center has grown from six partner schools in 1995 to over 600 schools participating in K20 Center initiatives.

The K20 Center's internal structure consists of 12 full-time staff including a director, five associate directors, an administrative assistant, two technology coordinators and three field coordinators. In addition, the K20 Center employs three student assistants, 25 NSF fellows (13 graduate,

12 undergraduate) and 40 learning coaches representing teachers, principals and superintendents.

In 2001, the K20 Center received approval from the university's Board of Regents to become a university-wide research centre. As a result, the K20 Center receives a percentage of indirect costs returned to the university, and the director of the K20 Center reports directly to the Vice President for Research.

In order to develop sustainability, the K20 Center develops phases and institutes in partnership with state professional organizations and governing bodies including:

- Administrator and teacher organizations (i.e. Cooperative Council for Oklahoma School Administration and the Oklahoma Education Association)
- Oklahoma State School Boards Association
- Oklahoma State Department of Education
- Oklahoma Educational Technology Trust
- Department of Career and Technology Development
- Governor, State Attorney General and the Oklahoma Legislature.

In addition, regional and national partners include: Southwest Educational Development Lab, National Science Foundation, Noble Foundation and the Howard Hughes Medical Institute. Through the K20 Center's internal and external structures and partnerships, we hope to sustain and nurture professional learning communities in Oklahoma.

The K20 Center's critical friends have raised issues about the sustainability of the K20 Center's work. Several issues pertaining to the K20 Center's partnerships exist. These include: How active and 'real' are the partners in the K20 Center's work? Do they simply provide moral support? Are they political more than substantive? That is, do they provide substance, or do they simply provide additional resources, credibility (for example, with administrators) and access (for example, to events, such as state-wide conferences, where further work can occur)? What is the ideal role for partners? How does the K20 Center reconcile competing agendas of partners and K20 Center philosophy? For example, how does the K20 Center reconcile a partner's agenda that schools improve standardized test scores with the K20 Center's agenda of increasing the use of more authentic forms of pedagogy in schools? Should competing agendas be subjected to democratic inquiry and discourse processes (for example, at partner and/or K20 Center board meetings) and not simply deference and lobbying? Indeed, what is the K20 Center's role in educating the designated leadership of the various partners (for example, CEOs, Executive Directors, boards, etc.) in significant and sustained ways that go beyond simply inviting them to attend institutes – which partners may often interpret as putting in a half

hour token appearance or making a few welcoming remarks at the beginning of the meeting? Since partners sit in positions of power in education
and society, might the education of partners not be an untapped resource
for impacting the state (and perhaps, national) education agenda?

Our response to this is that democracy is built on bringing differences of
perspectives and opinions together to solve problems and serve the common
good. We strive to listen and understand competing agendas and to move
ahead together to support student learning. It is not always easy or comfortable. As Beane and Apple (1995: 8) concur, 'Such contradictions and
tensions point to the fact that bringing democracy to life is always a
struggle. But beyond them lie the possibility for professional educators and
citizens to work together in creating more democratic schools that serve the
common good of the whole community.' We believe, as do our partners,
that it is worth the struggle as we continue to develop structures that allow
for the 'open flow of ideas, regardless of their popularity' (Beane and Apple
1995: 6) to be heard and considered through constant inquiry and discourse. One example cited was the competing agendas of improving test
scores versus using authentic forms of pedagogy. By examining research
and having informed discourse about our own practices, we concluded that
these in fact are *not* competing agendas, but rather are complementary
agendas since authentic pedagogy does increase standardized test scores
(Newmann and Wehlage 1995).

In order to encourage inquiry and discourse that informs our practices,
we have established state-wide and local partnership boards to advise our
work. These boards represent diverse and often conflicting perspectives.
They help us to deepen our work and to maintain our focus on what really
matters – identifying, analysing and addressing educational issues important to Oklahomans. State leaders and citizens from education, business
and government, including the First Lady of Oklahoma, serve on our
partnership boards. Over the past few years, we have discovered that active,
real partners must first develop trust and understanding of differing perspectives through constant inquiry and discourse opportunities. As a result
of establishing trust, our journey in becoming professional learning communities is accelerated through constant critical reflection and analysis of
our practices, problems and plans of action.

Conclusion

We believe that we have developed a significant and substantive agenda for
the K20 Center for Educational and Community Renewal in the past few
years. Clearly, issues of in-depth learning, capacity building and sustainability remain. While remaining unresolved, these are some of the

dimensions that keep our work both interesting and challenging. What we have not addressed in this chapter are the years we struggled to find any funding and how we finally stumbled into some insights into this process. But that's another story for another time. For now we leave you with some final thoughts: Why are common-sense efforts like the K20 Center's, which focus on authentic, in-depth learning and building the schools' capacity to continually renew themselves and sustain their growth over time, such uncommon sense? Why do they remain peripheral to the mainstream work and funding of schools?

References

Allen, L., Rogers, D., Hensley, F., Glanton, M. and Livingston, M. (1999) *A Guide to Renewing Your School: Lesson from the League of Professional Schools*. San Francisco: Jossey-Bass.

Allen, R. (2002) 'Big schools: the way we are' *Educational Leadership*, 59 (5): 36–41.

Beane, J.A. and Apple, M.W. (1995) 'The case for democratic schools' in M.W. Apple and J.A. Beane (eds) *Democratic Schools*. Alexandria, VA: Association for Curriculum Development and Supervision.

Bernhardt, V.L. (2002) *School Portfolio Toolkit: Planning, Implementation, and Evaluation for Continuous School Improvement*. Chico, CA: Eye on Education.

Cate, J.M., O'Hair, M.J. and Vaughn, C.A. (2002) 'As red bud grows'. Presentation at the Annual Meeting of the University Council for Educational Administration.

Cushman, K. (1998) 'How schools can work better for the kids who need the most' *The Journal of Annenberg Challenge*, 2 (2).

Darling-Hammond, L. (1997) 'The quality of teaching matters most' *Journal of Staff Development*, 18 (1): 38–41.

Darling-Hammond, L. and McLaughlin, M.W. (1995) 'Policies that support professional development in an era of reform' *Phi Delta Kappan*, 76 (8): 587–604.

Eaker, R. and DuFour, R. (2002) *Getting Started: Reculturing Schools to Become Professional Learning Communities*. Bloomington, IN: National Educational Service.

Epstein, J.L. (1995) 'School/family/community partnerships: caring for the children we share' *Phi Delta Kappan*, 76: 701–12.

Fullan, M. (1993) *Change Forces: Probing the Depths of Educational Reform*. Bristol, PA: Falmer Press.

Fullan, M. (1995) 'The school as a learning organization: distant dreams' *Theory into Practice*, 34 (4): 230–5.

Fullan, M. (2001) *Leading in a Culture of Change*. San Francisco: Jossey-Bass.

Glickman, C.D. (1993) *Renewing America's Schools: A Guide for School-Based Action*. San Francisco: Jossey-Bass.

Goffee, R. and Jones, G. (2000) 'Why should anyone be lead by you?' *Harvard Business Review*, 78 (5): 63–70.

Hargreaves, A. (2003) *Teaching in the Knowledge Society: Education in the Age of Insecurity*. Maidenhead: Open University Press.

Joyce, B. and Showers, B. (2002) *Student Achievement Through Staff Development*. Alexandria, VA: Association for Supervision and Curriculum Development.

Killion, J., Hord, S., Moller, G. and Hirsh, S. (2004) *Building for Success: A Study of State Challenge Grants for Leadership Development funded by the Bill and Melinda Gates Foundation*. National Staff Development Council.

Kouzes, J. and Postner, B. (1999) *Encouraging the Heart: A Leaders' Guide to Rewarding and Recognizing Others*. San Francisco: Jossey-Bass.

Kouzes, J. and Postner, B. (2003) *The Leadership Challenge*. San Francisco: Jossey-Bass.

Lambert, L. (1995) 'Toward a theory of constructivist leadership' in L. Lambert, D. Walker, D.P. Zimmerman, J.E. Cooper, M.D. Lambert, M.E. Gardner and P.J. Slack (eds) *The Constructivist Leader*. New York: Teaching College Press.

Lee, V.E. and Smith, J.B. (1994) 'High school restructuring and student achievement: a new study finds strong links' *Issues in Restructuring Schools*. University of Wisconsin: Center on Organization and Restructuring of Schools.

Lewis, C. (2002) *Lesson Study: A Handbook of Teacher-led Instructional Change*. Philadelphia: Research for Better Schools.

Lewis, C. and Tsuchida, I. (1997) 'Planned educational change in Japan: the shift to student-centered elementary science' *Journal of Educational Policy*, 12 (5): 313–31.

Lieberman, A. and Grolnick, M. (1996) 'Networks and reform in American education' *Teachers College Board*, 98 (1): 7–45.

Meier, D.W. (1996) 'The big benefits of smallness'. http://ascd.org/readingroom/edlead/9609/meier.html (accessed 10 April 2003).

National Association of Elementary School Principals (2001) *Leading Learning Communities: Standards for What Principals should Know and be Able to Do*. Alexandria, VA: National Association of Elementary School Principals.

National Research Council (2002) 'Studying classroom teaching as a medium for professional development' in H. Bass, Z. Usiskin and G. Burrill (eds) *Proceedings of a U.S.-Japan workshop*. Washington, DC: National Academy Press.

Newmann, F.M. and Wehlage, G.G. (1995) *Successful School Restructuring*. Alexandria, VA: Association for Supervision and Curriculum Development.

Newmann, F.M. and Associates (1996) 'Authentic pedagogy and student performance' *American Journal of Education*, 104 (4): 280–312.

O'Hair, M.J., McLaughlin, H.J. and Reitzug, U.C. (2000) *Foundations of Democratic Education*. Orlando: Harcourt, Inc.

O'Hair, M.J. and Reitzug, U.C. (1997) 'Restructuring schools for democracy: principals' perspective' *Journal of School Leadership*, 7: 266–86.

Patterson, J.L. (1993) *Leadership for Tomorrow's Schools*. Alexandria, VA: Association for Supervision and Curriculum Development.

Pennell, J.R. and Firestone, W.A. (1996) 'Changing classroom practices through teacher networks: matching program features with teacher characteristics and circumstances' *Teachers College Board*, 98 (1): 46–76.

Printy, S.M. (2004) 'The professional impact of communities of practice' *UCEA Review*, 20–30.

Reitzug, U.C. and O'Hair, M.J. (2002) 'Tensions and struggles in moving toward a democratic community' in G. Furman (ed.) *School as Community: From Promise to Practice*. Albany, NY: State University of New York Press.

Sirotnik, K.A. (1989) 'The school as the center of change' in T.J. Sergiovanni and J.H. Moore (eds) *Schools for Tomorrow: Directing Reform to Issues that Count*. Boston: Allyn & Bacon.

Sizer, T.R. (1992) *Horace's School: Redesigning the American High School*. Boston: Houghton Mifflin.

Starr, L. (2002) 'It's the principal of the Thing!' http://www.education-world.com/ a issues/issues 347.shtml (accessed 12 October).

Wasley, P.A. (2002) 'Small classes, small schools: the time is now' *Educational Leadership*, 59 (5): 6–10.

Wenger, E. (1998) *Communities of Practice: Learning, Meaning and Identity*. New York: Cambridge University Press.

Wood, G.H. (1992) *Schools That Work: America's Most Innovative Public Education Programs*. New York: Penguin Books.

Wood, G.H. (1999) *A Time to Learn: The Story of One High School's Remarkable Transformation and the People Who Made It Happen*. New York: PLUME.

Yee, D. (1997) 'Developing educational leaders for the 21st century'. http:// www.acs.ucalgary.ca/~dlyee/edlecontext.html (accessed 3 September).

Part 2

Starting a network

six

Developing an empowered vision of teaching within networks

Joan Rué

In this chapter we reflect on creating networks in the context of a changing cultural concept of professionalism in a political process of changing education in Catalonia. The context of educational change is relevant to understand the role of teachers who became involved in the network. The network has focused its reflection on one of the many problems teachers have faced: 'school absenteeism' or 'disaffected pupils'. In the process of work within the network two questions troubled us: When will the teachers from the participating schools take over a project led by a university team? What conditions are necessary for this to happen?

The reflection on this process allows us to consider the network as a strategic and collective agent for innovation and development, and emphasizes the concepts of creativity, freedom and responsibility. The network is a powerful agent of exchange at the knowledge reconstruction level. Nevertheless, our proposal for a cultural change is not easy, not even in our educational context that is managed by an administrative and political system that intends to regulate the curricula, time and work and professional agendas.

The following overview shows the basic reference of the work in our network.

The focus of the network in the 2003–2004 academic year

The objective of the network in the 2003–2004 academic year focused on analysing the educational intervention for students with difficulties in academic and social matters. This objective was made concrete in a series of exchanges based on the following agenda:

- managing the diversity of the students
- specification of the basic domain in the development of the curriculum
- conflict resolution and mediation
- exchanging ideas with other local educational non-formal networks.

The procedure that was followed during the meetings of the network meant that each of the teams at compulsory secondary school level presented their different action programmes to the other teams, and they were later discussed.

The people involved were:

- teachers representing the teams from the following secondary schools: IES 'Duc de Montblanc', 'Bernat el Ferrer', 'Escola Industrial', 'Celesti Ballera', 'La Mallola' and 'Can Mas'
- secondary school teachers appointed by the Universitat Autònoma de Barcelona, the network organizer: Lourdes Balaguer, A.M. Forastiello, Alicia García, Carmen Núñez, Francesc X. Moreno and Gloria Valls.

Where are we coming from?

Over the past 15 years there has been intensive debate in Spain about education, which was followed by legislative initiatives to introduce changes in this field. As a whole, the measures adopted were basically of a structural nature and they were all derived from the extension of the obligation to attend school until the age of 16 through a unified curriculum for all students. One of the most remarkable effects of this new structural situation is that it has generated new bases for the development of teaching professionalism. The two basic reasons are as follows:

1   all teaching staff in the new compulsory secondary schools (called ESO in Spain) have had to face the challenge of working in comprehensive and not in selective conditions, in heterogeneous classes and not in academic homogeneity
2   the extension of the school attendance age, as well as the social and economic changes that took place in the same period, have introduced different kinds of problems for teachers, such as the inclusion of students from other cultures, the youth culture transformation, and so on.

Due to its socio-economic structure, these latter changes have been very important in Catalonia.

Nevertheless, the changes and the human and economic resources required for these changes, which should have had a significant influence on the professional changes, were not always in line with the objectives intended by the ESO. In fact, this entire general innovation process has, for a number of different reasons, had contradictory elements. One of the most important reasons is that the various different driving forces behind the educational changes were not aware of the challenge that those changes would mean for the dominant conception of the way professionalism is practised and for how teachers are organized in the schools. As a result, while structural changes were introduced, other elements that affected the preceding conceptions remained untouched or were even reinforced, as, for example, the organization of the teaching staff by subject area. To sum up, we could say that the stocktaking of the process shows how structural changes have been introduced while other basic conditions needed to stimulate a cultural change among the teachers remained stable. Obviously, the whole process was much more complex during this time because there were a number of different governments with different programmes, and education has been managed and legislated in a decentralized manner within the different autonomous regions, within the same legal framework.

Starting with a project

The brief notes that we have just presented about the situation of the professional culture in the context of educational change are relevant for understanding the role of teachers who became involved in the network. This network has focused its reflection on one of the many problems teachers have had to face: 'school absenteeism' or 'disaffected pupils' (Elliott and Zamorsky 2002). By using these terms, we want to refer to those students who decide, either passively or actively, to leave school before completing compulsory education. The analysis of this reality and its characteristics, as well as the developing procedures and resources for educational participation with these students (plus the establishment of an important degree) is what led us to form this network. A team from the Universitat Autònoma de Barcelona (UAB) heads the network project. This team consists of university staff and collaborating teachers who work in the ESO, and teams from five different schools that share the common concern of being able to deal with this problem. These schools are located in similar socio-economic areas, all of them are public schools and share a common socio-cultural student profile.

Although the initiative to work in the network was welcomed favourably by the different school teams, there were two questions that troubled us: Will teachers from participating schools take over a project defined and led by a university team? How do we avoid a hidden power relationship on the basis of the 'common project'? We must not underestimate the fact that it is highly likely that a project from 'the university' is seen by teachers in schools as being both a *theoretical* problem, focused on academic interests and not on something that interests them, and as something that will require more work from them. Being aware of this, we can attempt to deal with teachers on the basis of a project rooted in their own reality. But there is still a problem here: what conditions are necessary for this to happen?

Without having an accurate idea of how to answer these questions, we started from three main ideas that seemed essential to us:

1   Specify the collective action through relevant specific actions in each context, according to the characteristics of each situation and the conditions in each school.
2   Focus reflection on the analyses of the different types of knowledge required by teachers in order to develop their practice: the proper representations of the phenomenon, the institutional mediations to face it, the specific proposals, etc.
3   Specify a priori the methodology for reflection. We followed a four-step rationality model: What is happening to us? How can we explain it? And what could we do to participate, and modify it?

We have perceived the network as a space that provides everyone with the opportunity to reflect on and to discuss and communicate about our work as it develops. But how can we define this opportunity for reflection and encourage adequate participation in each school? How can we define this *space of opportunity*? From our working perspectives, the opportunities disappear when the methodology, the regulatory systems of the proposed activities, or the time, sense and value of the activities are not favourable for the interests or the needs of the agents involved. If we want this space of opportunity to be relevant and effective for the network components, we should understand that it is necessary to carry out actions and reflections that strengthen the members involved in the network. This implies the development of awareness on the part of the agents involved. In this sense, the methodology of the work must take into account at least the following aspects related to the activity: the roles and functions of the initial leadership coordination and the technical leading of the process; the activities for the network's maintenance; the internal elaboration and performance of the project, in each school; the development of self-awareness and self-confidence (as an empowering process), by the different members and by each institution involved.

Cultural and political conceptions of school improvement

Before considering the methodological options of the work in our network it is important to reflect on the conceptions of the 'improvement' concept. These conceptions would be located between two large models of cultural and political management in the educational field, although not restricted to this alone. The first model is based on the autonomy principle, in a political principle of confidence and co-responsibility on the part of the agents so that they act in a self-regulatory manner, improving their actions, according to the principle that the action aims for its improvement. From this point of view, teams will find the way to improve and develop positively. In this sense, Barth (1990) is right when he points out that schools have the capacity to improve themselves, *if the conditions are right*. But political and cultural systems are not always based on this general principle of confidence towards the agents involved (Kember 2002). In fact, often the opposite idea to the principle stated above is at work, a political principle of distrust towards the local agents, seen just as technicians. It illustrates the deep roots of the technical rationality models, well spread in the field of the educational management. Having estimated the distance between both models, where are the different agents in our network located? What is the reference parameter that will define the action improvement of the different schools and agents involved in the network? What are the *right conditions* for our situation?

In our educational context, professionals develop their work within an educational model that is administered 'top-down', according to the intensification planning of the teaching staff work by the educational administration. It is ruled under a curricular and administrative pattern that attempts to define the agenda for improving the teachers' work. A second example involves believing in the different research syntheses about school improvement. In fact, different models of improvement programmes present a repertoire of common ideas about the conditions that 'good schools' might have. Elliott (1998) and other authors have indicated the enormous epistemological limitations of these investigations. To summarize, these repertoires of conditions are not particularly useful since the emphasis is on excessively general aspects of interest, and because we do not know if these conditions are a *cause of* 'good practices' or an *effect of* other actions or preceding 'good' practices.

Instead of the previous model, we propose a different working approach for the teaching staff and schools that are linked to our network. This approach demands a cultural change because it is based on the elaboration of its own criteria, internal cohesion and the expectation of progressive changes. When one works with school teams that are not put under any sampling of previous excellence, as in our case, but rather they are linked to the network project because they can and wish to share certain concerns, values or problems, the referents that come from those improvement programmes are not very useful as a point of departure. On the contrary, it is important for the network to elaborate its own framework. In this sense, we have remarked on four main aspects in our methodology:

- The first aspect consists of defining a specific agenda based on a specific problem, recognized and shared by all. We have learned that any shared plan for improvement requires sharing the concern about its importance, a certain field of values to face its solution, and the will to share the reflection process.
- In the second aspect, we have worked from the perspective of redefining, perceiving and trying to solve the general problems of each school on a local scale, through a network approach.
- The third essential aspect has been to emphasize the role of the network as a space for *cooperative deliberation* for the action. When this happens, the network becomes a space for visualization and evolution, a space for leading improvement and change projects, as well as a space for seminal tasks of initiatives and ideas.
- In the fourth aspect, we have tried to develop a reflection modality and an action adapted not only to the previous conditions and necessities of the participants in the network, but also to the conditions and necessities that have merged during the development of the work.

The previous aspects allow us to consider the network as a collective agent for innovation development, with the emphasis on the concepts of creativity, freedom and responsibility. However, this simply refers to the attitudes. On the other hand, the network is a powerful agent of exchange at the knowledge reconstruction level.

In a situation of social and cultural accelerated changes, such as the one we are currently experimenting with, it is important to remember that Margaret Mead (1977) considered co-figurative situations to be a fundamental way of learning. She defined them as horizontal learning situations, being shaped by exchanges among youngsters in a process of adaptation to the new necessities without any significant influence of the elders. Adapting this meaning to our case, this co-figurative relationship works because of the teaching staff interest in both, to reconceptualize and redefine their working tools, facing the new problems and challenges according to the needs perceived by themselves. This is a teaching model in action, compatible with the knowledge construction characteristics of the Internet era: knowledge developed from multiple connections, open to new experiences and interpretations by people who are learning and are willing to let their project and action ideas be regulated by reflection.

As stated above, we have considered this reflection process as a process of *cultural change*. Ebbutt (2002: 125) has reminded us of two definitions about culture: the first one deals more with anthropology – 'a constellation of both written and unwritten expectations, values, norms, rules, laws, artefacts, rituals and behaviours that permeate a society and influence how people behave socially'. The second definition leads us to remember what Lawrence Stenhouse proposed in 1967, something that was rooted in a more psychological basis: 'Consisting of a complexity of shared under-standings which serve as a medium through which individual interact. Culture, then, is a matter of ideas, thoughts and feelings'.

This point of view about culture provides us with two interesting ele-ments with which to understand the way to approach the practices that are carried out in the school teams from our network project. First, it emphasizes the necessity of using, in an explicit manner, the representation systems that are part of the work of the teaching staff. A cultural repre-sentation that arises from the characteristics of the schools, which are understood, at the same time, as contexts for micro cultural generators of processes, specific patterns and values. Second, this conception provides us with the basic orientations to act and manage the interaction process in the network. Throughout its performance and development, any network generates an interactive process among peers which allows one to visualize different variations with regard to certain practices. But it also allows interactions from different values and representations, to open a process of debate about other types of evidence that are different from the more tra-ditional ones, and so on. This kind of process will generate complex psy-chological processes among the participants such as, for example, comparison, self-perception and cognitive assertion or dissonance.

It is through these complex processes that ideas spread, are assimilated, and penetrate the experiences enriching them. All this is not done through processes of technical rationality, which only lead to simple behavioural accommodations when they succeed, without deepening or giving a major impulse to the changes among the agents involved. Our proposal of a cultural change is not easy, not even in our educative context that is managed by administrative and political systems whose objective is to regulate the curricula, the time and the work and professional agendas.

Metaphors from the methodology

Based on the previous explanation, we are attempting, in our network, to develop a methodology which goes back to the etymological root of the word. The classical Greek meaning of the word shows us that *methodos* means *to be on the way*, *to be moving* or *to be placed in time*. With this etymology in mind, we can explore two metaphors that help us to go more deeply into the methodology to be followed.

In the first metaphor, the *way* is seen as a specific route between departure and arrival. From this perspective, the working method in a project or in a specific proposal will depend on how the parameters are defined and how and where we wish to arrive. Therefore, the method is not independent of the content and the aims, but it is intrinsically related to them. Nevertheless, the direct way is not necessarily the best way, nor is it even the way that the guide knows best, but rather it is the one that allows you to reach the arrival point under the right conditions, and in line with specific proposals. This metaphor reminds us that the way is not the instrument of the trip. On the contrary, it can often be the main aspect of a trip. This notion links the idea of *way* with an open route that allows one to alter or modify the first intention during the process. This would not detract from the interest of the itinerary, on the contrary, it could even become relevant. The method can then be conceived of as a process that does not necessarily have to take us to a pre-established place if there are relevant alternatives. The way does not always pre-exist, it creates itself during the process.

The conclusion of what we have just said is that the reflections on the decisions about the methodology and its role in the development of the educational activities is neither secondary nor independent of all the other decisions made beforehand. The important aspects are not the principle claims or the degree of precision of the objectives, but the fact that the chosen way to carry out the reflection and action process is consistent. Therefore, when we talk about *methodology* we do not consider so much an action model established a priori as a collection of relevant and functional activities, resources and situations in a specific circumstance. This is why we consider the methodology to be an essential aspect in advancing towards the achievement of the goals that came together at the network's birth.

The methodology of work in the network can become both a learning context and a social-constructivist learning process in itself and that is why the methodological variations of the same proposal can be quite different. Taking the above aspects into account, we propose that the following points of reflection on the methodology be followed:

- Learning to contextualize the information, the ideas, is essential for the work in the network.
- Understanding a phenomenon from different and wider points of view, from other contextual perspectives and from different experiences, with a greater diversity of evidence provides a greater range for its solution.
- Defining the temporal and functional limits of the action in a reciprocal

social context favours not only the efficiency but also the commitment and consolidation of the reflection.

- Starting from the necessities, the representations and the time of the participants is a key element for progress.

In progress, or the 'god of the small things'

While working in the network, a few aspects emerged that became relevant. We treated these aspects with special care and developed the following responses. First, the social dynamics that arise from public appearance, the role of self-esteem, the public assertion processes of each participant teacher and the reactions they elicit from others in the workshops. Second, the language, the points of view, the referents and concepts used in the communication. We have to remember that in every context, the concepts do not lead to general abstractions but to elaborations of one's own situation under specific influences. The concepts refer to the elaborations used, and at the same time to communicative objectives and to a specific group of people who share the same referents and codes. Third, the proposed agreements about the objectives of the work in the network, the communication, the information feedback, the modalities and the characteristics of the preparatory work for the network meetings.

Whereas the latter aspect requires, in a special way, precise coordination, the first two aspects demand special attention. To understand exactly what we are saying, we have to remember that, in fact, we are at the beginning of a working process in a network, a process that is shaped by unique circumstances. First of all, the different agents involved do not always meet each other since not everybody is involved in the regular network meetings. It would, in fact, be quite difficult for all the participants from the different schools to meet regularly for practical reasons (time, type of involvement, etc.). Therefore, this means that there is a second crucial trend: we are dealing with a process in which people do not know who the others are in professional terms, and they do not have direct experience with or knowledge about what they are actually doing. All they know about each other's institutions are from discussion documents and the explicit commitment of their representatives at the regular meetings on the basis of the shared documentation, timing, goals and objectives, and the direct narratives from those representatives that interpret everything.

Moreover, it is a process in which participants share their own (private) experiences, expectations and objectives. A teacher's culture is both global and personal. We can see any school culture as a kind of triangulation between three different points of view: the teacher's personal conceptions that emanate from concrete experiences; the shared representations of them as a group working and living professionally in the same context; and the formal transparency of this common experience, expressed through the official narratives (i.e. formal documents, principals' explanations, formal group decisions, and so on). Nevertheless, all these different angles merge when people meet together in a shared project, and all that must be considered – from the initial contact to negotiating each institutional involvement in the work in progress – in the network coordination.

We should remember that teachers work in institutions that have social and micro-cultural contexts. In other words, teachers and schools belong to a general culture and at the same time they generate their own variations and adaptations to that culture and to the official patterns. Therefore, this means that the teaching staff participants have learned to behave within the micro-politics of their school environment. The teachers have developed more or less explicit frames of reference to communicate among themselves, and they have also developed ways of conceptualizing the phenomena and the specific practice of this context, and have accepted some specific values as their own reference values as well as certain communicative habits.

All the above provides conceptual, affective and relational security for certain members of staff. Security that can become insecurity when a shared relationship starts in a network, due to the fact that the interlocutors are not only individuals who are representing themselves (individuals who can apply their own personal strategies in their interaction with others), they are also institutional agents who feel attached to the group formed by their own staff. In other words, they are individuals who place their own values, concepts and references that circumscribe the corresponding practices under public scrutiny. In our opinion, this difference is very important in order to understand certain behaviour, and especially when starting to develop a working process in a network.

In the early contacts, public participation and regulations are important elements since all the individuals develop their own ideas about these issues, about other participants and about the specific work to be developed from what they have actually seen and heard. The confidence, the personal and collective interest and the validity of the implication in the network of the school and one of its specific agents, are put to the test in these initial sessions. One additional aspect to be considered is the emotional nature of participation when it comes to personal or collective experiences that generate professional or personal challenges. This makes it difficult to regulate the time allowed for certain contributions and for information processing by the rest of the interlocutors, since it is more difficult to undo the facts and their general value when this information is emotionally loaded.

Bearing this observation in mind, in the first sessions we had to move away from our initial intentions that focused on the development of a topic, to other demands such as network consolidation. This was something that was developed through an invisible and demanding process in which mutual needs regarding the common topic were negotiated, the corresponding expectations were assessed, the different requests were appraised and the extent to which one was actually understood was gauged. It is only from achieving a number of common values that the network will advance towards specific goals. It is only when this has been achieved that the goals, objectives and time available move on from coordination by the network promoters to actual coordination by the network itself.

Despite the aspects mentioned above, during the time working in the network, we have seen how the participants saw themselves as interlocutors. We felt the necessity to develop mutual agreements on exploratory terms and the different concepts used in a remarkable process of language objectivation and a common appropriation of the field of meaning of the shared project. In fact the network also developed into a micro-cultural arena.

Generally speaking, the process developed nine months ago has allowed us to discover that tools and conceptualization, participation and pupil control instruments can be exchanged by discussion and peer analysis. In this sense, the network becomes a collective agent for improving educational action.

Learning from the shared experience within a network: the teacher's voice

We can summarize what we have learned from this experience as much from its opportunities for improving teaching action (Rué 2001) as from its limitations. The following statements serve to explain:

- The concept of debate, analysis or problem solving in the network is comparable with the characteristics of knowledge construction in the Internet era: multiple connections, open to new experiences and interpretation linked to the interest of those who wish to improve their understanding or practice.
- The notion of project and shared action is much more complex than the simplified version imposed by technical rationality (Schön 1983), which is still a dominant theme as a way of thinking about problem solving. At the same time, it is a much more functional and operative modality because it starts with observation and the notion of regulation (Allal 1988) in its three possibilities: retroactive, interactive and proactive.
- A network is also a *network of opportunities* for professional development, for discussing, reflecting or communicating on the work at a

certain distance from one's own specific context. It can open up opportunities in a range of different senses: methodological, access to resources that are different from the ones traditionally applied, the observation of other ways of regulating activities and time, the discussion of the self and other's values, and so on.

- The network is formed, throughout its development, as a critical collective agent that combines shared action with debate.
- It appears to be an *atmosphere* of specific learning, focused on empirical knowledge and on its mutual community validation. This knowledge management increases the notion of the participants' accountability.
- While the participating teachers generate a process of personal empowerment, the participating schools involved in a network also change, they modify their frames of reference and introduce dynamic transformations in their practices.
- When starting a network it is essential to have recognized that a project functions as a leader for reflection and action. This kind of project must have the explicit and effective support from principals at the schools linked to the network.

Despite the previous explanations, work in the network does encounter a number of significant obstacles that are firmly rooted in both our educational culture and in our organizational background:

- The difficulty of generating reflection processes within the secondary schools that go further than the agenda of the work intensification introduced by the educational administration.
- This difficulty generates the necessity to adapt the work in progress in the network to both the time and the needs of the diverse participants, which involves introducing progressive adjustments to the agenda.
- The internal organization of the teaching staff, grouped by departments, gives priority to the main concern of *what to teach*. We should not forget that most of the problems with recent educational culture stem from how the school academic departmental staff are organized.

The members of the school should be responsible in their representations and work to ensure that the work of the network actually does enter the school. In this sense it is important that, in addition to the official involvement of the school management, other members of the staff get involved as well. Although the role of the official members is essential, it can replace other representations and certain discussion dynamics within the schools. One problem that has still not been solved is the problem of increasing the number of people involved within the school in the work of the network. The pressure of the technical culture surrounding the development of tools and frameworks for action can lead to the illusion of simply searching for practical resources. Instead, we propose elaborating the tools and frameworks within the school, in a deliberative process of taking account of the specific context and considering and discussing the previous criteria for the action.

Evaluating the first steps forward

We wished to have a closer approach to the analysis above in order to validate it from the teachers' opinions. For that purpose we asked the teachers who had participated regularly in the project about their feelings for and personal experience with the network. As a result, from the perspective of the different experiences accumulated in their participation in the network project, they could take stock of their real involvement in the project.

The groups of teachers developed this summary independently in their respective centres, starting from the proposals that were worked out and formulated in our last meeting. Before continuing, it is important to add that, while some groups actually continued to participate in the network project for all three years, for others the last academic course had been their first experience of the network.

Once the different ideas that were sent to us in writing had been collected, they were placed in different categories according to their central tenet. Our work was simply to classify and to link the different scripts, neither changing the information nor their evaluation. For this reason the reader will observe some slight subtleties in the different sections which relate to the reply from different teachers or teams. The teachers' evaluation of their own work in the network project was developed in line with the following guidelines:

1. Institutional and political context

The political context, the present educational system and its organizational structure affect experiences and the work's atmosphere in schools. There are expectations of progress or attitudes to change things which are not fulfilled, and which created gaps in the core of the school management team. Consequently, a general statement arises: our educational system obstructs the professional commitment that a network requires. Let us look at some examples of those obstacles:

- The difficulty to find time within school-scheduled time to work on the proposals of the network; for this reason it is usually necessary to plan this work outside the official school schedule.

- The difficulty to get a commitment from other teachers for the work on the network project since the school is organized mainly around subject departments.
- The absence of self-regulation and control in relation to professional behaviour.
- A lack of any institutional rewards for or public recognition of the professionals that are engaged in these kinds of projects and, consequently, it is difficult to prevent these professionals from losing interest once they are involved in the network process.

2. The network as a space for sharing

Nevertheless, in spite of the obstacles set out above, there was progress in the culture of collaboration. Working together within the schools started to bear fruit. Once this is achieved the work itself turns out to be very useful. Teachers feel that learning to share in the network is a necessary experience for them: it helps them to incorporate new experiences and new directions in the way they currently work. The concept of networking provides a space in which to work and reflect on their own actions: 'when such a space is not available it hampers improvement'.

One notices that the exchange of experiences in itself enriches all the members of the working group and facilitates the emergence of new points of view, new reflections and improvements to the daily work simply as a result of the number of schools participating. This contributes new perspectives, and the very act of meeting with a large group of people with different points of view makes the discussions about the present topics more valuable.

3. The kind of analysis that the network makes possible

The network allows one to step back from problems, thereby creating distance to analyse these problems. The network also provides emotional distance and sufficient criteria to analyse some problems in a better way than would have been the case in the school context. In order for this to happen, it would seem crucial that an explanation is given in the network of what kind of work is done in each particular school. When that is done, the network functions as a 'critical, collective mediator' in the most positive sense, as a tool that can be used to reproduce and to put forward present experiences for critical analysis and to come up with solutions in the shape of tangible action. The very size of the network helps to 'introduce it' to the school team and to project its image as a positive working place.

Among its participants, the network generates a positive attitude towards constructive criticism, which allows them to reach their goals, which is something that does not necessarily happen in the daily work of schools. It provides the space for difficulties the school teams are encountering to be discussed openly and frankly. It is possible in the network to analyse the different school performances in a comprehensive and positive manner, simply because the people who participate in the meetings are motivated and open to ideas about new methods that help them to deal with their own particular problems. Therefore, sharing experiences both with members of the same school and with network participants is a source of ideas for the pedagogical and structural renovation of school practice. In short, participation in the network allows everybody to expand his or her vision of the future and helps one decide where the focus of effort and professional resources should be placed, and to face the new requirements in educational work.

4. The methodology of working in the network

Working in the network requires working from a thematic nucleus, from a situation that follows a guideline, which allows the work of reflection and exchange to develop. Of course, 'exchanging experience' with different sources is something that has to be learned since the teaching profession is well-known for its levels of individualism. The logic of the network is something that has to be learned since it is about learning from others and with others, and about trying to apply general solutions in a concrete way in each of the schools involved in the network. The real challenge is to be able to transmit the spirit of the network, and what has been learned in the network, to other people who do not attend the network meetings.

The network, its methodology and the way topics are presented and discussed, support the theory that makes shared experiences better understood. At the same time, it facilitates the improved development of the practice on the current topics. This working method transforms itself into a sort of in-service training course for all the members involved in the network.

5. Participation

Although having a 'promoter group' for the network would seem to be obvious, the real challenge is to get more teachers from the participating schools to commit themselves to network projects, even though their participation in the network is only indirect. This is because, as we have already pointed out, the topics of interest reflect the reality of the centres, and are, in many ways, of crucial concern to all since they are aspects that worry us all. The self-recognition outcome that is generated by being involved in the network is a personal and collective building process, even though there is still a long way to go before it can be considered satisfactory enough for the school and thereby for participation by all teachers. Taking part in the network means seeing oneself as a key participant.

The case of one school showed that the network encouraged working on certain matters (to investigate, to be responsive to certain topics dealt with, to be more aware of ...), even though the level of enthusiasm of the teachers had been rather variable. In fact, we observe different levels of participation regarding network involvement:

- **Direct**: some representatives, usually those present at the inter-school meetings.
- **Indirect**: teachers who do not assist but who identify with the first group or with the projects in which they are involved.
- **Indirect on a second level**: depending on the level of involvement and the action of the others in the centre in matters relating to the project.

As one network participant has stated, 'In our school we try to involve more people in the network agenda and therefore we suggest certain groups of teachers to assist in the exchange-meetings; these people are selected according to their particular practice and level of experience, so that they can represent the experiences which they would like to share with the other participants in the exchange meeting.'

6. The process of change

The concept of cultural change can explain one of the fundamental challenges of the present situation for the participants in this project. 'Networking' points to another way of expressing oneself, of working and participating, and that what is needed is a new way of doing things, a certain kind of cultural change. Although the work in the network has not yet been totally incorporated, the correlated topics are dealing with the problems that we face every day; that is why the network model has to be integrated into our professional practice.

7. The impact of the network

Evidence of the impact the network has had on different contributing centres includes the following.

- In spite of the difficulties, i.e. for teachers to meet together for purposes in schools and to work from the network agenda, once this hurdle has been overcome it proves to be very useful. In A (one of the schools involved), an institutional hour has been set aside once a week for network coordination.

- From the very beginning we believed (in B), that it was necessary that the people who participated in the network should represent the different departments, involving a higher number of teachers and, in this way, providing a better transmission of the concurrence and the suggestions in the network.
- The process of self-recognition, as being a very real part of the network, is on the increase, but in the core of the school team (in C), the concept of the network still lacks support from all the teachers.
- Participation in the network involves seeing oneself as a key participant. Therefore, the joint project in the network has motivated teachers to work (in D) on certain issues, such as developing action research and becoming more aware of some issues that should be considered, even though the teachers' level of involvement does vary.
- We (those usually present at the meetings) used to explain (centre A) to our colleagues what we were actually doing in the network project and the difficulties that we were facing in the process. We actually started an open discussion.
- Progress is important in ensuring that the concept of the network is integrated in the working dynamic of the school (in E), because except for the people who are actually involved in the project the rest of teachers are not very responsive to what is happening. Some teachers know that the network exists but they 'don't live it'.
- With the objective of involving more people with the work of the network (school B), we have been chosen, in addition to the regular participants, to represent the team in the network meetings, and therefore function as representatives of the dynamics in the school.
- Though much is still required to consider it a team within the centre that works fully in the network (in C) and due to the limited commitment of the teachers working in the centre, we use the coordinator's meeting to develop the chosen topics for the network schedule.

Epilogue

The evaluation of our work from the participants' perspective concludes this account in which we have covered the project from the initial doubts of the network experience to the synthesis of evaluation regarding the work accomplished during the past year. Once the statements by the members of the participating teams were sorted out, we observed some overlap with the views that were stated previously. These coincidences converge to point out an important basic contradiction. While the teachers considered the work in the network as a methodology that enriches them, similar to a purposeful methodology of reflection and vital for sustaining the action all the way, they also observed how the institutional culture, the kind of political management and the administration of the educational system – at the limits of legislation – had posed important limitations on extending participation in the network by other associates and for the proliferation of this methodology.

This is a main feature of the final reflection. Our educational system has moved towards being a functional model, a collection of learning methods that are in a profound process of transformation due to new and important social and cultural challenges, a reality the teachers are confronted with in their daily work. For this reason, the reflections of these professional teams are very valuable. It alerts us to the danger of obsolescence, which confronts them with a system that does not synchronize with the requirements of the *new modernity* (Hargreaves 2003).

There is currently no point in expecting significant changes in the management of the educational system if we do not develop new evidence of pioneer experiences that point towards a workable cultural change in the educational organization; experiences that depend, as we often experienced, on the consolidation of individual and combined initiatives. Experiences that are well founded, both in a general context and in their own working environment. Experiences, in conclusion, that could be developed in a positive way for the students, while generating new perspectives and professional opportunities for the teachers who, in this context, develop positive self-esteem within their profession. This is the task the participants of this network intended to assume in the present context of education in Catalonia.

References

Allal, L. (1988) 'Vers un élargissement de la pédagogie de maitrise: processus de régulation interactive, rétroactive et proactive' in M. Huberman (ed.) *Assurer la réussite des apprentissages scolaires. Les prepositions de la pédagogie de maitrise* (pp. 86–126). Paris: Delachaux et Niestlé.

Barth, R. (1990) *Improving schools from within*. San Francisco: Jossey Bass.

Ebbutt, D. (2002) 'The development of a research culture in Secondary Schools' *Educational Action Research*. 10 (1): 123–40.

Elliott, J. (1998) *The curriculum experiment*. Oxford: Open University Press.

Elliott, J. and Zamorsky, B. (2002) 'Researching disaffection with teachers', special issue, in *Pedagogy, Culture and Society*, vol. 10(2).

Fisher, G.N. (1990) *Les domaines de la psychologie sociale: le champ du social*. Paris: Bordas.

Hargreaves, A. (2003) *Enseñar en la sociedad del conocimiento*. Barcelona: Octaedro.

Kember, D. (2002) 'Long term outcomes of Action Research' *Educational Action Research*, 10 (1): 83–103.

Mead, M. (1977) *Cultura y compromiso*. Barcelona: Granica Ed.

Rué, J. (2001) *La acción docente en el centro y el aula*. Madrid: Síntesis.

Schön, D. (1983) *The reflective practitioner, how professionals think in action*. New York: Basic Books.

Stenhouse, L. (1967) *Culture and Education*. London: Nelson.

seven

Introducing school–university networks in the Middle East

Elaine Jarchow, Barbara Harold, Tracey McAskill, Robin McGrew-Zoubi and Ian Walker

A comprehensive, cohesive renovation of the structure, content, and tools of education would release creative potential and revitalize Arab society. The following policy could bring about this renovation: ... Effective participation of various societal groups in learning ... Families, NQOs, the business sector and local communities should be able to take part in policy-making, finance and supervision.

(UNDP Report 2002: 59)

Networks that link schools and universities in the Middle East are relatively new. Indeed, the United Arab Emirates itself, the focus of this chapter, is only 40 years old. The United Arab Emirates (UAE) is a federation of seven independent states with a central governing council and is located on the northeast corner of the Arabian Peninsula. The states, also called the Emirates, are Abu Dhabi, Ajman, Dubai, Fujairah, Ras Al Khaimah, Sharjah and Umm Al Quwain. The federation was established in 1971. In the UAE Constitution the importance of education is established by the statement that education is essential to the nation's progress, and it is free from elementary level through to post-secondary nationals. The Ministry of Education and Youth supervises the education in all K-12 government-supported schools. The same curriculum is taught throughout the country. The education system in the UAE has made great progress in its relatively short history. The total number of students in UAE government K-12 schools in 1972 was 32,000. A total of 340,000 students began the 2002–2003 academic year. At the post-secondary level there are three govern-ment-supported universities. The United Arab Emirates University was established in 1977 at Al Ain and has produced some 17,000 graduates since its establishment. The Higher Colleges of Technology is a network of ten colleges established in 1988; they provide courses in business administration, accounting and engineering. Zayed University is the newest government institution established in 1998 for national females. More than 75 percent of all nationals attending universities are enrolled at these three institutions. Others attend various private universities in the UAE or study abroad.

Methods of instruction and assessment in schools have been modernized, and the old emphasis on memorization of facts is being replaced with a broad range of outcomes. The Ministry of Education and Youth wishes to enhance student learning by ensuring that systems of assessment monitoring, accountability and reporting are in place. The expectation is that educational opportunities will be improved for all students and that the Ministry will have available to it a programme of quality assurance. In this chapter, the authors review the literature, paying particular attention to the Middle East and the UAE. Zayed University, a new outcomes-based university for UAE national women, is used to provide a context for the analysis of networks. All of the authors are associated with this university. Finally, the authors discuss future directions.

Networks in theory

Discussion about and descriptions of university and school networks, among other forms of educational networks (such as corporate–school, interschool and school–home networks), is appearing in the literature at a rapidly increasing rate. Essentially, a university–school network is a form of partnership that underlies the way a university and school relate to each other for specific educational purposes (see, for example, Goodlad 1991). The concept is frequently linked to a variety of other terms related to educational change such as educational renewal, school restructuring, collaborative renewal and educational reform. It also encompasses some very specific contexts such as professional development schools and learning communities. What is needed, given the range of activity included in discussions about networking, is for the purposes and meanings of university–school networks to be made more transparent, so that their benefits to education can be more readily determined.

The purpose for establishing a university–school network varies from network to network. Teacher professional development (Myers 1995, 1997; Murrell 1998; Bowman and Ward 1999), improvements/changes in classroom and school practice (Myers 1995; Martin 2000), technology in education (Reising and Pope 1999; Skeele and Daly 1999), improvement of teacher pre-service education (Myers 1995; Birrell *et al.* 1998; Mayer 1999;

Friedland and Walz 2001) and conducting research are common reasons why such networks are established.

Although a university–school network may take different forms from place to place and may differ in its purpose and development over time, it will involve some form of collaboration between the institutions involved. It is worth considering in more detail the nature of the collaboration between universities and schools, to help achieve a clearer understanding of the meaning of any particular network and to identify the specific factors that are more likely to lead to a successful partnership and outcome.

A useful analysis of public/private school networks in the United States (Shinners 2001) contributes much to our understanding of the type of partnership that might exist between various educational organizations or institutions including universities and schools. Shinners identifies three major types of partnerships that she links to the level of network success:

1   those that involve education institutions simply cooperating with one another on some venture
2   partnerships that involve a greater degree of coordinated activity
3   those that involve a collaborative working relationship.

She found that the third type of partnership was more likely to lead to a successful network than either of the other two types (see also Myers 1997). She also found that the greatest block to success were the tensions that existed between the different cultures of organizations involved in an educational network. Collaboration between institutions rather than either simply coordination or cooperation was the most effective means of reducing such tension (see also Birrell *et al.* 1998).

The university–school partnership concept has been in action for long enough now that many other writers have identified key factors for success. These include a clearly articulated structure, recognition of mutual self-interest, trust, respect, information sharing and commonly agreed upon goals (Thorkildsen and Stein 1996), high quality school sites, well-qualified university and school personnel, and sound planning and preparation (Van Zandt 1996). Goodlad (1991) provides a useful summary of the major attributes of successful university–school partnerships when he outlines the characteristics of such partnerships, considers the purposes for their formation and identifies some strategies to overcome the many critical problems facing them.

It would seem that what is really critical for the success of a network is the degree of equality existing among the members involved (Murrell 1998). This raises key issues of power and legitimacy that, Kirby and Meza (1995) argue, must be understood if partnerships are to develop fully. They maintain that, as external agents, university facilitators hold no legitimate power in schools, but must work to establish this through their expertise and the development of respect in their relationships with school personnel. As a consequence, there inevitably needs to be a close working relationship or network operating between the school and the university as learning communities.

While much is known about the factors leading to success in school–university partnerships, the development of networks has also highlighted some problematic issues. Myers (1995), for example, notes that the development and maintenance of school–university partnerships can be affected by a variety of inhibiting factors including organizational obstacles, inertia, personal resistance, and the time and effort such networks take to establish. He argues for a change in the way both schools and universities see the relationship between pre-service and in-service teacher education. He suggests that rather than seeing student teachers as the apprentice and teachers as the artisan passing on to the student-teacher his or her skills, educators need to view the whole process of teaching as an ever-developing activity. Van Zandt (1996), in an evaluation of a school–university partnership, noted that issues of quality in the teacher education coursework, school and university personnel, and the school sites also had an important influence on the outcomes of the partnership. Finding a suitable 'match' among students, faculty members and mentor teachers was crucial to the success of a programme and was not always easily achieved.

A recent trend in school–university partnerships has been the development of Professional Development Schools (PDS). Field (2002) draws an analogy between these and the 'teaching hospital'. This concept goes a step further than the traditional links between universities and schools by emphasizing a more holistic approach by the school community to the development of pre-service teachers, and providing better opportunities for mentor teachers to teach in the university programme and to continue their own study. Field notes that early findings from PDS sites indicate higher levels of achievement for both students and interns.

The Middle East and the United Arab Emirates

Dan Davies, founder of the Institute for Responsive Education, in his opening remarks to the proceedings of the fourth annual conference of the Emirates Center for Strategic Studies and Research identified four themes that would be pervasive throughout the conference about educational change in the Arab world.

1. Education and training are the keys to both national and individual development and progress.

2.   Globalization is a fact and will have a major impact on education and training as well as on most other aspects of life on this planet.
3.   Technology is an important tool for education and training but is not a magic bullet with all of the cures for educational ills.
4.   Poverty is the enemy of social and educational development and reform (Davies 1999: 2–7).

He described the importance of learning the skills and attitudes needed for collaboration for productivity. Mograby (1999) documented the progress of the UAE educational programmes over the past 30 years and noted that the development of human capital capable of being good citizens at home and in the workplace is paramount. Benjamin (1999), director of RAND's Education Programme and President of the New York-based Council for Aid to Education, called for a comprehensive audit of UAE education and training classes to review gaps and misalignments with these goals. He asserted that in the merging global economy, the quality of a state's workforce (human capital) is the only asset that will count. In 2002, the *Arab Human Development Report* was published by the United Nations Development Programme (UNDP). It stated that limited current research found:

> the key negative features of the real output of education in Arab countries is the low level of knowledge attainment, and poor deteriorating analytical and innovative capacity. The most worrying aspect of the crisis in education is education's inability to provide the requirements for the development of Arab societies. This could mean not only that education loses its power to provide a conduit for social advancement for the poor within Arab countries but also that Arab countries become isolated from global knowledge, information, and technology. If the current situation is allowed to continue, the crisis can only worsen – this at a time when accelerated acquisition of knowledge and information of advanced human skills are becoming prerequisites for progress. Comprehensive action to reform education systems is therefore urgent.
>
> (UNDP Report 2002: 54)

The need for collaborative networks throughout the Middle East and the world is significant. Education and training will contribute to diversification of the Middle East national economies as they move away from the dependence on the oil industry. Productivity and competition in a global and interdependent world requires that all children and youth must achieve both academic and social success. Clearly, ample fodder for university–school partnerships are present to support their development.

In this century, teachers will be the primary determinant of the quality of education at all levels. Technology will increase, not decrease, the need for good teachers and skilled teaching. Significant educational improvement requires substantial involvement of families and communities. Students from homes where parents take an active interest in their schooling, where there are discussions about a wide range of subjects, where there are books and a culture of inquiry, have been clearly shown to do better academically than do students from homes where these advantages are not available. Lifelong learning will be a hallmark of the most successful and productive societies.

The ten principles of reform offered by the UNDP Report (2002) form the skeleton of partnership projects at work between Zayed University and the Ministry of Education and Youth. These principles are:

1. The individual should be central to the learning process. Without implying indifference to the community or absence of cooperative behaviour, the dignity of the individual should be respected.
2. Modern knowledge is power. The critical faculties of Arab youth should be encouraged as both a guide and an approach to better social structures.
3. Without denigrating higher values and established creeds, intellectual and cultural heritage should not be immune to criticism and change in the face of scientific evidence. Dialogue should be valued.
4. Creative human effort lies at the heart of progress. Arab education systems should be restructured to give precedence to creativity and the dignity of productive work.
5. The spirit of challenge should be stimulated in the Arab people, who should shape their future through creative responses to their natural and human surroundings.
6. Equal educational opportunities should be made available to all children.
7. Education should aim at promoting, in a cohesive and harmonious manner, students' physical, emotional and societal well-being as well as their acquisition of knowledge.
8. Education should help children and youth to understand themselves and their own culture, past and present, creatively and in the context of a world where cultures can flourish only through openness and dialogue.
9. The objectives of the educational process should be derived from the global vision of twenty-first century education. Education should integrate the Arab people into the age in which they live, an age governed by the exactness of science – its causality, rigour and method.
10. Education should help the young to cope with a future of uncertainty, acquire flexibility in the face of uncertainty and contribute to shaping the future.

The most effective relationships between education and society will be partnerships or collaborative connections between educational institutions and the families and communities they serve. UNDP (2002: 55) states that the strengthening of educational programmes in the Arab countries requires action in the enhancement of human capability, creation of strong synergy between education and socio-economic systems, and the formulation of programmes for educational reform at the pan-Arab level.

Zayed University

Zayed University, a government-supported institution, was founded to prepare women leaders who will foresee the possibilities and capture the opportunities that will create the future of the United Arab Emirates. Although it is a young nation, less than 40 years old, the UAE is destined to command a significant position in the Middle East because of its strategic location, the forward thinking and far-sighted vision of His Highness President Sheikh Zayed bin Sultan Al Nahayan and other leaders of the country, and the quality of its modern infrastructure.

Zayed University's mission is to produce graduates who, in addition to excelling in Arabic and English, are masters of the computer, well grounded in the academic disciplines, fully prepared in a professional field and capable of providing leadership in the home, community and nation.

The university offers a comprehensive educational programme. A readiness programme ensures that students meet proficiency standards in Arabic, English, mathematics and information technology. Special individualized programmes are provided to assist students to meet proficiency standards before enrolling in General Education courses. The General Education programme provides a foundational curriculum in five domains: creative expression, culture and society, humanities, language and communication, and science, mathematics and technology. Also, students choose a major in one of the university's six colleges: Arts and Sciences, Business Sciences, Communication and Media Sciences, Education, Family Sciences and Information Systems.

The colleges began accepting majors in autumn 2000 and graduated the first class in June 2002. The unique aspect of the university and its teacher education programme is the commitment to nurturing a learning community that integrates learning outcomes throughout the general education and the professional education components.

Zayed University's vision is to be a learning community where students will develop the knowledge, skills and abilities they will need for meaningful and successful twenty-first century life. In a successful learning community, faculty, staff and students work together to achieve learning goals. They share the opportunity and responsibility to learn from and teach each other in an environment of trust, respect and mutual support. They are jointly engaged in the pursuit of excellence and the development of human potential.

The College of Education

Designed to prepare teachers for leadership roles, the teacher preparation programme at Zayed University is characterized by international standards, work in schools, technology projects and a close connection to the Ministry of Education and Youth.

The College of Education has identified six learning outcomes. They are introduced in the early courses, reinforced in subsequent courses and mastered during student teaching. They are:

1. Engage and support all students in learning.
2. Create and maintain effective environments for student learning.
3. Understand and organize subject matter for student learning.
4. Design and implement learning experiences for all students.
5. Assess and evaluate student learning.
6. Develop continuously as professional educators.

The Zayed University educational experience for teachers begins with the aspiring teacher observing student-centred schools and learner-centred classrooms as she considers her own experience in K-12 education. She works with teachers from the UK, USA and Canada as she takes her first steps in planning a lesson and teaching. The potential for education to maintain the status quo is strong and compelling, but it is the interaction of the optimistic and altruistic national student with the experienced teacher that allows her to see how to turn the theory she is learning at the university into meaningful practice with children. The future she wants for her own children is the future she wishes to make available to all children by graduating with the ability to make significant change in her classroom. As students progress through the programme, they are given more and greater responsibility for planning, teaching and assessment of students. During the last two semesters they complete their practical experience in government schools. While her methods may be different from the mentor she is assigned to, she has the opportunity to learn and to share what she knows, making the experience productive to both. The intern teachers, during their last semester of training, are placed with teachers who are open to the possibilities of using other approaches to teaching but who may not have had the opportunity to study them.

Students at Zayed University are coached on leadership skills and skills of group interaction as they learn about ways of teaching that are very new to

them. While they experience instruction about the learner-centred strategies, they observe them in action when they enter classrooms where these
are used. They are encouraged to reflect upon their own interactions with
the learner-centred strategies that they experience first hand as students at
Zayed University. They will be pioneers of best-practice methodology as
they enter schools where faculty are interested in teaming, but who may not
have had the opportunity yet. Interns are often asked to share their lessons
or to teach their colleagues about a particular method that they may have
used and that looked interesting to the other teachers. The Zayed University
interns are often requested to show other teachers how to use technology in
teaching and learning, as each student is fluent in the use of her laptop as an
instructional tool.

In summary, the literature on school–university partnerships indicates
that such a relationship is worth pursuing, and that they may take a variety
of forms. While the realities of establishing such a relationship may prove to
be 'complex and messy' (National Network for Educational Renewal
2002), there is clear evidence of which strategies are more likely to be
successful and which issues should be addressed to avoid failure.

School–university networks

Eight examples of existing networks provide a context for current efforts.
Each of these, in time, must be concerned about quality assurance. The
importance of these networks to education reform is aptly pointed out in
the UNDP Report, which calls for:

> quality enhancement of all phases of education to pave the way for
> renewal, excellence, and creativity and incorporate modern knowledge
> and technology into Arab Societies. Education should become a con-
> cern for society as a whole, for government agencies generally and for
> business and civil society, particularly in local communities. This
> synergy is particularly important with respect to institutions of higher
> education. There is little here for education reform unless a strong
> synergy emerges between schools and local communities.
>
> (UNDP Report 2002: 56)

Ministry of Education and Youth partnership

In March 2000, the Ministry of Education and Youth and Zayed University
formed a partnership for the advancement of education in the UAE. The
partnership included these objectives:

1. Developing a programme for teachers and other personnel in the education sector to develop and execute in-service training and professional development programmes.
2. Updating methods of teaching, school supervising, assessment, school administration and any other matters related to education in accordance with current international trends.
3. Supporting applied educational research that aims at advancing methods of performance in the education system.
4. Improving students' academic achievement standards and developing their abilities for the development of teaching and learning.
5. Making technology, information systems and communication resources available for the development of teaching and learning.
6. Supporting institutional planning and assessment, and enhancing planning authorities and units responsible for evaluation and assessment of achievement standards.
7. Providing Faculty of Education students with practical training opportunities to prepare them, in the best way possible, for teaching positions.

The partnership also called for the establishment of two demonstration schools and the offering of graduate degrees. These two projects are currently on hold. Progress on other elements of the partnership has been slow but steady. A strong trust relationship has been established, and Zayed University is often called upon to provide in-service workshops and advice. The language barrier does inhibit progress but simultaneous translation helps to overcome this barrier.

Center for the Professional Development of UAE Educators

Building upon the Ministry partnership, in 2002, Zayed University established a Center for the Professional Development of UAE Educators. The Center's mission is to assist UAE K-12 teachers and administrators in developing their practice so that they may, for example, participate in the reform of the UAE educational system. The Center provides programmes and consultancies, and conducts research. The Center's ambitious goals include staffing the Center and developing certificate, incentive and reward plans. The College of Information Systems has agreed to develop a client database. Several networks with other government universities have been forged.

Two secondary schools, one near each campus, receive assistance to enhance their English curriculum. Other K-12 schools offer faculty-led workshops in cooperative learning, classroom management and literacy development. Ministry of Education supervisors join classes in instructional supervision and educational leadership. The Center sponsored a conference on educational standards for nearly 1,000 education personnel. Experts from the USA, the UK and Australia keynoted the two-day event, and 60 concurrent sessions were offered. Another conference for Abu Dhabi school personnel resulted in the production of both English and Arabic versions of the sessions.

In December 2002, a bilingual journal entitled *Teacher, Learners, and Curriculum* was published and provided free to 30,000 teachers and education personnel. Each of the articles offers practical teaching ideas. The Center also launched a First Year Teacher Induction project for all English teachers in the Emirates.

Four Ministry of Education research projects will be completed by the end of 2003. These concern the evaluation of private school curricula, the evaluation of school libraries, the evaluation of the primary school and its curriculum, and the evaluation of a secondary integrated curriculum.

Two specialized training courses are underway: one to teach English, computer and measurement to the Ministry's Testing Center staff and one to provide insights into best practices for the senior curriculum supervisors staff. Courses such as these will result in numerous educational improvements in the UAE.

Inter-university cooperation

There are three public higher education institutions in the UAE. They are Zayed University, the United Arab Emirates University and the Higher Colleges of Technology. Personnel from the three institutions meet regularly to accomplish the following goals: coordinate field placements; plan workshops for Ministry and K-12 personnel; and share international speakers. The activities to date have resulted in a strong desire to collaborate and to act as change agents.

National Advisory Council

Zayed University has two National Advisory Councils – one in Dubai and one in Abu Dhabi. Each includes Ministry, public and private school representatives. The Council serves as a network to address such matters as ways that the college can: best serve the needs and interests of the community and nation; provide students learning experiences in community and professional settings; assist graduates to obtain and succeed in professional positions; assist the Emiratization of employment in the UAE, and promote the development of UAE business and societal interests through research and professional service.

Inter-college networks

The efforts of each of Zayed University's colleges has led to networks which impact the College of Education. An Institute for Technological Innovation was established to provide a forum for all colleges to engage in research and outreach activities. An Institute for Applied Social Research defines research projects of interest to the UAE and these include College of Education researchers. A Child/Family Studies Project will result in research and outreach efforts in the area of Early Childhood Education. The College of Family Sciences places school social workers in the schools. Zayed University English Language Center faculty provides advice to the K-12 schools on curriculum and best practice. The journal entitled *Teachers, Students, and Curriculum*, to be published by the College of Education, will include articles from faculty in other colleges. A number of interdisciplinary research projects includes College of Education researchers.

Assessment panels

Establishing comprehensive networks between the College of Education and the wider educational community is an important component of the evaluative process. A guiding principle in the development of this process is strengthening the relationships and shared responsibilities among the Ministry, schools, the College of Education and Zayed University in the professional development of pre-service teachers. In addition to establishing networks and evaluating teacher preparedness, the creation of assessment panels embraces a number of broader objectives. By seeking the input of educational practitioners within the UAE context, these panels aim to improve the readiness and quality of graduates. A further underlying goal is to demonstrate the mutual value of education partnerships and to improve the ability and inclination of future educators to engage the community in the education process.

   Assessment panels are utilized by the College of Education to determine the readiness of pre-service teachers prior to their internship and graduation. Members of the panel are empowered to make decisions on students' readiness to advance to the next stage of their professional development. Each panel is comprised of faculty from the College of Education, a representative from the Ministry, a representative from a private school, a discipline studies specialist from Zayed University and a member from the Department of English Readiness. The members in the panel assume joint responsibility throughout the summative assessment process. This process is underlined by a commitment on the part of all members to true collaboration. Schrage (1990: 40) defines collaboration as the 'process of shared creation: two or more individuals with complementary skills interacting to create a shared understanding'.

Collaborative efforts are directed towards maximizing evaluative feedback for students and reinforcing standards for pre-service teachers. The learning outcomes of the College of Education guide the evaluation process. Members of the panel individually assess students on their achievement of learning outcomes and collectively make recommendations on whether the student is ready to begin teaching. The student's role in the process includes the development and presentation of an electronic portfolio. The goal of the presentation is to showcase selected artifacts that demonstrate competencies in the learning outcomes. The portfolio presentations offer an evolving portrait of students' growth as prospective teachers, while the artifacts exemplify this reflective development and specific competencies.

The goal of developing and managing education partnerships through the formation of assessment panels has met with a degree of success. Assessment panels were employed at the end of the autumn semester, 2001, to determine the preparedness of students for internship. Invited representatives from the education community engaged in educational dialogue with faculty and were active participants in the decision-making process. Equally important was their participation in the learning process. The students were provided with valuable feedback on areas that would benefit their growth and development as professionals. This same cohort of students presented to assessment panels in Spring 2002 to demonstrate they were ready to take their place in the teaching profession. The quality of presentations was considerably improved and suggested that targeting learning experiences during internship had paid dividends. The College's initial experience with assessment panels underscores the mutual value of education partnerships.

However, the continued development and management of the education networks established by assessment panels presents several challenges. One of these is ensuring that the stakeholders work together to set and reinforce consistent messages and standards for students. The marriage, between the university and the wider community, must be strengthened. Only by working together can these partners fulfil the goal of excellence in teaching. A further challenge is to harness the strengths of various stakeholders to build on the success of the current model. To this end, the College of Education must continue to harness and analyse the evaluative feedback of participants, identify best practices and modify its programme to meet the needs of its education partners.

The practical and internship programme

The main purpose for the development of links between the College of Education and the schools has been to provide the best possible school-based experiences for student teachers. More recently the network has been used for additional purposes of professional development and to introduce some small-scale research studies.

School practical and internship programme structure

The teacher education programme at Zayed is a two-year one that utilizes a range of methodologies integrated with modern technologies, that emphasize a more learner-centred approach to teaching in schools. Students are encouraged to implement these approaches in four practical experiences. The programme links a teaching methods strand with a practical strand for each of the first three semesters, culminating in a ten-week internship in the fourth and final semester. The first practical experience runs for one morning a week for ten weeks. During this time student teachers have an opportunity to make detailed observations of classroom practice across a range of school types and grade levels. The second and third practicals run for a similar time frame, but allow for increasing responsibility for student teachers to plan, teach and assess individuals, groups and full classes.

The school placement programme is based on best practice from international contexts, within the framework of the National Council for Accreditation of Teacher Education (NCATE) guidelines. The programme is underpinned by two guiding principles, a *developmental* perspective and *flexibility*. The first assumes a view of teacher development that is cumulative and characterized by ongoing growth in professional skills and capabilities. The second takes into account the knowledge that the programme model and content is relatively new for some schools, and perhaps entirely new for others. It also takes into account the variation in structure, policy and practice across schools and districts.

Faculty roles in development of networks

The College of Education faculty play a key role in the development and maintenance of school–university networks. Oversight and administration of the practical and internship programme are carried out by the School Placement Coordinator (SPC) whose role encompasses liaison with school personnel, organization and placement of student teachers in schools, development of policy and practice, and organization of support and training for mentor teachers. Links between College of Education, Ministry and schools are also maintained by other faculty who carry out school visits and supervision. They provide the ongoing liaison and relationships with individual mentor teachers. The College of Education has tended to use a specific group of schools for the practicals and internships, thereby, building a stronger relationship with schools' personnel. Some faculty have been invited to assist the school staff in development of new ideas and practices.

Other university links with schools

While the majority of links with schools and the Ministry are undertaken by the College of Education, some other faculties also have such connections. The College of Information Systems (CIS), for example, allows a choice of institutions where its senior students can apply their skills during their internship. Some of these interns choose to work in local schools to assist in the development and implementation of information systems (for example, for administration). These students are placed and monitored by faculty in the College of Education. This includes meeting and discussing the type of project the students are going to be working on, explaining the information systems internship paper work, developing the university Blackboard site and tracking of the students (via weekly reports) from daily logs based on the work agreement. In a current project, a group of CIS students are working in a local secondary school to develop new administration systems based on leading edge technology. Principals and teachers are highly supportive of this kind of programme as the university students are very knowledgeable about current technology systems and practices.

The English Language Center (ELC) is another group of faculty who have developed some continuous relationships with local schools, particularly the teachers of English. During the inaugural semester of Zayed University, the ELC welcomed groups of Ministry of Education supervisors and local teachers to observe English teaching methodologies used by faculty. A group of ELC teachers volunteered to welcome visitors to their classes, met the visitors over coffee and discussed their lesson plans. Up to three teachers/supervisors visited these classes, then during the next break, linked up with another teacher to visit a different class and level. This first event instigated a chain of visits, discussions, workshops and mini conferences over the next three years. These served to cement relationships and enhance awareness and understanding, and in the opinion of faculty, have led to shared professional development in both institutions.

For the past two years, both the Head of the ELC and the Dean of the College of Education have been approached by the Ministry of Education to provide professional development activities for Ministry personnel. This has meant an even richer professional development experience as the ELC, the College of Education and the Ministry of Education have worked to improve English teaching standards in the region in an atmosphere of shared responsibility.

Development of relationships with principals, teachers and Ministry personnel

A variety of methods are used to build relationships with principals, teachers and Ministry personnel. The School Placement Coordinator (SPC) makes regular visits to schools to meet with principals and teachers to share information about the programme, and also maintains close links with Ministry of Education zone advisors, who assist with understanding of school policy and practice, and with the placement of student teachers. Each zone has a senior advisor responsible for liaison between the zone and the local tertiary education institutions. The SPC is in regular contact with these key people to discuss school–university related issues. Regular phone contact and face-to-face meetings are used to maintain communication. Faculty advisors interact more closely with specific mentor teachers during the placement programme and are also frequently invited to be involved in professional development for the Ministry advisors. Feedback and ideas are actively sought from the school and Ministry personnel to 'fine tune' aspects of the programme. Another means of maintaining relationships is through the use of support documents (English and Arabic) that are provided to principals, mentor teachers, Ministry supervisors and student teachers. These give details of the respective roles and responsibilities of those involved in the practical and intern programmes, and provide a common understanding of the university's goals and activities. The initiative for the development of these support documents has been taken by the College of Education faculty but it is envisaged that schools' personnel will have a more active and collaborative role as relationships develop.

Developing a shared culture of teacher development

It is important to align the development of links with schools to improve practical and internship experiences with support and information for the personnel involved. The Zayed University teacher education programme aims to introduce classroom practices that may not necessarily be familiar to teachers in some schools, and the school-based requirements themselves may be unfamiliar to schools. The introduction of a ten-week internship, where interns were expected to be based full-time in classrooms, was not readily accepted by all the schools and much negotiation and information was initially required before principals and teachers accepted the interns in their schools. One strategy used was a full-day information and training session for principals, mentor teachers and Ministry advisors, where these groups were encouraged to raise questions and concerns and to share experiences in mentoring.

The development of a 'shared culture' of teacher development remains an important goal in the university–school relationship. Some valuable moves towards this have already been taken. For example, principals in some schools have invited faculty supervisors to return outside the programme to assist school staff in professional development (for example, reading programmes, behaviour management, special education). This is often done as a goodwill gesture by faculty and serves to further a spirit of collaboration between the institutions. The new Center for Professional Development in the College of Education will provide a more focused programme for such development. Reciprocity is also evident where principals and mentor teachers have been invited to participate in the campus-based programme as guest lecturers.

Social occasions have also provided a means of furthering a shared culture between the university and schools. For example, the student teachers organized an end-of-year afternoon of celebration, including food, certificates and gifts, to thank all those who had provided support to the practical and internship programme. An occasion like this also provided opportunities for taking the university–school relationship further towards a 'network' rather than individual links.

Issues with the programme

The College of Education's links with local schools have been positive and effective in the main, but nevertheless, some challenges and issues have arisen. The first category is that of language and communication. The faculty of the College of Education is entirely made of native English speakers while the majority of principals and teachers have Arabic as their first language and vary markedly in their knowledge and use of English. It has thus been necessary for faculty to take Arabic-speaking support staff with them to schools on several occasions. Recently an Arabic-speaking faculty member from another college has been assigned to work with College of Education faculty in the evaluation of student teachers when lessons are delivered in Arabic. Support documents are also prepared in English and Arabic but a related problem is that good translators are not always readily available for this important work. College of Education administrative staff have played an important support role on a number of occasions (for example, with phone calls, communication and translation of documents). Another strategy is to ask the bilingual student teachers to assist in communication between faculty and mentor teachers but this may not always be appropriate (for example, in some evaluative contexts).

Some cultural issues have arisen during practicals and internship. For example, the bulk of the students are placed in girls' schools staffed by female teachers. In a Muslim society this entails some restrictions on male faculty access to discussions with some teachers and to some classrooms. The student teachers are comfortable in their interactions with male faculty but some teachers are not. In these cases, the SPC must be sensitive to school and staff cultural expectations.

A third issue in the development of relationships with schools has been a logistical one. For example, the school timetables vary considerably across sectors. University and school timetables do not always overlap, and it can be difficult for faculty to keep a balance between their supervision roles and other teaching responsibilities. Schools often open and close early (i.e. by midday or early afternoon) and this restricts the time available to do multiple visits to interns, especially those working in schools at a distance from the university.

Student–mentor teacher interactions

Student teachers are a key element in the development of school–university relationships and the evolutionary nature of Zayed University's links to schools has allowed for some interesting opportunities for some students to extend their interactions with school staff. Senior interns are often entrusted with higher levels of responsibility than their western counterparts enjoy, where principals recognize their particular skills. During a recent internship, for example, a group of students who majored in computer and information systems was invited to participate in the development of a school-wide curriculum plan and the professional development of teachers. Student teachers have also been involved in resource development and demonstration of the uses of technology in classroom programmes. Such opportunities allow student teachers to develop the leadership skills that are part of the overall learning outcomes for their university programme.

Future directions

The eight school–university networks, outlined above, provide some understanding of the challenges to improving the quality of education in the UAE. The efforts to date are quite encouraging and provide an impetus to improve upon what exists and to forge new networks.

The College of Education at Zayed University has embarked on a number of mutually beneficial arrangements that involve all education stakeholders in the UAE. Contributions from the Ministry of Education and Youth, supervisors, private and public school teachers, tertiary institutions and faculty from other university colleges have been harnessed in a number of partnership and network agreements. By taking advantage of the special strengths of each of these stakeholders, synergies can be achieved that allow the needs of all to be met. These mutually beneficial alliances are designed to bring the community together in pursuit of common educational goals. Formal partnerships provide the structure needed to effect beneficial changes to the current system.

While the formation of these partnerships is complete, the partnerships themselves are very much in an embryonic stage. For example, partnerships with parents, while important, have yet to be established. Some effort to involve parents in committees is under way. The College of Education must continue to take a leadership role in the development and maintenance of these networks. The problems commonly associated with partnerships need to be overcome: inertia, resistance, inefficiency and unequal power relations. Attempts to address these and other related problems will shape the future directions of these partnerships in general and the College of Education in particular. In endeavouring to maximize the benefits of networks, the College of Education plans to:

1. Engage in ongoing dialogue with stakeholders to formulate and review common goals and expectations.
2. Determine, in negotiation with stakeholders, mutually beneficial priorities.
3. Negotiate processes for democratic management.
4. Promote equitable selection and ensure that all stakeholders share in the decision-making process.
5. Design a sustained system of evaluation.
6. Harness the feedback of stakeholders to measure future outcomes for the College of Education.
7. Analyse, evaluate and identify best practices and modify its programme to meet the needs of its education partners.
8. Promote discourse on the future directions of partnerships and the College of Education.

The task of improving education through the creation and maintenance of networks has barely begun. These partnerships must be structured to maximize the benefits for all stakeholders. The biggest obstacle facing their success is the divergent backgrounds of various partners. While the Ministry of Education has embraced a mission towards modernizing methods of instruction and assessment, the process of modernization will take time. Thus, strengthening the relationship between teachers and students during internship and practicals is a major priority. As Myers (1995) argues, a close working relationship between the school as a learning community and the university as a learning community needs to take place. In the long-term, the effectiveness of partnerships that have been formed between various stakeholders in the UAE education community will rely on joint planning, steady focused attention and a sustained system of evaluation. It is hoped that a spirit of involvement and mutual respect will develop between these partners as they work together to achieve common goals.

References

Benjamin, R. (1999) 'Developing the united Arab workforce for 2015' *Education and the Arab World: Challenges in the next millennium*. Abu Dhabi, UAE: The Emirates Center for Strategic Studies.

Birrell, J., Young, J., Egan, M., Ostlund, M., Cook, P., Tibbitte, C. and DeWitt, P. (1998) 'Deinstitutionalizing teacher preparation in a collaborative, school-based program' *Professional Educator*, 20 (3): 25–36.

Bowman, C. and Ward, P. (1999) 'Extending the vision: Mentoring through university–school partnerships' *Mid-Western Educational Researcher*, 12 (4): 33–7.

Davies, D. (1999) 'Introduction' *Education and the Arab World: Challenges in the Next Millennium*. Abu Dhabi, UAE: The Emirates Center for Strategic Studies.

Field, T. (2002) Partnerships to improve teaching and learning. http://www.scre. ac.uk (accessed).

Friedland, B. and Walz, L. (2001) 'Pre-teachers evaluate university–school partnerships for curriculum adaptation and access for students with disabilities in rural classrooms' *Growing Partnerships for Rural Special Education Conference Proceedings*. San Diego, CA.

Goodlad, J. (1991) 'School–university partnerships' *National Digest*, 58 (8), 58–61.

Kirby, P.C. and Meza, J. (1995) 'University-district-school, collaboration for school restructuring'. Paper presented at the annual meeting of the American Association of Colleges of Teacher Education. Washington DC.

Martin, C. (2000) 'University outreach and affirmation action' *ADE Bulletin*, 125: 57–8.

Mayer, D. (1999) 'Preparing secondary teachers: Building professional identity within the context of school/university/community partnerships'. Paper presented at Initial Teacher Education Forum. RMIT University, Melbourne.

Mograby, A. (1999) 'Human development in the United Arab Emirates: Indicators and challenges' *Education and the Arab World: Challenges in the Next Millennium*. Abu Dhabi, UAE: The Emirates Center for Strategic Studies.

Murrell, P. (1998) *Like Stone Soup: The Role of the Professional Development School in the Renewal of Urban Schools*. Washington DC: American Association of Colleges of Teacher Education Publications.

Myers, C. (1995) 'Building and sustaining school-university collaborative learning communities: Overcoming potential inhibiting factors'. Paper presented at the Annual Meeting of the American Association of Colleges for Teacher Education. Washington DC.

Myers, C. (1997) 'Reconceptualizing learning, teaching and schools as the next stage in teacher education reform and school renewal'. Paper presented at the Annual Meeting of the American Association of Colleges for Teacher Education. Phoenix, AZ.

National Network for Educational Renewal (2002) Telling our story: Unravelling the lessons from a complex change initiative – Agenda for education in a democracy. http://mse.byu.edu/nner/main/history7/htm (accessed).

Reising, B. and Pope, C. (1999) 'Technology in language arts teacher education' *Clearing House*, 72 (4): 196–7.

Scharge, M. (1991) *Shared Minds*. Random House: New York.

Shinners, K. (2001) 'Public/private school partnerships: What can be learned from the corporate school partnerships'. Paper presented at the Annual Meeting of the American Educational Research Association. Seattle, WA.

Skeele, R. and Daly, J. (1999) 'Symbiosis: University–school partnerships' *Journal of Interactive Instruction Development*, 12 (1): 31–40.

Thorkildsen, R. and Stein, M. (1996) 'Fundamental characteristics of successful university–school partnerships' *School Community Journal*, 6 (2): 79–92.

United Nations Development Programme (UNDP), Arab Fund for Economic and Social Development (2002) *Arab Human Development Report 2002: Creating Opportunities for Future Generations*. New York: United Nations Development Programme.

Van Zandt, L.M. (1996) 'Assessing the effects of reform in teacher education: An evaluation of the MAT programme at Trinity University'. Paper presented at the Annual Meeting of the American Educational Research Association. New York.

eight

Networking as a strategy for restructuring basic and further teacher education

Tero Autio and Eero Ropo

Introduction

Networking in teacher education can be discussed from at least two different perspectives. First, there is the pre-service perspective and the second perspective relates to in-service teacher education and school development. We will address both perspectives, although our main focus is on the first perspective of networking in pre-service teacher education.

Our starting point in this chapter can be expressed by Fullan's (1993) idea that student learning cannot be improved without improving teacher learning (see also Chapter 1 in this book). We also agree with the belief that teachers need to network in order to cooperate and communicate, share ideas and see different approaches applied in teaching (O'Hair *et al.* 2000). Our purpose is to review and elaborate theoretical perspectives related to teacher learning in networks. We consider this to be particularly important for enhancing the learning effects of networking for the individual and institutional participants.

The chapter is divided into two parts. We first discuss some of the trends and forces that affect education and curricula in the current societal situation in Western societies. We argue that globalization and individualization, as a result of the processes involved, have permanently changed the arena of education and are also making themselves felt in teacher education. Consequently, networking has become a way of life and living. It is, therefore, important to study the theory related to learning in networks.

We propose an autobiographical approach to thinking about learning, education and the curriculum. This framework offers a way of thinking about learning as an essential part of the life course. We argue that from the perspective of life course, learning can best be described as auto-biographically individualized. This approach may be applied to both individuals and organizations. Our point is that autobiographical learning is enhanced by interaction with the social context. Networking at its best provides an arena for interaction. Networks are formed by institutions, and they provide forums for people to meet, engage in discourse, exchange ideas and communicate. At the mental level, networking means reflecting on the experiences of social interaction. In short, we may say that an auto-biographical approach promotes the cultivation and preservation of individual multiple identities in accordance with the ineluctable wider social heterogeneity of postmodern, multicultural society.

In the last part of the chapter we describe a curriculum studies oriented teacher education programme (CuSto), developed and ongoing at our institution. This programme aims to promote our theoretical ideas on individualization as a social structure. This conceptualization relates individualization to networking. Networking is seen in the CuStu programme as an organizational locus for individualization in order to provide, according to critical postmodern curriculum theory, informed and enriched options to identify practical problems and to find creatively situated and viable solutions to them. Although we describe the curricular ideas of the programme thoroughly, a description of the network operations and the institutional participants can be found at the end of this chapter.

The globalized context of education

The term globalization is often used to describe the myriad changes in trade, production, mobility and access to information. For instance, Gibson-Graham (1996: 121) defines globalization as:

> a set of processes by which the world is rapidly being integrated into one economic space via increased international trade, the internalisation of production and financial markets, the internationalisation of a commodity culture promoted by an increasingly networked global telecommunications system.

Globalization as a term has been used increasingly to refer to a number of changes in economy and trade, culture and politics. The 'global world' described as a unified 'economic space is increasingly connected to cultural influence and to political relations that are also global in nature' (Stromquist and Monkman 2000: 4). It is quite clear that these changes have implications well beyond the aim of developing an individual self to adjust (Burbules and Torres 2000). How much and the extent to which globalization changes education and what consequences those changes have for education is, however, debatable. Burbules and Torres (2000: 14) have listed a few of the characteristics of globalization they consider to be related to education.

- in economic terms, a transition from Fordist to post-Fordist forms of workplace organization; a rise in internationalized advertising and consumption patterns; a reduction in barriers to the free flow of goods, workers and investments across national borders; and correspondingly new pressures on the roles of worker and consumer in society
- in political terms, a certain loss of nation-state sovereignty, or at least the erosion of national autonomy, and correspondingly, a weakening of the notion of a 'citizen' as a unified and unifying concept, a concept that can be characterized by precise roles, rights, obligations and status
- in cultural terms, a tension between the ways in which globalization brings forth more standardization and cultural homogeneity while also bringing more fragmentation through the rise of locally oriented movements.

In this chapter we have adopted the same position as Burbules and Torres (see Burbules and Torres 2000: 18–19). They believe that it is hard to see any single answer to the question of how globalization changes educational policy or practice worldwide. They think that 'national and local economy, political and cultural changes are affected by, and actively responding to, globalising trends within a broad range of patterns' (ibid.: 18). New models of education can emerge from careful and critical analyses of these trends.

It is also important to analyse the influences and pressures of globalization on teacher education. We approach this question from the perspective that teacher education, being typically part of the national strategies for reforming education, is and will continue to be affected by globalization and its various side effects. Therefore, it is necessary to contemplate perspectives for reform strategies. Those strategies need to involve networking as an essential element.

Networking and individualization

We referred above to some of the findings researchers have emphasized about the globalization process. We will now focus on two of them, namely networking and individualization.

During the past two decades, networking has become not only a fashionable way of speaking of institutions and organizations but, in fact, a predominant feature in the change of societal institutions. The hierarchical order has been replaced increasingly by flat horizontal networks in managing the growing flows of knowledge and information and the accompanying distributions of power and authority. This process refers to the networking inside companies and organizations. Subsequently, new forms of power stratification have emerged, but the nature and identity of the new organizational constellations have not necessarily relied on the top-down model.

The proliferation of novel information and communication structures, supported and facilitated by information technology, has made the top-down model increasingly dysfunctional and ineffective. In a situation where information technology has enabled the knowledge and information explosion, hierarchical models of knowledge and power exchange of the industrialist epoch, the 'first modernity' in Beck's (1994) terms, simply do not work. The development has been accompanied decisively by changes in the power climate in most Western societies. There is hardly an unequivocal authority in any human sphere to decide on behalf of the majority. These effects have been reinforced by the fact that practices and relationships are no more primarily dependent on physical proximity. Consequently, the power to 'choose' has been transferred closer to the actors themselves or to the respective institutions. The quintessence of 'second modernity' lies in the novel interconnectedness between macro- and micro-structure: the free flow of information with all its effects, known as the process of globalization, and the simultaneous individualization of society.

The partly paradoxical interplay between globalization and individualization might also be a relevant point-of-view given the recent educational policies and respective reform pressures in educational settings. In general, the non-traditional individualist ideology of post, late or second modernity derives its importance from the novel social intensity of the individual (Autio 2002: 159).

> A number of properties, functions and activities attributable to the nation-state, the welfare state, the hierarchical firm, the family, and the centralized trade union have been otherwise located. Some of them have been extensively displaced onto global instances, while others have been intensively displaced, onto the individual, to conscious or unconscious subjectivity: in any sense more private instances.
>
> (Lash, in Beck and Beck-Gernsheim 2002: xi)

When the individual in the 'first modernity' was constituted in consonance with a set of roles in a variety of institutions, the functions that were once taking place at the interface of institution and individual in the role are now taking place much more intensively and closer to the individual (see Lash, in Beck and Beck-Gernsheim 2002: xi). Thus, by the outsourcing of the functions of the first modernity, globalization has effected a radical shift in the relationships between individuals and institutions.

What has happened is that there has been a de-normalization of roles. The individual has become 'nomadic'. There has been a move toward complexity, indeed toward 'chaos'. But it is somehow a regularisable chaos. The 'roles' of the first modernity depended very much on what Kant called determinate judgment; on prescription, on determinate rules. Now the individual must be much more the rule finder himself. Determinate judgment is replaced by 'reflective judgement'. Reflective judgment is not reflection because there is now no universal to subsume the particular. In reflective judgment the individual must find the rule. Reflective judgment is always a question of uncertainty, of risk, but it also leaves the door open much more to innovation.

(ibid.: xi)

This way individualization has become a structural characteristic of highly differentiated societies (see Autio 2002: 160). In the field of education and curriculum, the process of individualization has yielded two contrasting outcomes. In curriculum theory, the theoretical expanding of the understanding of the epistemological, cultural and social constitution of the individuality is markedly enhanced by postmodern theory and critique by its methodological and epistemological relativism. In curriculum planning and practice, this expanded understanding is squeezed yet again by the exploitation of this very individualization for managerial and political uses by standardizing the desirable learning outcomes and by burdening the individual with new loads previously belonging to institutions (for example, teacher accountability). For instance, regarding the work of the teachers, 'restructuring of education' or 'devolution of schooling' have not only meant an increase in the power to 'choose', or to decide about one's work but, paradoxically, these efforts have arguably resulted in the further intensification of teaching from without. What is at stake could be succinctly defined as a struggle for the teacher's soul (see, for example, Goodson 1998; Klette *et al.* 2000; Whitty 2002).

We argue that those sweeping developments in economy and material production but also in politics and in the identity of the nation-state (Giddens 1990; Crook *et al.* 1992), in culture and identity formation (Beck *et al.* 1994) have irreversibly changed the context of education and teacher education in particular. The accompanying processes of globalization and individualization have implications that challenge the traditional institutional isolation of schools and teacher education. The introduction of new educational agendas reflecting those changes while emphasizing devolution and deregulation as new forms of educational governance, has far-reaching impacts on teaching and teachers' work that may not have been clearly recognized in the traditional curricula of teacher education or teachers' in-service training.

As a partial and local response to the need to review the current practice of teacher education we discuss the networked teacher education model developed and applied in some programmes at the University of Tampere, Finland. We describe the basic guidelines of the model and then discuss the experiences with its application. We argue that the networked teacher education model also addresses many of the current problems of quality and access to teacher education. We do not claim that the questions teacher education is facing are ubiquitous or similar or even related as they draw heavily on national, historical and local idiosyncrasies and imageries. Consequently, our experiences from our own model may prove helpful in different local contexts while rethinking teacher education and attempting collaborative and networked responses to uncertainty.

The Finnish case

The overall interest in the content of teacher education has increased in Finnish society in the past decade. The reasons for this have been largely uncovered, but we may speculate that at least one of the reasons is the predicted lack of workforce from 2007 onwards. Consequently, industry leaders have, in their public appearances, stressed the strategic importance of teacher education. This indicates that teacher education is no longer a monopoly of the universities but is done in the ideological, practical and theoretical context of an information society and its myriad stakeholders.

The context of teacher education is an information society. Such a society, described, for instance, by Castells (1997) is rich in technology and networking, having the values advocated by the globalized economy and emphasizing social networks and technology-enhanced communication in establishing and maintaining human relations. Education has experienced the same invasion of information and communication technology.

Concurrently with the global trends, the importance of local culture and local issues has increased in teacher education. Serving the local communities and schools is a new task of the Finnish universities mandated by recent legislation. This aim is political in nature, but influences the directions university education will take in the future. In teacher education this means participation in school development networks, teacher in-service training, and curriculum development and assessment in the schools.

The challenges to teacher education are said to be huge. In Finland those challenges have been addressed with nationally coordinated development agendas. The following goals have been listed in the most recent of them (Ministry of Education 2001):

- give every teacher the basics of instructional and communication technology skills
- offer every teacher mandatory courses on special education
- provide pre-service teachers with better skills in multiculturalism and multicultural teaching
- prepare teachers to design school-level quality systems and quality assessments
- offer teachers a better conception of school-level curriculum development
- provide pre-service teachers with knowledge of the issues of human relations in the workplace, teach them to work in teams and provide them with basic knowledge of school administration and management
- equip teachers with skills and experience in working with students' parents and families, and other stakeholders of the school.

The above are just examples of the goals listed in the national development programme, but suffice to show that there are a lot of pressures when it comes to developing teacher education. Since our purpose is not to analyse the reasons for the pressures and trends, we only remind ourselves and readers that there is a need to analyse past policies and trends, and the current contexts of teacher education, to understand the origins of the programmes such as the one above. Adopting the globalization framework that we have sketched above might prove fruitful in those analyses.

In the Finnish context, teacher education and secondary teacher education, in particular, have been under considerable pressure to incorporate the above goals in the relatively short, one-year programme. The solution is not to increase the number of courses or credit points (hours) of the teacher education component of the Master's Degree. It is, consequently, necessary to redesign the current programme to respond to the new requirements and challenges.

Our programme at the University of Tampere has been designed over the past five years. It is an early attempt under careful scrutiny that aims to gather the experiences of new forms and procedures in teacher education.

Networked model of teacher education at the University of Tampere

The principles of Finnish teacher education have been drawn up throughout the long tradition of European teacher education. The ideas are initially from the 18th century when *Normalschulen* ('normal schools') in German speaking areas and the Paris *École Normale* were established. Both teacher education models were intended to set standards by which teaching competence could be assessed. The structure of teacher education has since then remained by and large intact. In Finland, we still have 'normal schools' as an institutional monopoly with their privileged status in the field of teacher education.

The curricula of Finnish teacher education aimed both at primary and secondary teaching, have revolved around a clear division of labour between theory and practice. In secondary teacher education, theoretical studies have consisted mainly of elementary notions of educational science, most notably educational psychology and the so-called subject matter didactics. The purpose of those studies has been to provide the student teacher with the basic skills of syllabus and lesson planning, the skills of presentation and classroom management, and other traditional virtues of the teaching profession. The task of the 'normal schools', in turn, as the sole place for practice teaching, has been to familiarize student teachers with the routines of the normal school classroom.

The typical model of teacher education considers teaching and curriculum largely as technical matters to be transferred unreflectively in the form of skills and routines by the 'normal school' system. Instead, we have created a programme that attempts to take better account of the changed context of education, teaching and curriculum planning. Those shifts in the programme reflect, for their part, the two major and inseparable trends of the changed world: globalization and individualization. Globalization has made the taken-for-granted presuppositions and imageries of the national curriculum as a purely domestic issue as questionable, as is the case of the national economy. For instance, Spring (1998) observed that global economic pressures have caused the national curricula to become more homogenous in many Asian and European countries. An important question related to this concerns the kind of changes needed in teacher education.

For the teacher education curricula, this would mean a new challenge to rethink and redefine the competencies teacher education has traditionally promoted. In the current restructured practice of education there is a tendency to reduce the full participation of teachers in curriculum planning and limit their agency to the implementation of curricula designed without the input of teachers themselves. Additionally, assessment and external control together constitute an attempt to achieve this limited teacher role. The neoliberal policy has become increasingly obvious for countries like Finland, which have traditionally put considerable effort into the professional freedom and autonomy of the teaching profession and school practice.

The teacher education curriculum will play a key role in identifying the alien and often arbitrary demands of educational stakeholders and becoming aware of the increasingly open politicization of the curriculum (cf. Kelly 1999). The previous view of teaching and teacher identity as a unified nationally-mandated project has been disturbed by the processes of globalization. Klette *et al.* (2000: 18–21) argue that the restructuring context of teaching and curriculum will require of the teachers new kinds of competences, such as a greater ability to cooperate with parents and other local authorities and partners, the ability to design local versions of national framework curricula, the ability to adapt their work with increased planning, and coping with the pressures of new evaluation and assessment systems. Succinctly, then, the teacher education curriculum must help prospective teachers not only to cope successfully with the situations in the classroom, but also provide them with sufficient literacy of the surrounding world to interpret how the 'globalized' world is shaping their professional practice.

The aim of our revised programme (the CuStu programme) is to provide students with a comprehensive curricular matrix that includes a rich variety of theoretical approaches to education, curriculum and instruction. This is not only theoretical, but is also intended to encourage students to explore and experiment in their teaching practice during their year in teacher education. The CuStu programme, which is currently available to students majoring in philosophy, psychology, social psychology, sociology, political science and other social sciences, is theoretically organized around the discipline of curriculum studies.

Curriculum conceived of both as an intellectual and organizational centrepiece of education aims at providing not only tools for classroom practice in different educational settings (from primary to higher education), but also an arena for perceiving and reflecting education, culture and society at large. Curriculum is indicative with regard to power and political relations in society, economic tides and turns, gender relations, multicultural and racial issues, and the ideals of self that society will promote through education. Curriculum studies is useful from the perspectives of subject matter. Students benefit from it while reflecting the various views of sciences and disciplines. It is also helpful in recognizing the nature of science as a vital mode of learning, perceiving the reciprocal relationships between sciences and identifying their educational relevance. Curriculum studies also provide an approach to contemplate internal and historical developments and disputes within the provision of education drawing on different theoretical and geographical roots (for example, the Anglo-American curriculum studies versus the German didactics tradition).

Theoretical networking of teacher education across historical and contemporary intellectual and scientific traditions by curriculum studies is complemented by teaching practice. The guiding principle of practice is to familiarize the prospective teachers with the working cultures in different educational settings, from basic education to higher and university education, from general to vocational education. This kind of multi-focused and networked approach serves at least two goals. First, the prospective teacher is able to see what happens to her or his subject matter as it is taught and learned in the university lecture halls and seminars or transferred to other educational settings and institutions. Second, these hands-on observations during teaching practice may enhance a student's competence and the development of expertise in general. It is also probable that subject matter competence would be improved, and similarly the awareness of what obstacles or difficulties there might ensue when some pieces of science or discipline are to be conveyed into non-expert, school pupils' minds. Professionally, this kind of approach during basic education training might help the student to find a professionally and personally suitable working arena and provide better options in future to move from one level to another or to make one's way in an unstable job market. More generally, the ultimate aim of our networked teacher education approach is to find ways to cope with the increasingly fragmented cultural, social and personal reality with the official and often rigid system of schooling. One way out might be to take more serious account of the social intensivity of the individual, also in the field of teacher education, where individuality has traditionally been interpreted in terms of collectivization and standardization, in the spirit of the traditional guiding beacons of educational psychology: 'conformity of wills' and 'predictability of behaviour' (see Autio 2002: 110).

In the CuStu programme we have attempted to address, on a minor scale, some other major challenges that teacher education is currently facing. The first is the discourse between the universities and the community. Teacher education can and should perhaps be thought of as a mode of discourse that universities have with the local community. Schools should not be left alone, and schools should not work alone. Networking with the university and each other is necessary. However, from the university point-of-view, it is equally important to be networked to the schools and community. Networks differ, but it is necessary to build and support them. In our case, developing a network of local schools and pre-service teaching has been one of the major challenges.

Networks are also an important tool for in-service teacher education. Teachers' continuing education, education at work, has not been a main obligation of the universities in the past. However, it is important to keep school teaching and instruction up-to-date and that it should be based critically on the latest research. Teaching in teams, the use of technology and multicultural education are just some examples of research-based innovations that diffuse optimally through the networks of schools and universities.

Individualization and the autobiographical approach to teacher education

We have described above the basis of our programme mainly from societal and sociological points of view, orienting from global frameworks. Our programme and ideas for developing it also rest on another historically important cornerstone – individuality and individual learning.

Psychology has advocated an instructional model in which learning is the key process and term. Theories of learning have come and gone, but the process remains, in the focus of every teacher, student and administrator. We have incorporated an implementation of the so-called autobiographical model of human learning and development into our programme. This model is not an established method, but rather an attitude in the making. The main idea comes from the concept of 'currere' (Pinar and Grumet 1976; Grumet 1980; Pinar 1994). The concept of 'currere' (infinitive) is a Latin word meaning to run, to move quickly (on foot, on a horse, by ship, etc., to hasten, fly, sail, flow). The first person singular form in Latin is 'curro' (I run). Slattery (1995) argues that educators forget that curriculum is an active process; not only a lesson plan, guidebook, a list of goals and purposes or a textbook. Curriculum, according to Slattery (1995), is a holistic life experience, the journey of becoming a self-aware subject capable of shaping his or her life path. In this sense our autobiographical model of teacher education advocates 'curro', the processes of one's own 'running'.

> As a perpetual struggle, the curriculum in Pinar's currere is never a finished product that can be finally mastered and passed along to an awaiting new generation. Such a perspective protects the curriculum from the all-too-common fragmentation of modernist pedagogies, as it focuses our attention on the lived realities, socio-political encounters, and the identity formation of individual human beings.
>
> (Kincheloe 1998: 130)

The autobiographical approach emphasizes the need for reflective practice in which the main element to reflect upon is one's own existence and its relation to the contexts of life and time. For classroom teachers, currere insisted that the self should never be collapsed into subject matter, that self and identity should be cultivated in relation to the learning processes (Kincheloe 1998: 130). According to Pinar (1994), in a 'currere' guided classroom, planning should be informal and personal, allowing teachers room to adjust to the idiosyncrasies and needs of students. What is special about teaching is the moment-by-moment experience of specific teachers and students in a particular place at a particular time (Kincheloe 1998: 136).

The autobiographical approach to teacher education celebrates teaching in which the teacher identifies issues that the participants may be unaware of but that are related to the current classroom situation and participants' past experiences and future prospects. Learning as an autobiographical experience relates its content to those issues that are personally meaningful because of one's personal history, current experiences or plans and expectations for the future. Development of self (edification) and identity are the key processes of teaching and education in which all learning can and, in our view, should be anchored. In teacher education students are encouraged to develop their own self-knowledge and identity while learning how to teach school students to do the same (see Kincheloe 1998: 135).

The adoption of an autobiographical approach or, as we call it, being inspired by hermeneutic tradition has many currently unexplored implications. We have probably more questions than answers. However and therefore, it is important to learn and continue by applying the theoretically rich literature that appears to inspire multidisciplinary oriented researchers in many countries.

Implementation and experiences of the model by networking

The developments in the psychological and sociological conceptions of the narrative nature of personal identity, autobiography and 'curro' are all inspiring from the perspective of teacher education. Yet, it could be maintained that the culture of the school institution still adheres to the individualization concept of the 'first modernity'; at least in the sense of institutional and professional isolation. This predilection for the organizational and institutional encapsulation of schooling has naturally long roots in history, theories and practice. It has been embodied, for instance, in the strict organizational boundaries between the school levels, between the separation of general and vocational education, in subject matter divisions and in the individualistic working culture of a teacher. All these features are maintained and reproduced in teacher education programmes that traditionally and mainly focus on enhancing the methical competence of an individual teacher.

Most recently, the emphasis on individualization in terms of the first modernity has been fuelled by the assessment-led reforms which, through the accountability discourse, have stressed the performativity of a single and isolated 'unit' of the system, a teacher or a school. The ideology behind these principles is based on the hope of increasing the effectiveness of the system. However, one of the intended or perhaps unintended results has been increased, which is separation where the units of the system have been pitted against each other by invoking choice and competition. In fact, this mainly managerial stress of educational stakeholders on results has engendered scholarly concern about the possible deterioration of intellectual standards of schooling and educational outcomes at large (see, for example, Kelly 1999; Whitty 2002).

The basic bureaucratic structure of the school institution has effectively defied any attempts at large-scale and lasting change. The change has often been sought not through structural and organizational experimentation but through the working habits of single teachers – with frustrating results. The reform efforts to break out of the individualistic culture of schooling by top-down ventures might have resulted in caricature-like formations such as 'contrived collegiality' (Hargreaves 1994: 195–6).

In this sense, the idea of networking in education is not only to buck the trend, but an attempt to find a solution to a lasting organizational crisis. Change cannot be initiated in the first place by planning, but it should rather take place *reflexively*, through individuals. Hence, the creation of space for individual and collective exchange and creativity would be the main organizational and administrative principle in the educational settings of highly educated and advanced societies.

In order to attempt to convey these kinds of theoretical ideas into teaching practice, we have built a networked context basically for the learning environment for student teaching. The basic idea consists of a kind of matrix, which we think could be useful for new teachers for at least three reasons. First, our aim was to enhance the skills of new teachers in different levels of schooling. Second, we wanted to create space for student teachers' reflection about teaching and educational issues at large across different institutional contexts. Third, there has been a need to give opportunities to reflect upon what level of schooling or what kind of schools would be best suited to a student's present personal and professional aspirations, needs or dreams. The networked community consists of schools and institutions comprising both general and vocational educational settings: the junior high school and the high school of the Tampere Normal School, two polytechnic colleges (one focused on the secondary level education in technology, the other primarily on social work and health care), the Tampere High School for Adult Learners, the Police School of Tampere, the Tampere University of Technology and the University of Tampere. The exchange of ideas between different teachers and schools to arrange the educational environment for the practice of student teachers has led to many kinds of organizational and curricular experimentations and as such, as an unintended consequence, this networked practice has also proved to be an informal but much appreciated arena for the further learning of supervising teachers. At the individual level, the network is comprised of mentoring teachers and the official representatives of the institution (typically rectors or vice rectors). The University of Tampere is represented by the authors, one in the role of programme coordinator and the other as a department head.

The network has been initiated, its basic theoretical ideas established and operation in different levels has commenced. Initial experiences are very promising both from the university point-of-view and from the institutions' point-of-view. What this kind of organizational experimenting would mean, for instance, for the life of schools, for the organization of basic and further teacher education, for curricular innovation and cooperation in and across different settings will be seen in future. What is promising is that this type of networking is not only about meeting people, it is also meeting with ideas and thoughts that may have a great impact on teachers' individual thinking and the practices at the institutional level at the same time.

References

Autio, T. (2002) *Teaching under siege: beyond the traditional curriculum studies and/or Didaktik split.* Tampere: Tampere University Press.

Beck, U. (1994) 'The reinvention of politics' in U. Beck, A. Giddens and S. Lash (eds) *Reflexive modernization.* Cambridge: Polity Press.

Beck, U. and Beck-Gernsheim, E. (2002) *Individualisation.* London: Sage Publications.

Beck, U., Giddens, A. and Lash, S. (eds) (1994) *Reflexive modernization.* Cambridge: Polity Press.

Burbules, N.C. and Torres, C.A. (2000) 'Globalization and education: An introduction' in N.C. Burbules and C.A. Torres (eds) *Globalization and education: Critical perspectives,* pp. 1–26. London: Routledge.

Castells, M. (1997) *The power of identity. The information age: economy, society and culture.* Volume I. London: Routledge.

Crook, S., Pakulski, J. and Waters, M. (1992) *Postmodernization: change in advanced society.* London: Sage Publications.

Fullan, M.G. (1993) *Change Forces.* New York: Teachers College Press.

Gibson-Graham, J.K. (1996) *The end of capitalism (As we knew it): A feminist critique of political economy.* Cambridge, MA: Macmillan.

Giddens, A. (1990) *Consequences of modernity.* Cambridge: Polity Press.

Goodson, I. (1998) 'Storying the self: life politics and the teacher's life and work' in W.F. Pinar (ed.) *Curriculum: Toward new identities,* pp. 3–20. New York: Garland Publishing.

Grumet, M. (1980) 'Autobiography and reconceptualization' *Journal of Curriculum Theorizing,* 2 (2): 155–8.

Hargreaves, A. (1994) *Changing times, changing teachers: teachers' work and culture in the postmodern age.* London: Cassell.

Kelly, A.V. (1999) *The curriculum: theory and practice.* London: Peter Chapman Publishing.

Kincheloe, J.L. (1998) 'Pinar's currere and identity in hyperreality: Grounding the post-formal notion of intrapersonal intelligence' in W.F. Pinar (ed.) *Curriculum: Toward new identities*, pp. 129–42. New York: Garland Publishing.

Klette, K., Carlgren, I., Rasmussen, J., Simola, H. and Sundkvist, M. (2000). *Restructuring Nordic teachers: an analysis of policy texts from Finland, Denmark, Sweden and Norway*. University of Oslo, Report no. 10.

Lash, S. (2002) 'Individualisation in a non-linear mode' in U. Beck and E. Beck-Gernsheim *Individualisation* pp. vii-xiii. London: Sage Publications.

Ministry of Education (2001) *Opettajankoulutuksen kehittämisohjelma* (The development programme for teacher education). Available at http://www.minedu.fi.

O'Hair, M.J., McLaughlin, H.J. and Reitzug, U.C. (2000) *Foundations of Democratic Education*. Fort Worth: Harcourt College Publishers.

Pinar, W. (1994) *Autobiography, politics and sexuality: Essays in curriculum theory, 1972–1992*. New York: Peter Lang.

Pinar, W. and Grumet, M. (1976) *Toward a poor curriculum*. Dubuque, IA: Kendall/Hunt.

Slattery, P. (1995) *Curriculum development in the postmodern era*. New York: Garland Publishing.

Spring, J. (1998) *Education and the rise of the global economy*. Mahwah: Lawrence Erlbaum.

Stromqvist, N. and Monkman, K. (eds) (2000) *Globalization and education: integration and contestation across cultures*. New York: Rowman & Littlefield Publishers.

Whitty, G. (2002) *Making sense of educational policy*. London: Paul Chapman Publishing.

Part 3

Networking of networks

nine

Quality education initiatives in Hong Kong: school networks in transition

William Y. Wu, Dennis W.K. Chan and Victor Forrester

In response to the impact of globalization and the demand for a knowledge-based workforce, many countries have a shared vision to strive for excellence in education through education initiatives that specifically address the market-defined needs of the twenty-first century. In Hong Kong, there were both governmental and non-governmental education initiatives to promote quality education at both the community level and the school level. This chapter aims at describing these quality education initiatives and examines the impact of these initiatives with respect to fostering school partnerships and school networks. These initiatives include: the Quality Assurance Inspection (QAI), the Quality Education Fund (QEF), the Outstanding School Awards (OSA), the Thinking Curriculum Project (TCP), the Thinking Project for Secondary Schools (TPSS) and the Thinking Project for Primary Schools (TPPS). Finally, it concludes with reflections on these school partnerships and school networks, and raises questions for future research.

There have been changes and reforms throughout the documented history of education in Hong Kong (Bickley 2002). Most recently, a series of reports issued by the Education Commission of the Hong Kong Government have led to the implementation of various educational policies to address societal needs and demands (see, for example, Cheng 2000; Cheng and Townsend 2000). Schools either individually or collectively have to make adjustments to address these changes.

The school sector has to be responsive to meet the current needs of Hong Kong's knowledge-based society. Students not only are trained to master generic skills, for example, literacy, numeracy, and life skills (UNESCO 1999), they are also expected to be conversant with the developmental needs of an information society, to be competent in information processing, and to be adaptable, flexible and pro-active in a changing and dynamic environment. Thus, the question of how to promote quality education in the school sector has posed a challenge to all educators world-wide and has been given top priority among attempts to improve education.

To foster quality education, the Curriculum Development Council of the Hong Kong Government proposed a series of short-term (2001–2005), medium-term (2006–2010) and long-term (beyond 2011) plans for the Hong Kong school curriculum. The goal for the new school curriculum to be implemented within the first decade of the twenty-first century is to enable students to attain all-round development and lifelong learning. The focus of the implementation strategies is to accumulate experiences gradually and to build up partnerships. Different forms of partnership have also been identified and established. Some of the important partnerships include:

1   university partnership projects
2   District Teacher Networks (DTN) formed by professional associations
3   self-initiated networks of principals and teachers
4   learning communities in research and development projects organized by the Curriculum Development Institute
5   Regional Education Offices networks established by the Education Department
6   curriculum expert groups formed by the Government of Hong Kong and mainland China
7   international educational networks (Curriculum Development Council 2001).

This chapter seeks to provide an overview of some of the recent quality education initiatives in Hong Kong and to examine the impact of these initiatives on initiating school partnerships and school networks in the school sector. Though it is understood that a network or networking is not a well-defined concept, it is possible to identify school networks as entities which have similar concerns and a common educational philosophy but with differences in practice, experiences and new ideas (Veugelers and Zijlstra 2002). The term 'school network' in this chapter is in line with this working definition. It refers to a number of loosely coupled schools working collaboratively together on a very informal basis with a common interest to accomplish specific tasks in their coping with changes and in their quest for quality education. Similarly, the term 'school partnership' also refers to such collaborative relationships, but it is on a smaller scale and may only involve two schools.

This chapter comprises three sections. The first section entitled 'Governmental quality education initiatives and school networks' describes three recent educational initiatives of the Hong Kong government. It examines these initiatives with reference to what they have done to foster quality education at the school level and their impact on initiating school partnerships and school networks at the community level. The second section entitled 'Non-governmental quality education initiatives and school networks' examines three thinking-skills projects of Hong Kong Baptist University designed to promote quality education. The impact of these non-governmental initiatives are examined at both the school level and at the community level. The concluding section reflects on these school partnerships and school networks and raises questions for further research.

Governmental quality education initiatives and school networks

As part of Hong Kong's response to the impact of globalization, there has inevitably been concern about the ability of the education system to meet the market-demands for a knowledge-based workforce (Mok and Chan 2002; Lee and Gopinathan 2003). The government-initiated attempts to promote quality education in Hong Kong represent a systemic approach to encourage schools to improve themselves and to prove their worth in positively contributing to the social and economic development of Hong Kong. Three quality education initiatives are described below. They are:

1   the Quality Assurance Inspection (QAI), put forth in the Education Commission Report No. 7 (Education Commission 1996)
2   the Quality Education Fund (QEF), set up by the Chief Executive of the Hong Kong Special Administrative Region Government (1998)
3   the Outstanding School Awards (OSA), launched in June 1999.

Fostering a network of model schools through school inspection

Under the Quality Assurance Inspection (QAI) scheme, school inspections are described as 'open and transparent, identifying the strengths and weaknesses of individual schools, recommending improvement measures and taking appropriate action to assist those under-performing ones' (Education Commission 1996: 21). The QAI has adopted a whole-school approach and enlisted support from an array of officials, professionals, practitioners in schools and lay-persons from the community to help in the implementation of the scheme. This approach helps to build partnerships between the tertiary and school sectors on the one hand, and to foster a network of model schools covering planning and administration, teaching and learning on the other.

In the QAI process, performance indicators (PIs) are used as references to evaluate school performance under four domains of school work. The four domains are: Management and Organization, Learning and Teaching, Student Support and School Ethos, and Student Performance. The PIs can be used to facilitate schools to conduct self-evaluations and be used by the QAI teams to assess the effectiveness of individual schools. The Education and Manpower Bureau has published the PIs for secondary, primary and special schools and, in collaboration with the Social Welfare Department, the PIs for pre-primary institutions.

The success of a QAI depends on a mutual understanding and acceptance of the PIs by both the QAI team and the inspected schools concerned. Upon announcement of the inspection results, the improvement of quality is assumed to result from each individual school actively seeking the provision of professional and financial support. Judged from the QAI's perspective, the scheme has achieved its intended purpose in promoting quality education and improvement. Follow-up attempts on the part of the inspected schools are left entirely to the schools. As a result of the QAI, some inspected schools will naturally form collaborative partnerships in order to learn from one another's experiences, to seek advice from schools with a more satisfactory performance, and to sustain their quest for quality improvement. Though no systematic research has been conducted among inspected schools to enumerate the number of collaborative relationships formed, it is observed that in various degrees the QAI has occasioned such informal relationships between and among schools.

Promoting quality schools through diversified funding

The Quality Education Fund (QEF) represents the second systemic initiative of the government to foster quality education. It is an ambitious endeavour to identify and promote current 'good practice' in the school sector. When the QEF started in 1998, it was endowed with a sizeable budget of US$700 million. From 1998 to 2003, 4889 projects (US$350.82 million) have been approved.

Established as one of the major recommendations of the Education Commission Report No. 7 (1996), the QEF supports non-profit making initiatives within the ambit of basic education, i.e., pre-primary, primary, secondary and special education. Funding is directed to projects within five broad developmental categories: Effective Learning, All-round Education, Implementing School-based Management, Exploring Education Issues and Application of Information Technology (http://www.info.gov.hk/qef/object/index.htm). It is important to note that the first four categories of the QEF are re-statements of the QAI four inspection domains. In effect, the QAI identifies school 'quality needs' and application to the QEF, where approved.

The QEF represents a paradigm shift that attempts to resolve the negative reaction commonly generated by 'top-down' change initiatives. This paradigm shift involves placing responsibility for change initiatives in the minds and hands of front-line personnel at school. Where the QAI may identify school strengths and deficiencies, the QEF may offer funding to address these needs in the terms of that school's own personnel. To formulate these terms and to successfully apply for QEF funding, both universities and schools are encouraged to form consulting partnerships to satisfy the competitive and increasingly rigorous vetting imposed on QEF applications. In harmony with the QAI initiative, QEF is managed by a steering committee consisting of educators, practitioners and lay-persons from the community. One of the market-orientated criteria of the QEF vetting process requires participating parties to provide evidence of their project's value-addedness.

The experience of the QEF indicates that there is ample evidence showing that many schools did form collaborations and consulting partnerships with universities in securing QEF support. These collaborative networks or partnerships have to come to an agreement on what counts as quality education and on how to assess what they regard as having value-addedness. Based on the fluctuating number of cross-sector projects and observations, various forms of informal school partnerships and school networks have come into existence as a result of the financial incentives offered by the QEF to promote quality education. These emerging or newly established collaborative relationships can only be described as loosely-coupled informal entities with common interests to cope with changes and to promote quality education at both the school and the community levels.

Establishing Outstanding School Awards

The third 'quality in education' initiative is the Outstanding School Awards (OSA), launched in 1999. The declared objectives are threefold – first, to give recognition and encouragement to schools with excellent performance; second, to promote and disseminate schools' excellent education practices; and third, to cultivate a quality culture within the school sector, to strive for excellence while considering the schools' unique conditions.

The OSA comprised two award levels – full awards and Certificates of Merit (COM) – to be earned by providing evidence of attainment across any one the QEF's five domains: Effective Learning, All-round Education, Implementing School-based Management, Exploring Education Issues or Application of Information Technology. The OSA results were announced in July 2001 with a total of 21 schools receiving 24 awards, including six full OSA and 18 COM.

The OSA scheme has been regarded as an ongoing quality school movement with a view to enhancing a culture of quality education.

Nominated schools are held not to be competing with one another, but against pre-determined standards – a process aimed at facilitating schools' reflection, self-learning and improvement, and thereby enhancing a culture of quality education.

The OSA frame of reference includes awards for fostering students' all-round development, effective management and school organization, self-set school goals, process standards and value-addedness. Notably, in certain key respects, the OSA frame of reference rephrases the four domains common to both the QAI and the QEF. In effect, schools gaining OSAs serve as QAI and QEF exemplars. By this systemic approach, the 'change-process' becomes a self-generating one. As a self-generating process, schools are left free to retain, strengthen or reform and renegotiate their current networks. With newly found freedom to choose to develop into a quality school, together with the financial incentive furnished by QEF, it is natural to assume that each school will be highly motivated to pursue quality through alliances and networks.

The impact of quality education initiatives on Hong Kong schools

In this section, the QAI, the QEF and the OSA have been described as governmental attempts to promote quality education in Hong Kong schools. These three initiatives have required schools to self-regenerate and accordingly have empowered the creative and critical thinking of the concerned parties. The combined effects of these three initiatives indicate that a systemic approach can promote and generate changes for better quality among schools. For example, the demands and evaluation of QAI, the increasingly rigorous criteria for vetting project proposals applying for the financial support of QEF, and the 'model-effect' of the awarded schools of OSA have, either separately or in combination, posed challenges to schools to pursue quality education and to demonstrate their accountability. Though opponents of monitoring performance of schools by external parties criticize the government for aligning school quality with seemingly quantifiable outcomes, these initiatives have nevertheless aroused, in various degrees, awareness of and a quest for quality education in the school sector. In addition to their impact at the school level, these initiatives have also generated collaborative school partnerships involving self-initiated networks of teachers and principals, partnerships with universities, and loosely-coupled school networks at the community level with a view to pursing quality education. These collaborative partnerships and school networks also serve to engage schools in critical self-reflection and self-improvement.

Non-governmental quality education initiatives and school networks

In the following section, attention will be focused on three non-governmental quality education initiatives, which aim at promoting quality education by equipping in-service and practising teachers with critical and creative thinking skills. It first examines the broader and the more specific contexts of these 'Thinking Teachers Initiatives', with particular reference to the local curriculum reform, and then briefly describes these initiatives all of which are targeted at training teachers with respect to higher order thinking skills.

Fostering quality education through curriculum changes

In promoting quality school education, the Government of the Hong Kong Special Administrative Region has put forth a number of proposals to review education. For example, re-examining the aims of education and revising the school curriculum (Curriculum Development Council 2000) are two of the most recent comprehensive reviews. While the former proposal focuses on reviewing the educational aims at all levels of education, the latter proposes a curriculum framework for curriculum development – *Learning to Learn* – in the school sector. The underlying rationale for curriculum development is well explicated in the following quotation from the Chairman of the Curriculum Development Council.

> In preparing the curriculum framework for Learning to Learn, which is a student-focused curriculum developed in the best interest of students, we firmly believe that all students could learn, and that they have different intelligences. We provide them with opportunities to learn. We identify key learning experiences and key learning areas, integrating the generic skills, values and attitudes that are essential to their whole person development. We help them to become more aware that there are different ways of learning. What is important is to enhance their quest for knowledge, their awareness and responsibilities in advancing the frontiers of knowledge.
>
> (Curriculum Development Council 2000: 1)

In the proposed curriculum framework the three components include:

1   eight key learning areas
2   nine generic skills
3   values and attitudes (for details of each component, see Curriculum Development Council 2000).

Of particular relevance to the three Thinking Teachers Initiatives described in this chapter is the component of generic skills. 'The component of generic skills is fundamental to help students learn how to learn. They are to be developed through the learning and teaching in the contexts of different subjects or key learning areas, and are transferable to different learning situations' (Curriculum Development Council 2000: 35).

Of the nine types of generic skills identified, three of them, in various degrees, are considered to be relevant to the Thinking Teachers Initiatives in promoting quality teacher education. They are: critical thinking skills, creativity and problem solving skills.

> Critical thinking skills help students to draw out meaning from given data or statements, generate and evaluate arguments, and make their own judgements. Creativity is the ability to produce original ideas and solve problems appropriate to the contexts. Problem solving skills help students to use thinking skills to resolve a difficulty and determine the best course of action.
>
> (Curriculum Development Council 2000: 36–7)

In the following section it is within the above-mentioned context of curriculum changes that the three Thinking Teachers Initiatives are described. These quality education initiatives have not only contributed to quality education in the midst of school curriculum reform, but also to initiating and establishing loosely-coupled thinking school networks in the pursuit of teaching thinking skills.

Fostering quality education through teaching higher-order thinking skills

There are clear examples of government initiatives to promote thinking schools. For example, in America the 1990s was declared by the US Congress as the 'Decade for Thinking'. In 1997, the Singapore Government established the goal of 'Thinking Schools, Learning Nation' (Chang 2001). In Hong Kong, this 'thinking movement' has found expression in some non-governmental initiatives. For example, the Thinking Curriculum Project (TCP), the Thinking Project for Secondary Schools (TPSS) and the Thinking Project for Primary Schools (TPPS) are Thinking Teachers Initiatives of Hong Kong's Baptist University with a focus on equipping teachers with higher-order thinking skills.

The first initiative (1993–1998), the Thinking Curriculum Project (TCP), involved training a total of 85 in-service student-teachers in a 20-hour course entitled 'Critical and Creative Thinking' (Centre for Educational Development 1999; Wu and Chan 1999). The second initiative (1998–2001) entitled 'Thinking Project for Secondary Schools' (TPSS) aimed at equipping more than 400 secondary school teachers and principals with thinking skills for improving the quality of their teaching at school. These teachers had to attend a 30-hour workshop series (Centre for Educational

Development 2002). The third initiative (2000–2003), the 'Thinking Project for Primary Schools' (TPPS) targeted for training 700 plus schoolteachers and principals and monitored six schools in their implementation of thinking lesson plans (Centre for Educational Development 2003). While direct teaching of thinking skills was found in all three thinking initiatives, infusion of thinking skills in subject instruction was a unique feature of the third initiative (Wu and Chan 2003).

In response to the call for quality education and school curriculum changes, the three thinking initiatives have made a significant impact on in-service and practising teachers by equipping them with the ability to apply thinking skills in their teaching at the school level. In addition, at the community level, they have initiated and fostered school partnerships as well as informal school networks among participant schools, who show a keen interest in teaching thinking skills to students across different grade levels. Examples of these networks are those formed by teachers and principals who were the workshop participants of the TCP, the TPSS and the TPPS. Some of these school networks share a common interest in focusing on direct teaching of thinking skills, others on infusion of thinking skills in content instruction, and still others on a combination of both. In these school partnerships and school networks, there is sharing of resources and experiences among teachers and an exchange of ideas on the teaching of thinking skills in seminars and conferences organized both formally and informally by professional associations and societies.

Cultivating a culture of thinking in informal school networks

If students are to learn to think critically, to access and evaluate information effectively, and to solve problems creatively in order to meet the challenges of the twenty-first century, it is essential that the teaching of thinking skills are promoted and practised at the school level. This is in line with the direction of curriculum reform as proposed by the Curriculum Development Council (2000) mentioned in the previous section of this chapter. The experiences obtained from equipping teachers with thinking skills in the thinking initiatives have provided valuable insight into the teaching of higher-order thinking skills in local schools.

In order to promote the teaching of thinking skills, initiating informal school networks with schools interested in higher-order thinking is just the first step. Equipping teachers with the skills to teach meta-cognitive skills is important, but no less important is the fostering of a classroom culture of thinking among schools. According to Tishman *et al.* (1995: 2), a classroom culture of thinking refers to 'a classroom environment in which several forces – language, values, expectations, and habits – work together to express and reinforce the enterprise of good thinking'. Just teaching thinking skills to students is not enough. If this teaching is to be successful, it has to take place in a learning environment where high-level thought – skills, attitudes, values and habits of mind – of both students and teachers are encouraged, supported and reinforced.

Tishman *et al.* (1995) define a culture of thinking as consisting of six dimensions of good thinking. These six dimensions include: a language of thinking vocabulary, thinking dispositions, mental management or meta-cognition, the strategic spirit, higher-order knowledge, and teaching for transfer. To what extent are these key dimensions of good thinking found in local schools? According to the observations of practising teachers participating in the thinking initiatives, few of these dimensions of a thinking culture were found in their schools. This suggests that more effort needs to be expended in fostering a thinking culture among schools.

Though the three initiatives have done very little with respect to cultivating a culture of thinking among the schools of the teacher participants, they have at least made a start in this direction. As a result of these quality education initiatives, it has been observed that informal school networks consisting of schools interested in promoting the teaching of thinking skills have emerged. Building on these school networks, the next step is to cultivate a culture of thinking among these schools in the short term and to sustain such a learning environment in these schools in the long term.

Concluding remarks

This chapter described three governmental and three non-governmental education initiatives put forth in Hong Kong for promoting quality education and their impact on schools, particularly with reference to the establishment of partnerships among schools and the emergence of informal school networks. While the former initiatives include the Quality Assurance Inspection (QAI), the Quality Education Fund (QEF) and the Outstanding School Awards (OSA), the latter comprise the Thinking Curriculum Project (TCP), the Thinking Project for Secondary Schools (TPSS) and the Thinking Project for Primary Schools (TPPS).

The QAI, the QEF and the OSA are governmental attempts aimed at promoting quality education among schools. While the QAI and the OSA tend to be systemic, the QEF adopts a non-systemic approach. To what extent are these initiatives successful in achieving their intended objectives? To what extent have they made an observable and significant impact on the quality of education at the school and community levels? Both questions are open to debate and to different interpretations. So far, no systematic research has been conducted to address these questions. Nevertheless, observations show that these initiatives, in various degrees, have occasioned partnerships among schools, collaboration between schools and universities, and informal school networks, all of which attempt to pursue quality education at the school level. These collaborative efforts, particularly those between and among schools themselves, are new or emerging networks in the local school sector with a clear and well-defined focus on striving for quality education.

The TCP, the TPSS and the TPPS are non-governmental efforts to promote quality education by equipping in-service and practising teachers with higher-order thinking skills. Unlike the governmental attempts, which are large-scale and cover a wide range of domains with respect to promoting quality education, these thinking initiatives are relatively small-scale with a narrow focus on the teaching of thinking skills. To what extent are these thinking initiatives successful in achieving their intended objectives? To what extent have they made a difference in teacher participants' teaching at school? These two questions are far less controversial. The feedback from teacher participants and principals indicated that these initiatives have made a significant impact on their thinking dispositions and their teaching at school. Like the governmental initiatives, both have generated partnerships among schools and informal school networks, and both have empowered the practice and the teaching of higher-order thinking skills.

The initiation and formation of informal collaborative relationships, whether they are between schools or among schools, in the local school sector have raised a number of questions. These questions include:

1   What is the potential impact of these partnerships and informal school networks on promoting quality education in Hong Kong?
2   What is their impact on individual schools in the short term and in the long term?
3   Will they become transient and dissolve in the short term?
4   Will they become more formalized and structured as they evolve in the long term?
5   If they become more formalized, what role will they play in the school sector?

This list of questions is by no means exhaustive. Systematic research is needed to address these interesting questions.

References

Bickley, G. (2002) *The development of education in Hong Kong 1841–1897: As revealed by the early education reports of the Hong Kong government 1848– 1896.* Hong Kong: Proverse Hong Kong.

Centre for Educational Development (1999) *The Thinking Curriculum Project report*. Hong Kong: Centre for Educational Development.

Centre for Educational Development (2002) *The Thinking Project for Secondary Schools report*. Hong Kong: Centre for Educational Development.

Centre for Educational Development (2003) *The Thinking Project for Primary Schools report*. Hong Kong: Centre for Educational Development.

Chang, S.C.A. (2001) 'Implementation of the "Thinking Schools, Learning Nation" initiative in Singapore' *Journal of Southeast Asian Education*, 2 (1): 13–41.

Cheng, Y.C. (2000) 'Educational change and development in Hong Kong: Effectiveness, quality, and relevance' in T. Townsend and Y.C. Cheng (eds) *Educational change and development in the Asia-Pacific region: Challenges for the future*, pp. 17–56. Lisse, The Netherlands: Swets and Zeitlinger Publishers.

Cheng, Y.C. and Townsend, T. (2000) 'Educational change and development in the Asia-Pacific region: Trends and issues' in T. Townsend and Y.C. Cheng (eds) *Educational change and development in the Asia-Pacific region: Challenges for the future*, pp. 317–43. Lisse, The Netherlands: Swets and Zeitlinger Publishers.

Curriculum Development Council (2000) *Consultation documents on learning to learn: The way forward in curriculum development*. Hong Kong: Curriculum Development Council, Hong Kong Special Administrative Region of the People's Republic of China.

Curriculum Development Council (2001) *Learning to learn: The way forward in curriculum development*. Hong Kong: Curriculum Development Council, Hong Kong Special Administrative Region of the People's Republic of China.

Education Commission (1996) *Education commission report no.7: Quality school education*. Hong Kong: Government Printer.

Lee, M.H. and Gopinathan, S. (2003) 'Convergence or divergences? Comparing education reforms in Hong Kong and Singapore' *Journal of Southeast Asian Education*, 4 (1): 71–103.

Mok, J.K.H. and Chan, D.K.K. (2002) 'Introduction' in J.K.H. Mok and D.K.K. Chan (eds) *Globalization and education: The quest for quality education in Hong Kong*, pp. 1–19. Hong Kong: Hong Kong University Press.

The Hong Kong Special Administration Region of the People's Republic of China (1998) *Address by the chief executive the honorable Tung Chee Hwa at the legislative council meeting on 7 October 1998*. Hong Kong: The Hong Kong Special Administrative Region of the People's Republic of China.

Tishman, S., Perkins, D. and Jay, E. (1995) *The thinking classroom: Learning and teaching in a culture of thinking*. Boston: Allyn and Bacon.

UNESCO (1999) UNESCO Task Force on Education for the Twenty-first Century. Retrieved on 3 December 2002 from http://www.unesco.org/delors/.

Veugelers, W. and Zijlstra, H. (2002) 'What goes on in a network? Some Dutch experiences' *Journal of Leadership in Education*, 5 (2): 163–74.

Wu, W.Y. and Chan, D.W.K. (2003) 'Thinking teachers initiatives in the Hong Kong context: Planning, implementation, and concerns' *Journal of Southeast Asian Education*, 4 (1): 30–47.

Wu, W.Y. and Chan, J.C.K. (1999) 'Exploring thinking curriculum in Hong Kong secondary school: A five-year retrospect' in M. Wass (ed.) *Enhancing learning:*

Challenge of integrating thinking and informal technology into the curriculum, Vol II, pp. 642–7. Singapore: Educational Research Association.

ten

From networking to school networks to 'networked' learning: the challenge for the Networked Learning Communities Programme

Mark Hadfield

In this chapter I want to discuss a movement, an arc, which maps out where much of the theory and practice around school networks, at least in the UK, currently appear to be leading. It is a movement where a value of professional networking has moved onto stressing the need to create more formalized networks of schools. At first, bringing schools into networks was primarily a means of helping deliver central and local government initiatives more effectively. Now the agenda is shifting as the power of networks which have come together around local interests is being harnessed as a mechanism for system-wide change. This is the movement from networking, to networks, to what we have termed, in the Networked Learning Communities Programme, 'networked learning'.

Networking has been around for sometime in the UK where there has been a number of school network structures arising from both central government initiatives and a plethora of local initiatives developed by schools and local education authorities. At this point, networks are being discussed as a means of dealing with a range of policy concerns from how to deal with the flattening performances of central improvement initiatives, such as the national Numeracy and Literacy Strategies, enhancing the leadership of schools, to dealing with broader multi-agency agendas encapsulated in the recent Green paper, Every Child Matters (DfES 2003). As an academic currently working within a national 'network of school networks' initiative, the Networked Learning Communities (NLC) Programme, my work spans this arc both practically and theoretically as we work with school networks that have arisen from both central as well as local initiatives.

The practical challenge for those who work within the core team of this development and research programme is how to move a group of networks from their existing levels of networking, or current structures based on delivering external initiatives, to the point where they are capable of engaging in what the programme team has called 'networked learning'. ' "Networked learning" is a unique form of lateral engagement (between schools and networks) required for effective network and system learning' (Jackson 2004). It is a form of learning that encompasses the notion of building capacity within schools and networks (Hopkins and Jackson 2002) so that they promote not just school- or network-level learning but system-wide learning.

> Networked learning is at the heart of collaborative capacity building. It occurs where people from different schools in a network engage with one another to enquire into practice, to innovate, to exchange knowledge and to learn together. Unlike 'networking', perhaps, it doesn't happen by accident and, in order to happen by design, alternative organisational patterns, new professional relationships and different forms of facilitation, intervention and brokerage are required.
>
> (Jackson 2004: 2)

Or, in the terminology of the NLC programme, the aim is to establish new norms around learning within networks so that 'Learning from, with and on behalf of others' (NLC 2003) becomes a reality. This commitment to learning on behalf of others is not just a vague aspiration or simply an espoused value within the programme. Those advising the core team recognize that it requires very specific structures and processes to evolve between schools and networks if teachers are to develop a belief in the need not only to learn with others, or share their existing expertise, but to actually learn and innovative for the benefit of others. 'The existence of more formal structures via a network offers a means of the whole system learning from what is going on in that network. The content is almost like a public good and the formal structures offer a way in which to understand that content' (Demos 2004). Our challenge, then, is how to create the structures and processes that can not only support the development of school networks but also offer a means of developing 'whole system learning'.

The theoretical challenge is of a similar order of complexity. The tone of much of the current theoretical debate in the UK is that school networks will need to become more than loosely linked associations of individuals if they are to deliver the potential system-wide benefits that their advocates outline for them. This gives rise to a need to establish clear water between notions of professional networking, which has long been an aspect of teachers' lives, and the idea of networks of schools that have the potential to influence fundamentally schools both within and outside of the network. In establishing this clear water, the theoretical debate surrounding the value of professional networking, which has long been seen as a key part of organizational capacity building (Mitchell and Sackney 2000), has moved on to a qualitatively different argument about the potential of networks as a source of 'collaborative capacity', which can have an effect at a system level.

> A central idea of the English reform agenda is that of a world class system driven by the energy of the schools. There is an assumption that collaboration is one of the ways in which that energy is generated and sustained. Accordingly, we need to look at how the reform agenda can build collaborative capacity across the school system – hence there is a reciprocity, a virtuous circle, in which reform now both depends upon collaborative capacity and seeks to build it.
>
> (Bentley 2003: 10)

To complete the theoretical arc, described previously, two further theoretical stages need to be fully articulated. The first is what a network with a high degree of collaborative capacity would look like, the second is how to create such networks. Particularly when currently networks with a capacity to influence other schools in a local area are rare, never mind having sufficient in number to influence the whole system. Put simply, we need a theory of both the thing 'in itself' we wish to create, a school network with sufficient capacity to influence schools outside it, and a theory of the changes needed to move schools from where they currently find themselves to the point where they are part of such networks. Unfortunately, there appears to be rather more agreement as to what counts as an effective school network, whether focused on professional development or school improvement, than there is about how best to develop them.

Not only is there a theoretical gap in current theories of how to develop networks of the kind we are seeking to create, there is also an inherent weakness in the approaches being adopted. In that they tend to discuss how to create networks from the perspective of what an effective school network looks like in practice and then work backwards. In doing so, they are making exactly the same error as previously made by theorists in both school improvement and effectiveness movements. It is a serious theoretical flaw to conflate the process and structures that occur within an effective school network with those that need to be put in place to build them in the first place. If we should not rely solely upon established successful school networks, where else should we look to understand more about how to develop networks? Obviously existing accounts of successful school networks are a starting point but they are limited when considering how to develop networks across a whole education system. This is because they are often based around specific well supported initiatives that have impacted upon only a small cross-section of schools. They therefore don't necessarily provide us with generalizable, or adaptable, approaches when a whole education system is being brought into various kinds of networks, from school to school and multi-agency. This is, in part, why I am interested in how theories of 'naturally' occurring networking and networks can inform the development of 'artificial' networks of schools.

My interest leads to questions such as: How can we fruitfully apply the constructs currently employed when discussing our current social world as a 'network society' (Castells 2000) to the work of those trying to create and lead networks of schools? How similar are the processes and structures that underpin social networks with those that occur within closely knit communities of practitioners? Are there qualitatively different forms of networking or is it more a case of some being simply more 'formalized' than others? Or closer to home whether the 'communities of practice' (Wenger 1998) that arise between individuals who share 'relations of belonging that expand identity through space and time in different ways' (Wenger 1998) in large organizations can extend our understanding of how to get teachers spread across a whole local education authority to work together to change how they teach? In this chapter, I am not going to attempt to answer these questions, rather I want to argue that much of the current discussion around different forms of networks prevents these questions being answered properly. Which might seem a surprising claim considering the role that the study of communities and other social networks have played in the development of ideas about school networks (Kerr *et al.* 2003).

The theoretical arc – the relationship between systems, structures and individual agency

I want to start my theoretical discussion not with an account of what constitutes a successful school network but with two contradictory quotes. The first by Giddens refers to the broad notion of social systems, including social networks such as those based on families, friends, ethnicity and community. The second quote, from the research and consultancy group Demos, is focused on school networks and discusses the difference between networks and networking. I want to use them as a means of exemplifying how current conceptions of the differences between 'informal' networking and 'formal' networks are hindering our learning from the extensive forms of social networks that currently exist and applying this to how to develop school networks. Giddens believes that to function, social systems logically require structures, in order to 'regularize' the interdependent relationships that make up and maintain the system.

Social systems involve regularized relations of interdependence between individuals or groups, that typically can be best analysed as recurrent social practices. Social systems are systems of social interaction ... Systems in this terminology, have structures, or, more accurately, have structural properties. Structures are necessarily (logically) properties of systems or collectives, and are characterized by the absence of a subject.

(Giddens cited in: Callinicos 1988: 92)

For Giddens there is an inextricable link between the existence of interdependent relations (networking) and social structures (networks). In contrast the next quote, from a recent Demos publication on school networks, tries to separate the general idea of networking from the notion of being part of a school network.

It is very easy to treat 'networks' and 'networking' as interchangeable terms. They are not, and we need to be clear about how they are different. We can think about the differences in terms of structures. A network implies a more formal organisational structure within which collaboration and working together takes place. Furthermore, a network can exist between schools or institutions.

Networking describes an activity rather than a structure. It takes place between people. So, it could be used to describe the activity within a network; equally it could be used to describe two (or more) teachers meeting to exchange ideas or thoughts before going their separate ways again. This is an important difference ... Networking, on the other hand, will inevitably remain more tacit as there are not the structures to amplify or make explicit what is being discussed. Arguably you cannot have networks without networking, but networking does not require networks.

(Demos 2004: 12)

Demos are right in trying to make this distinction between the informal professional networking which has always occurred between teachers, some 40 per cent of teachers in the UK recently claimed to be part of some form of network (GTC 2003) and more formalized networks of schools. Because they are trying to draw both a historical and theoretical distinction between previous educational networking activities and those that are now being developed and introduced in the UK. Unfortunately, although this distinction is useful when considering school networks it does us a disservice when we try to learn from other forms of social and professional networking. I believe that making such a strong distinction between networking as an informal process and networks as a structured process results in us throwing out the theoretical baby with the bath water. Demos are not making an original distinction, it occurs in various other writings about networks,

> Confusion over terminology – there is particular confusion in the literature between the terms **network** [which is about *structure*] and **networking** [which concerns *process, action and activity*] and often the two are used interchangeably. It is important to distinguish between these two terms. One is about *network structure* and the other is about *networking and coordination process.*
>
> (Kerr *et al.* 2003: 32)

It has led to the creation of an orthodoxy within the theoretical discussions of school networks. This is that the most significant distinction between broader social networks and school networks is the absence of structures in the former or, if present, they are in some way more informal than those in school networks. An orthodoxy which either flatly contradicts Giddens' theory, that structures are a logic necessity within anything we want to call a social system including networks, or leads to a failure to recognize the nature and functioning of these structures within informal networking. This is the confusion that still seems to blight many discussions of networks and networking.

My argument is that differentiating between the concepts of 'networks' and 'networking' in this rather dichotomous manner unhelpfully separates social action from social structures, when they need to be brought together. It leads to a number of problems in learning from other forms of networks when considering how to develop school networks. One of the most important of which is that insufficient attention has been paid to how the differences in the origin of structures and relationships within networks affects how they develop, and how they can be developed. In the final section of this conceptual framework I want to argue that we should pay more attention to the reasons why people are drawn into networks, or are placed within them, if we want to understand how to develop them.

Now there are a multitude of reasons why networks develop and persist, from people choosing to become part of a social network based on a hobby or interest to the recognition that we all rely upon several networks each day to help us do our jobs and feed our families. All I can do in the space available is to take two overarching and contrasting reasons for networks to develop and discuss how these affect how people could set about developing school networks.

Let's argue for a moment, as Giddens does, that the processes and structures in social networks arise fundamentally from the 'necessity' of interdependence. Individuals in social networks are in multiple interdependent relationships with others, their origins vary depending on the network. These interdependencies could be based around physical need or economic survival and may or may not create a sense of being inter-dependent among the group, through some kind of shared identity. Individuals therefore may not have any knowledge of those they are dependent upon but they are aware of the structures through which they engage with them. The structures and processes that characterize a social network would therefore tend to originate from necessity, a state of interdependence which we often denigrate by terming dependence. Relationships built around the agency of people are secondary in the development of such networks and when they occur many are built on and affected by the 'necessity' of their interdependence.

Now let's argue that, in contrast, what characterizes the processes and structures in school networks is that they arise from the actions of individuals within the network, particularly school leaders. They therefore originate in the agency, or actions, of people who are interested in actively collaborating. Their commitment to collaboration is generally based on a value position they hold, rather than any impinging necessity. Although opportunistic, instrumental and resistant forms of collaboration to secure funding, resources and fight off local policy changes and so on are commonplace.

Now what could we learn from considering the role of 'necessity' and 'interdependence' in developing school networks? Well first of all we use them as a way of defining the problem for which networks are the solution. Is it because teachers within schools are not already in the right kinds of interdependent relationships with other teachers outside of their school that there is a need to create 'formal' networks of schools? Next, to what extent are current networks really based on voluntarism and collaboration? What forms of 'necessities', both benign and corrosive, influence people's decisions to take part in a network? Are they worried that their school will be left behind in the latest wave of change? Is it out of desperation to try and acquire new funding or help them to recruit new staff? To what extent do network leaders consciously 'manufacture' interdependence? Using rewards and their authority and power to influence others into more dependent relationships with other teachers.

One could argue that those leading school networks are, or should be, as much in the business of creating interdependence between professionals as they currently are in creating structures and processes based around collaboration and the transfer of knowledge. Could we improve the quality of school networks by studying the interplay of structures and processes that arise from both, 'necessity' and 'interdependence' as well as 'voluntarism' and 'collaboration'?

It may seem overly instrumental and controlling to talk of 'manufacturing' interdependence, especially in the context of a theoretical framework based on voluntarism and open collaboration. There are though examples of social networks where this could be said to be done in an ethical manner. Many political and social movements have to create a collective sense of mutual interest and interdependence as they organize campaigns and alternative forms of social provision. Could we profitably use studies of the nature of social movements to see how its leaders have set about building effective and ethically based networks, Melucci (1996)? Similarly could we use discussions of the decline and revival of social networks, for example Putnam (2000), to understand how to extend professional networking?

A rather more pragmatic argument for considering the potential role of manufacturing interdependence is that relying primarily on voluntarism and collaboration presents a number of problems for both practitioners in networks and policy makers interested in promoting the idea of networking as a system-wide solution. For practitioners in networks, voluntarism is seen as important in gaining acceptance of new ways of working, because of widespread negative reactions to previously imposed change, but also to help liberate the agency of teachers so that they contribute to the network. A major problem that this can lead to is that voluntarism may not create a sufficiently large critical mass of collaborative relationships to establish networking as a norm. Without this change networks may only draw in relatively few active members who can quickly become either a clique or burn out as the enthusiasts lose energy.

For policy makers, voluntarism as an underpinning tenant of network theory presents even more difficulties. If a policy is going to be inclusive and have a national reach, how are they going to deal with schools that are struggling and would benefit from networking but instead wish to focus their limited capacities internally? How are they to engage those schools who currently benefit from competition and have achieved a measure of success who can see little utility in employing their internal capacity for the benefit of others in a network?

Currently fostering collaboration and developing shared values is seen as the most successful approach to building networks. What though if creating interdependence based on different types of 'necessity' was the preferred approach? What would this mean in practice? It would mean removing some of the reasons why only very weak interdependent relationships currently exist between teachers in their network. Exploring all the reasons for this lack of interdependence would take another chapter to discuss adequately but in the UK context there are several significant influences, key among which is the external accountability system currently in place. This system currently holds head teachers responsible, and to a great extent determines their career progression, for just the achievement of pupils in their schools. Alternatively why not make groups of head teachers collectively responsible for the educational needs of their local community as a whole? This would make them interdependent upon each other's success in improving the quality of teaching and learning. This is an approach that is currently being adopted in some local education authorities in the UK. Currently though most attempts to develop interdependence have been based around removing structures that create competition and suspicion, they are therefore reactive rather than proactive.

If an education system creates competitive structures rather than those that foster interdependence, if the culture of most schools and the reality for most classroom practitioners is that they are only able to seek out help which is near at hand and immediate, and if practitioners feel no direct responsibility for the education of children within a whole community rather than just their classroom, then networking will fail. The key theoretical question at this point is which approach, or combination, will be the most effective? Fostering collaboration or manufacturing real interdependence?

The practical arc – the Networked Learning Communities (NLC) programme

Networks of schools and professional networking have become of such interest to governments, policy makers, academics and practitioners, in part, because they are seen as having the potential to create opportunities for sustained change and professional learning Chapman and Aspin (2002). Networks are therefore seen, in part, as a potential solution to several of the key problems facing schools. Particularly in coping with current issues such as staff recruitment and retention, and effective professional development in a context of multiple policy initiatives and rapid social change: 'In important ways education reform and professional development networks appear to be uniquely adapted to the rapid socio-economic changes taking place in society' (Lieberman and Wood 2003).

The Network Learning Communities programme (NLC) developed because of a belief in the power of networking and to demonstrate this to other schools. It also grew up with a bigger ambition, to use the power of networking to change the education system as a whole. To return to the previous theoretical discussion, although the programme mainly works on the basis of supporting voluntary collaborative arrangements within school networks, it is also trying to develop a greater sense of interdependence within and between networks. The area it is concentrating on is the professional development needs of teachers and school leaders. The NLC programme recognizes that because of the frequency and nature of change within the education system in the UK, and the strong impact difference in contexts between schools have on teachers' work, they are increasingly in need of very specific and rapid support. As large-scale top-down initiatives have juddered through the system, quicker and more focused approaches to supporting teachers have been sought, from the Advanced Skills Teachers initiative to Leadership Incentive Grants. Networks are part of this movement to more differentiated forms of support. Local networks with sufficient capacity to connect with schools in similar contexts and provide them with the timely support they need will create interdependent relationships, as they become the most effective source of practical knowledge that works in their classrooms. Before I elaborate any on this point, you need to know a little more about the programme, particularly its scope and its origins.

The NLC programme is essentially a 'network of networks', which currently involves some 5 per cent of all schools in England. Currently there are 109 networks, 85 of these joined the programme between September 2002 and January 2003, with a further 24 joining in September 2004. This made a total of 1259 schools across both primary and secondary phases, with some 70 per cent from the primary sector. The networks vary considerably in size, ranging from a minimum of six to a maximum of over 60, with an average of around ten. Not all of these are new networks indeed the majority, some 60 per cent, were already involved in some kind of networking arrangements before applying to be NLCs. These ranged from formal structures set up under previous central government initiatives which drew together schools into a range of network structures, such as Education Action Zones and Excellence in Cities, to networks that had arisen more organically through the enthusiasm and commitment of school leaders who came together with other local schools for a variety of reasons.

The NLC programme has brought together these networks, old and new, offering them a small amount of financial support for three years, providing them with support from a central team of facilitators, researchers and administrators, and creating opportunities and structures through which they can learn from each other. Pragmatically these include: national and regional conferences and workshops; e-newsletters and magazines; an online community; and access to range of resources created by the central team and in collaboration with the networks.

The NLC programme is an ambitious project, which in its early days sailed under the banner of 'Like no other initiative', in order to distinguish itself from central government school improvement initiatives. It did this by honouring some of the basic principles of effective school networks, such as voluntarism and commitment to local problem solving, and not enforcing a particular way of working or structure beyond a relatively broad set of non-negotiables and principles. In doing so, it tapped into a huge wave of enthusiasm among schools and school leaders for an opportunity to fashion both their own agendas for improvement but also to create local structures and processes, rather than having them imposed from central government. Not only is the programme ambitious in terms of its approach to working with networks of schools, it is also aspirational in working with so many networks and trying to create a 'network of networks'. To understand the programme's aspirations it is necessary to consider briefly its origins.

The origins of the NLC programme

As I write we are in the middle of the programme's second year and the complexity of working with such a wide variety of networks, in terms of their history, structure and purpose. While trying to support them to develop as networks, and particularly in their interactions with other networks, it is interesting to reflect that this was initially going to be a demonstration project of just ten or so networks. It turned into something much larger and more ambitious because of three factors: the internal logic of network theory, the passion of those involved in developing school networks at the heart of the programme, and the current state of the education system in the UK. It is worth discussing these in more detail before we move on to a description of how the programme has been designed to facilitate 'networked learning'.

As far as the internal logic of networking is concerned, there was a problem with the idea of a demonstration project which would impart the benefits of networking to the rest of the education system. The logical inconsistency within this idea is that part of the underlying commitment to the idea of networking was that it was not just a possible solution to providing effective professional learning and sustaining school improvement, it was also intended to overcome more systemic problems within education. These systemic problems (Hopkins and Jackson 2002) included the education system's failure as a whole to learn from the good practice it contained, its inability to draw on research carried out in schools and in academia, and the considerable lag in learning about new innovations and critically assessing their worth. If these problems were systemic, it raised the question of how the education system as a whole would learn from a demonstration project?

If the current education system in the UK is beset by the legacy of competition between schools, weakened cross school structures, ineffective relationships and the lack of expertise in transferring good practice then why have a demonstration project? Because even if it could show the potential of networking and networks to schools outside the demonstration, they would not be in a position to learn these lessons and put them into practice. How then to change the system as a whole so that it would be in a position to be able to take on board the notion of networking and learn the lessons about how to set up networks from the NLC programme?

If the internal logic of networking ran counter to the idea of a traditional demonstration project, on the grounds that it would have very little impact on the system as a whole, then what kind of programme would? This was when the logic of networking met the passion of those involved in setting up school networks to create the idea of the NLC programme as a 'network of networks'.

There are two beliefs about networking, treated as axiomatic by network enthusiasts, which were important in shaping the design of the current programme. The first is that to a greater or lesser extent we not only live in a networked society but that we learn much of what is important to us, and achieve much of what we do, via our relationships and social contacts. We construct our learning in a mixture of networks both formal and informal, personal and professional, large and small. Hence the links being made by the programme between theories of socially constructed learning, social capital, capacity building and networking. These linkages are not new and have been made both theoretically and practically in ideas such as 'communities of practice' (Wenger 1998) and networked-based initiatives such as Improving the Quality of Education for All (Hopkins 2002). The particular combination of these ideas which most influenced the development of the NLC programme was the idea of professional learning communities.

> An effective professional learning community has the capacity to promote and sustain the learning of all professionals in the school community with the collective purpose of enhancing pupil learning . . . An effective professional learning community may have an impact on . . . the capacity of those within the school community to engage with networking and other external opportunities.
>
> (Stoll 2003: 5)

The idea of a 'learning community' was attractive because, as set out above, it is not simply about transferring good practice or accessing research but taking collective responsibility and enhancing the internal capacity of a school community to engage with 'external opportunities' such as other schools in a network. If sufficient learning communities could be joined together or 'networked', it was believed they would have the capacity to change the education system as a whole.

Networked Learning Communities are purposefully led social entities that are characterized by a commitment to quality, rigour and a focus on outcomes. They are also an effective means of supporting innovation in times of change. In education, Networked Learning Communities promote the dissemination of good practice, enhance the professional development of teachers, support capacity building in schools, mediate between centralized and decentralized structures, and assist in the process of restructuring and reculturing educational organizational systems.

The NLC programme was therefore designed not only to help create networks which would help individuals schools to work together and coordinate and focus their improvement efforts but also by bringing a sufficient numbers together to fundamentally change the whole education system. The development path of the programme would be a series of incremental steps, which would lead to real transformation at the level of not just the school or individual network but the education system as a whole. One idealized path for its development would be for a school or group of schools within a network to create the necessary capacity to move from a situation where they networked to support the development of their own learning communities to the point at which they had sufficient internal capacity to influence the work of other networks. The next step would be for these networks to influence other existing networks so they, in turn, developed their capacity to become developed learning communities. As this process develops, then networks would evolve which would have the ability to draw new schools into them or create new networks of schools.

This leads us on to a second axiom of network theory, more metaphorical in nature than the last, and which is concerned with how ideas and practices move within and between networks. This is the notion that a network society consists of a multitude of overlapping networks, creating a meta-structure, which is particularly vulnerable to certain forms of change. Both technical and organic metaphors have been used to describe how change could affect such a structure. One recent example applied to schools, Hargreaves (2003) uses the growth of the Internet and 'hacker culture' to show how the combination of both technical development and cultural shift resulted in the simultaneous establishment of new forms of networks and networking. A shift that could only occur because networks created the structural opportunity for viruses and epidemics to spread.

> A key to transformation is for the teaching profession to establish innovation networks that capture the spirit and culture of internet hackers – the passion, the can-do, the collective sharing. Teachers could create an 'innovative commons' for education, ... a common pool of resources to which innovators contribute and on which any school or teacher might draw to improve professional practice. This requires an initial generosity and the taking of a risk that I might never get a return.
>
> (Hargreaves 2003: 3)

The 'architecture' of the NLC programme

How then has the NLC been designed to achieve its two main aims? To develop robust networked learning communities, generative of learning about the possibilities of networking, and to impact upon the system as a whole so that it would be in a better position to learn from these networks? In this chapter I don't want to go into the details of the programme, as it has been written about extensively elsewhere and is of limited relevance to other initiatives (Jackson and Leo 2003). What is of wider relevance is the shape of its internal 'architecture', by which I mean the overarching design principles that have been consistently applied to its internal structures and processes and its work with networks. These principles are of relevance to a whole range of organizations involved in supporting school networks, from local authorities and school districts to leaders in schools.

There are three building blocks that are the foundations of the architecture of the programme:

- It is based around key aspects of existing knowledge about networking, particularly in the areas of learning, capacity building and knowledge management.
- These principles are applied consistently to all aspects of the programme, from the work of the core team and the resources it creates to its interactions with networks.
- These principles have been converted into more metaphorical and generative forms, which allow them to act as 'boundary objects' (Wenger 1998). These 'objects', both processes and materials, have the ability to bridge the boundaries between not only the core programme team and the networks but also between networks and the wider education system.

The NLC programme has drawn much of its architecture from studies of capacity building initiatives and professional learning communities. This led to three non-negotiable items in its design principles:

Moral purpose – a commitment to success for all children
Models of shared leadership – for example co-leadership and distributed leadership
Enquiry – evidence and data-informed learning.

(NLC 2003: 1)

In addition, seven aspects of existing theories were seen as sufficiently generalizable to be built into the design of the programme:

People unite around compelling ideas
Values based networks are the most enduring
Networks require facilitation

Networks create new patterns of leadership – leadership is cross-cultural brokering
Networks balance insider and outsider knowledge
Leaders have to model the learning
'Joint work' projects form a foundation for sustained relationship building.

(NLC 2003: 3)

Although these non-negotiables and generalizations are set out in the documentation of the programme, used in contracting with networks, and frame the materials and resources used within it, they have had to be recreated in a different form to help practitioners build network to network connections. They have had to be converted into 'boundary objects' because as networks form they create boundaries around them, which define who is a member and who is not, giving them a sense of community, but as we wish to bring networks together we need to cross these boundaries in ways that 'bridge disjointed forms of participation', to use Wenger's phrase. Boundary objects do this by creating processes that cross boundaries and allow connections to be made. 'The boundary object does not in itself achieve the connection across boundaries, it enables the participative action that will enable the connection to take place' (Thorpe 2003: 34).

At the commencement of the NLC programme it was the core team that took on the role of brokers and connection makers, having to dance a particularly difficult line.

Brokers must often avoid two opposite tendencies: being pulled in to become full members and being rejected as intruders. Indeed, their contributions lie precisely in being neither in nor out. Brokering therefore requires an ability to manage carefully the coexistence of membership and non-membership, yielding enough distance to bring a different perspective, but also enough legitimacy to be listened to.

(Wenger 1998: 75)

There are two particularly powerful 'boundary objects' within the programme: the 'Levels of Learning' framework and the 'Three Fields of Knowledge', which illustrate how the programme team set out to dance this line between membership and non-membership of the networks, while trying to make connections between them.

The Levels of Learning framework

This framework was initially presented as a list of levels but has now become more commonly expressed as a series of nested areas of learning with the focus on pupil learning. This shift in emphasis is partially based around a growing understanding of the importance of focusing learning at all levels on pupils as a means of building cohesion of effort within a network. 'Ultimately, networked learning is only worth doing if it enhances pupil learning' (Desforges 2003). It also taps into the one necessity that is common to every network, they are all involved in pupil learning. The Levels of Learning framework is a way of expressing some of the key ideas within the learning communities and capacity building literature, and taking this into the area of networks by stressing the need to learn from school to school and across networks, and when applied to the plans of all the networks, allows them to make links at multiple levels. It only becomes a boundary object when it is used to focus interactions between networks, so how did we set about doing this?

The first instance the framework was explicitly used was at the point of networks applying to become NLCs. Every network in the programme had to submit an application for funding, £50,000 for three years, on the basis of a proposal to develop their learning at each level. This was done to familiarize themselves with the language of levels of learning and to help them integrate the range of activities in which many were already involved. Second, each year the networks in the programme take part in a Levels of Learning activity using questionnaires to gather staff perceptions about the quality of learning at each level. These are fed back to the network and their scores are contrasted with other schools in their network and programme averages, thus providing them with a baseline against which they can assess their progress in each level. This keeps the idea alive in the networks and allows them to discuss their development in relation to other schools and networks.

Initially the framework only truly came alive as a boundary object when the programme team acted as brokers. It was the facilitators within the core team, some 20 people, drawn from a wide range of backgrounds who most commonly undertook this role in the early days of the programme, increasingly it is individuals from within the networks who are now being supported to take on this role. The programme did this in a variety of ways including providing information about what networks were doing at each level of learning and examples of their work, and creating tools which would help them share their knowledge of what was working in their networks. These were modelled at the events and conference held throughout the first year of the programme. Getting practitioners from the networks to act as brokers was formalized by asking networks to appoint someone as a network-to-network facilitator who would formally take on this role. In addition, we have launched seven small scale development and enquiry projects, focusing on three levels of learning: pupil, adult and whole school. These projects aim to skill up small groups of networks who will then take on the role of working with other networks in these areas, creating their own mini-networks around key levels of learning.

The Three Fields of Knowledge

The NLC programme is a development and research initiative and therefore has fashioned an inclusive model of knowledge utilization and generation, which allows for the combination of existing public knowledge, the experiences of practitioners and the knowledge generated by the programme. The Three Fields of Knowledge have been applied to the architecture of both networks and the programme team in a variety of ways. Again at the proposal stage networks were required to have an access to the wider public knowledge base, mainly but not exclusively through existing or new partnership with local universities, contact with local education authorities and a range of consultants. As a non-negotiable, practitioner enquiry of some form had to be a strong element of their proposals whether termed as action research and enquiry or some form of experiential learning. The networks were also required to consider what 'artefacts' they could create from this work, which would then become part of their network-to-network activities. As a model of knowledge generation and utilization its biggest benefit has been to legitimate an inclusive approach to enquiry and research, bringing together groups as disparate as pupil researchers and full-time education researchers from research establishments both in the UK and internationally. It therefore helps cross the boundaries between these different forms of research and enquiry.

As a boundary object for network-to-network brokerage this model has been used in combination with the Levels of Learning to help shape the programme-level enquiries carried out twice a year by the core team in collaboration with networks. These programme-level enquiries cover all 109 networks and are carried out twice a year. They are initiated within the core team who then develop the central focus in collaboration with the networks. Each enquiry reflects the Three Fields of Knowledge. First, the existing public knowledge base is used to construct enquiry tools, which can be used by both the facilitators and network participants. They constitute another level of 'boundary object' which can cross the public knowledge base into the world of practitioners. These boundary objects have included processes such as appreciative enquiry methodologies, frameworks for analysing network structures and processes such as network maps (McCormick 2003), theoretical models of teacher professional knowledge bases (Shulman 1987), and empirically grounded criteria for assessing the quality of collaborative CPD. Each boundary object is designed in collaboration with the facilitation team whose overriding concern has to be the development to the network. They therefore treat each object as a means of developing the levels of learning within and across every network.

The next stage of development, as with other aspects of the design of the programme, is whether these boundary objects can travel outside the programme and cross into the education system as a whole. It is at this point we will know whether we have the architecture of the programme right.

Conclusion

We live in interesting times in terms of exploring the power of networks and networking. The interest in school networks, of various kinds, has shifted from dealing with issues faced by individual and groups of schools to the point where networks are being considered as an approach to dealing with system-wide problems. In this shift, the previous history of how networks have developed, and the knowledge this has generated, is being applied to a different order of problem. From specific problems such as adopting a multi-agency approach to complex community issues, to how to ensure the reach of networks across a whole education system. This shift in emphasis raises the question of the status of our current knowledge of networking. In this chapter I have tried to raise theoretical issues about the way in which we draw upon existing social structures and networks to aid our learning about schools networks.

The challenge for the NLC programme is to help networks not only to become more intentional and systematic in their learning at each of the levels, and to create an inclusive model of knowledge creation and management, but also to create sufficient internal capacity to create flexible and supportive relationships with other networks. I am arguing that along with other network-based initiatives it will need to draw on literature and theories that are not based on typical or innovative organizational forms or even those primarily concerned with learning and education. It may well be that the challenges we face have more in common with those faced by other forms of social networks, and the lessons learnt by political and community movements will be as rich a source of knowledge and new concepts as are studies of established networks of schools. Particularly if we believe there is a need to manufacture interdependence as well as foster collaboration in pursuit of transforming the ways in which teachers and schools think about their work.

References

Bentley, T. (2003) *The purposes of networks and their contribution to collaborative capacity*, unpublished policy discussion paper. London: Demos.

Callinicos, A. (1988) *Making History, agency, structure and change in social theory*. New York: Cornell University Press.

Castells, M. (2000) 'Toward a Sociology of the Network Society' *Contemporary Sociology*, 29 (5): 693–9.

Chapman, J. and Aspin, D. (2002) 'Networks of Learning: A new construct for educational provision and a new strategy for reform' in B. Caldwell and J. West-Burnham (eds) *The Handbook of Educational Leadership and Management*. London: Pearson Publishers.

Department for Education and Skills (DfES) (2003) *Every Child Matters*. Nottingham: DfES Publications.

Demos (2004) *What is Networked Learning*, briefing paper February.

Desforges, C. (2003) *Despatches*, LEA/HEI Conference May.

GTC (2003) Teachers and teaching: A survey of the teaching profession. General Teaching Council, England.

Hargreaves, D. (2003) *Education Epidemic – Transforming secondary schools through innovation networks*. London: Demos.

Hopkins, D. (2002) *Improving the Quality of Education for All*. London: David Fulton.

Hopkins, D. and Jackson, D. (2002) *Networked Learning Communities – Capacity Building, Networking and Leadership for Learning*. Nottingham: National College for School Leadership.

Jackson, D. (2004) *Networked Learning Communities*. Nottingham: National College for School Leadership.

Jackson, D. and Leo, E. (2003) *Knowledge Management in Networked Learning Communities*. Paper presented at the American Educational Research Association Annual Conference, Chicago, April 2003.

Kerr, D., Aiston, S., White, K., Holland, M. and Grayson, H. (2003) *Literature Review of Networked Learning Communities*. NFER, NCSL commissioned research.

Lieberman, A. and Wood, D. (2003) *Inside the National Writing Project: Connecting Network Learning and Classroom Teaching*. New York: Teachers College Press.

McCormick, R. (2003) *Learning and Professional Development: Networks*. Paper presented at the British Educational Research Association, Edinburgh, September 2002.

Melucci, A. (1996) *Challenging Codes: Collective Action in The Information Age*. Cambridge: Cambridge University Press.

Mitchell, C. and Sackney, L. (2000) *Profound Improvement: Building Capacity for a Learning Community*. Lisse: Swets and Zeitlinger.

Network Learning Communities (NLC) (2003) *Principles*. Nottingham: National College for School Leadership.

Putnam, R. (2000) *Bowling Alone: The collapse and revival of American community*. New York: Touchstone.

Shulman, L. (1987) 'Knowledge and Teaching: Foundations of the New Reforms' *Harvard Educational Review* 57 (1): 1–22.

Stoll, L. (2003) Presentation to DfES Collaborative Research Forum, December 2003.

Thorpe, M. (2003) *Communities of practice and other frameworks for conceptualising, developing and evaluating NCSL's network communities*. The Institute of Educational Technology, The Open University, NCSL commissioned research.

Wenger, E. (1998) *Communities of Practice: learning, meaning and identity*. Cambridge: Cambridge University Press.

eleven

Keeping progressive educational discourse alive during conservative times: Harmony Education Center and the National School Reform Faculty

Jesse Goodman

During the last 25 to 30 years a resurgence of conservative ideology has swept across United States' schools and society. This latest 'conservative restoration' began within the political realm of society with such events as Richard Nixon's 'southern strategy' that successfully incorporated the Dixiecrats into the Republican Party and the subsequent election of Ronald Reagan which, in turn, set the stage for the 'dixification of America' (Cummings 1998). Space does not allow for, nor is it necessary to present, a comprehensive review of the conservative ideology, policies and practices that have swept the United States during the last two decades of the twentieth century as others (see, for example, Wallerstein 1995; Barber 1998; Blau 1999; MacEwan 1999; Brock 2001) have already explored this phenomena from several perspectives as it has materialized within several realms of society. As Apple (2001) and others (see, for example, Miller 1995) recently discussed, the educational ramifications of this restoration included (among other things): public supported vouchers for children going to private schools, high stakes testing, legislation of curriculum content, emphasis on drilling and memorization, internal racial segregation through tracking, the deskilling of teachers, and a deepening of 'savage inequalities' (Kozol 1991) related to the inequitable resources provided to wealthy versus impoverished children.

One response within the educational sphere of US society to this turn of events has been the establishment of various networks designed to promote more thoughtful, authentic and meaningful discourses than that encouraged by current educational policy makers who are fixated narrowly upon the results of standardized test scores. These networks have been organized among various schools and school districts, as well as ad hoc groups of administrators and teachers. Unfortunately, many of these conversations lack an adequate historical context within which to place their work and deliberations.

In response, the purpose of this chapter is to present the work of the Harmony Education Center (HEC) and its current focus of attention: facilitating the work of the National School Reform Faculty (NSRF) in the United States. Towards this goal, we describe the structural and ideological framework that serves as the foundation upon which HEC has evolved during its more than 12 years of existence. Next, we will briefly present the history, basic activity and several auxiliary projects of the NSRF. We conclude with a discussion of a particularly difficult dilemma HEC faces as coordinators of this network of educators.

Harmony Education Center

The Harmony Education Center came into existence in 1990 and represents a collaboration between Harmony School and Indiana University. In this section, we briefly recount the origins of this center and provide an account of the historical tradition within which we place our work. This placement is crucial in establishing a context in which to situate our current efforts to make education more democratic and existentially meaningful to those who work in our schools. Following this historical review, we describe the HEC's organizational structure.

Origins and ideological orientation

Approximately 17 years ago, the author of this chapter conducted an interpretive study of Harmony, an independent, pre-k–12th grade school based upon a democratic ethos located in Bloomington, IN, USA (Goodman 1992). A few years after the fieldwork was completed, he proposed the creation of the Harmony Education Center (HEC) for the purpose of fostering conversations between the educators at Harmony and other reform-minded educators, policy makers and scholars. During the last decade, our understanding of this work and the society in which we live has continuously evolved. In broad terms, the ultimate purpose of the Harmony Education Center is to support and engage those who work in schools and who are interested in creating educational experiences and environments that will help foster the movement of society towards a more liberal, social and critical democracy. The term *critical* is used in the sense that it is unwise to take a given notion of democracy for granted (as many people do in our society). In a critical democracy, the meaning of democracy itself is always contested. In addition, every institution and organization, proposed and/or implemented policy, political party, public individual, law, ritual, social value and history is vulnerable and open to public critique. Within a critical democracy, class struggle is 'in the open'. Within such a polity, there is tolerance for a wide range of public commentary and action as long as it remains non-violent. As scholars and reformers, this commitment to open critique is central to our occupational endeavours. Ever since the scholastic tradition emerged within Western universities during the Middle Ages, public critique has been a significant component of academic and journalistic discourses within functioning democracies.

As most social scholars recognize, the adjective 'liberal' comes from the tradition of liberalism that swept across Europe, and its descendant states such as the USA, between the seventeenth and twentieth centuries. Although we reject the excessive individualism embedded in traditional, European liberalism which has been so dominant throughout the history of the United States (see, for example, Dewey 1920; Bellah *et al.* 1985; Nisbet 1990), its value as a social ideology should not be completely discounted in efforts to deepen our democracy through the education of our children. Liberalism's historical value continues to lie in the attention it gives to basic rights and liberties (for example, freedom to speak publicly, assemble, create political parties and organizations) that all individuals should have in a democratic society. Individuals must be not only free but also supported in their efforts to 'self-actualize' (Fromm 1956; Maslow 1976). The ability and freedom to focus on one's desires, fears, hopes, dreams and creativity in order to existentially 'know oneself', is crucial for any society that wishes to promote human dignity. A society that considers itself to be democratic also provides numerous opportunities for individuals to lead, as much as possible, self-determined lives. Individuals in a functioning, democratic society have the liberty to pursue their inner callings, to achieve beyond typical expectations, and to have those achievements recognized and rewarded. Most importantly, our conception of democracy is deeply rooted in the notion that society is actively tolerant of individual uniqueness and self-expression regarding such matters as religion, ethnic heritage, race, gender, sexual preference, emerging life-styles, social and political ideas, and the creative and performing arts. In short, human diversity is celebrated and embraced as a social value. Finally, our reference to the word 'social' comes from Dewey's (1946 [1929]) conception of social pragmatism. As Dewey (1927) argued, although democracy's primary function is to resolve class (and other types of) conflict without resorting to violence in a given society, it can also be viewed as a 'way of life' rather than merely a set of democratic societal rituals (for example, voting) and governmental structures (for example, congress, president).

A democracy is more than a form of government; it is primarily a mode of associated living, of conjoint communicated experience. The extension in space of the number of individuals who participate in an interest so that each has to refer his own action to that of others, and to consider the action of others to give point and direction to his [or her] own, is equivalent to the breaking down of those barriers of class, race and national territory that kept men from perceiving the full import of their activity (Dewey 1966: 87). This latter notion of democracy is particularly important since the primary focus of the Harmony Education Center is to bring collaborative values, structures and habits of interaction to schools and other educational communities for the purpose of educating children to find personal meaning within the context of a democratic community.

From Dewey's perspective, democratic living calls upon us to recognize our connection to others both inside and outside the particular polity within which we live, and calls upon our voluntary commitment to their general welfare. In this light, several scholars have called for a greater understanding of what Fraser (1997) calls the 'politics of recognition', that is, the connection between identity and social justice. Of particular importance is the dynamic of what Rorty (1989) refers to as our 'we' consciousness. In addition to having an individual identity, Rorty notes that we also have any number of collective identities rooted in our families, our ancestral heritages, our gender, our age, the colour of our skin, and our occupation, among other things. Typically, a given individual will feel a greater connection to other people who share one or more of their collective identities than to those who do not. As a result, this individual is more likely to care about the welfare of these fellow compatriots. Rorty (1998) and others (see, for example, Nussbaum 1997; Barber 1998) have recently advocated for the development of a collective identity based upon our national polity, to the degree that this collective identity acknowledges our diversity as a people (for example, ancestral, gender, physical/mental abilities) and is committed to the politics of democracy, inclusion and social justice. That is, they argue for a nationalism based, not upon a particular ancestral heritage, but upon a mutually recognized (although imperfect and contested) social contract, or what Habermas (1994) refers to as 'constitutional patriotism'. For example, Rorty calls for the left within the United States to justify our advocacy for democracy, equality, opportunity, inclusion, respect and care-giving not upon a particular economic class or system, but upon our national identity. If this identity took hold firmly among the electorate, then as Americans, *we* would not allow 20 per cent of *our* children to live in poverty or to attend grossly inadequate schools, for a significant number of our society to go without basic medical care, or for citizens to be marginalized or otherwise based upon their skin colour, ethnicity, body type, gender or sexual preference (because these differences pale compared to our bonds of nationhood).

Unfortunately, many in the United States view their 'we' in much more limited terms than suggested here. For example, the 'we' consciousness among most individuals within the bourgeoisie and many within the intelligentsia stops at their immediate or extended family members. For the most part, patriotism and national identity are called upon only when there are external threats such as those from Al-Queda rather than as a rationale to promote equality and social justice. Nevertheless, Rorty notes the potential power that this national identity could have as a catalyst for bridging our 'otherness'. This national 'we' would ideally create a foundation for members of different classes to embrace one another as 'us', rather than 'them'. In this way, classes can engage in struggle, but this conflict is modified by our union which is based upon geography and the imperfect social contract under which we agree to live.

Of special concern for the reformist left is the redistribution of wealth, power and other benefits that occur within a given society. As Rawls (2001) notes, the social contract that is the basis of a given polity is never generated by classes of equal power. As a result, all social contracts benefit some classes (elites) over others. In capitalist societies where the common denominator of power is wealth, the bourgeoisie and others (for example, the intelligentsia) with access to wealth form this elite. In the twentieth century Marxist/Leninist states, the elite was almost exclusively comprised of members of the intellectual and intelligentsia classes. The rewards that go to some classes are always disproportionate *vis-à-vis* other classes (Sen 1992). In any given culture, there will always be personal characteristics, structures and systems of power that will benefit some and not other members of that society. Since the former's 'success' is contingent, in part, upon these characteristics, structures and systems of power, it is only socially just to have a portion of this wealth, power and benefits redistributed for the purpose of creating opportunities and protecting basic necessities and rights for those individuals who, for whatever reason, have a difficult time being successful under these same characteristics, structures and systems (Rawls 2001). Recognition of our collective identity as the building block for promoting social justice was central to what Dewey (1927) called the 'great community'.

Organizational structure

Similar to Dewey, the Harmony Education Center views the education of children as a crucial site for the building of a more liberal, social and critical democracy. Along with religion, popular culture, news media, political and economic systems, friends and family, schools influence the ways in which children will come to view themselves, other people, the nation state in which they live, and the world at large. In return, the children of today will influence the type of society their children will inherit, creating an endless feedback loop (Dewey 1920).

We view educational reform as largely a matter of engaging in a variety of discourses in a diversity of settings. As a centre, we seek to initiate and/or participate in conversations among democratically reform-minded scholars (for example, university seminars, journals, books, conferences), school practitioners (for example, administrators, teachers, staff, parents, children), educational change agents (for example, Bay Area Coalition for Equitable Schools, ATLAS, Institute for Democracy and Education, Fairtest, League of Professional Schools) and philanthropic institutions (for example, the Bay Foundation, the Philanthropic Initiative, the Lucent Foundation, Gates Foundation, Lilly Foundation). To facilitate our involvement in these discourses, HEC consists of three integrated components:

- *Harmony School* (HS), an early childhood–12th grade school that is committed to democratic education, and serves as a demonstration site for school visits/debriefing sessions. Harmony teachers and students also get involved in the reform efforts of interested schools (for example, by establishing critical friends groups, demonstrating lessons and democratic student meetings, arranging student exchange visits and projects, participation in NSRF meetings). Recently, Harmony School was selected as one of 12 'First Amendment' schools in the country by the Association of Supervision and Curriculum Development in their effort to promote the freedoms of this amendment to children. Teachers and students from each designated school met during the summer of 2002 for their first seminar and planning session. Although the democratic ethos, governance structure, curriculum and pedagogy of the school has deepened since the publication of the previously mentioned ethnographic study (Goodman 1992), this study still provides a basic understanding of the educational experience found within its walls.
- An *Office for Outreach Services* (OOS), which is the main focus of this chapter, has provided a wide range of assistance to educators engaged in substantive reform projects. Examples of the Office's activities during the last 12 years have included: 1) Providing leadership and facilitation of school-wide reform projects. These projects involved the entire school community in an effort to substantively alter the ways in which the school was governed, and its relationship to the community and parents. In addition, there were significant efforts made to deepen the curriculum, pedagogy and learning experiences of the students. 2) Consulting or facilitating staff development activities on topics of progressive, democratic education; organizing meetings and conferences on topics of school reform; and collaborating with organizations that share our pedagogical and social ethos (for example, Bay Area Coalition for

Equitable Schools, Boston Center for Collaborative Education, John Dewey Center for Democracy).

- An *Institute for Research*, which is responsible for contributions to educational scholarship, supports the enquiry work of young scholars and Harmony teachers, and provides resources (for example, books, articles, films, speakers) to educators working with the HEC. Scholarship supported by the institute includes both collaborative and individual projects. Some of these projects included additional research into the lived experiences of Harmony School (see, for example, Kuzmic 1990; Goodman 1991; Bintz 1995; Heilman and Goodman 1996; Skulnick forthcoming), teacher/scholar research (for example, Goodman *et al.* 1994), reports on the ways in which the school has served as a catalyst for pedagogical changes in public schools in which the OOS has worked (for example, Goodman and Kuzmic 1997), and self reflective analyses on the Office for Outreach Services (see, for example, Goodman *et al.* 1999, 2001a, 2001b; Goodman 1994). In addition, the institute has supported several historical studies of education and progressive politics in the West (for example, Goodman and Holloway 2000).

Although each component of the centre has autonomy to conduct its work in the ways it sees most beneficial to its 'clients' (for example, scholars, children, educators, parents), a Budget Committee (comprised of two of the centre's directors, one member of the support staff and four of the school's teachers) oversees all financial decisions, and a Solidarity Committee (comprised of one of the centre's three co-directors, one member of the support staff and five teachers from the school) oversees and coordinates the activities of each of the previously mentioned components. Each of the centre's components also works collaboratively. For example, teachers and students have been involved in numerous school reform projects. Educational change agents who work for the OOS and the institute also participate in school functions, and as previously indicated, teachers and change agents help generate scholarship supported by the institute. The goal was to create an organization in which there would be a rich cross pollination of ideas emerging from both contemporary scholarship in a wide diversity of fields, as well as from actual human experiences working with educators and children.

National School Reform Faculty

The NSRF represents a network of approximately 40,000–60,000 teachers, administrators, support staff and school change agents located throughout the United States. Created in 1995 by the Annenberg Institute for School Reform at Brown University, NSRF relocated to Harmony Education Center in July 2000. The initial goal of NSRF was to create one or more ongoing staff development seminars, referred to as *Critical Friends Groups* (CFG) in schools across the nation for the purpose of authentically improving students' academic achievement (i.e., beyond quantitative notions of learning). However, after five years at Annenberg, NSRF selected the Harmony Education Center as their new coordinating centre. These coordinating responsibilities include:

1   being a steward of NSRF vision and values
2   developing and coordinating NSRF human and material resources
3   serving as a conduit for NSRF's financial resources
4   establishing and developing communication networks with other progressive educational organizations
5   convening conferences and meetings to support ongoing and emerging work of NSRF.

Shortly after assuming these responsibilities, HEC proposed altering NSRF's mission statement to more directly address issues beyond children's academic achievement. After approximately 12 months of discussion, the following mission statement was approved on 3 June 2001: 'The mission of the National School Reform Faculty is to foster educational and social equity by empowering all people involved with schools to work collaboratively in reflective democratic communities that create and support powerful learning experiences for everyone.'

CFGs are now viewed as small learning communities within a given school or school district that utilize student academic work, among other things such as scholarly and journalistic articles, as catalysts for substantive discussions around issues of authentic achievement, learning, curriculum content and pedagogy within the context of values such as equity, social justice, diversity, inclusion and democracy. These discussions are often guided by 'CFG Protocols', which are conversation activities designed to stimulate open dialogue, provide everyone in a given CFG an opportunity to share their thoughts (i.e., voice) and react to the ideas of their colleagues. The description below is but one of many examples.

Jason presented a paper written by Mirabella, a fifth grade, African-American student who was doing poorly in her school work and often resisted his efforts to help her. After presenting his case, each of the participants in the CFG asked him a 'clarifying question' about the situation. For example, one member asked if she had particular learning problems. Another asked if she resisted 'everyone who tries to help her'. A third asked if she had any close friends in the class who he might talk to about her resistance. This continued until all eight members asked a question. After

Jason answered these questions, each member shared their analysis of the situation and offered potential responses or ideas to consider. Finally, Jason asked several follow-up questions in light of the comments made and then offered an analysis based upon the feedback he received. His comments then ignited a free flowing conversation about ethnic heritage (Jason is Euro-American) and the struggles of cross ethnic teaching, and the racism young people of colour might face in society that gets acted out in classrooms. Although there was no 'answer' to Jason's situation, he left the discussion feeling supported and with several new ideas for him to consider in his reactions to this student's attitudes, feelings and academic work in his class (summary of CFG meeting notes).

Over the years, scores of these discussion protocols have been developed by members of the NSRF (McDonald *et al.* 2003). Those educators who become more deeply involved in the work and want to become seminar leaders (referred to as CFG coaches) participate in week long 'coaches seminars' that develop their talents for leading their own CFG in their school or school district. Currently, there are approximately 5000 coaches leading CFGs throughout the United States. The coaches seminars are offered by NSRF members (referred to as facilitators) who have been actively involved in the NSRF for several years and have developed their aptitude for leading CFGs, and helping others in their efforts to be effective coaches. In addition, to further support the work of CFGs and those who wish to learn more about NSRF work, a national coaches conference is held each year and is designed to support and improve the work of those who lead CFGs. There are also five regional conferences held in the spring of each year to introduce educators to NSRF work. In response to requests from members during the last year, we have established CFGs specifically for principals within a given district, superintendents within a region and school boards within given states. Finally, NSRF has begun working with administrators who want to conduct faculty meetings in schools and or administrative meetings within a district with similar values, foci and procedures found in CFGs.

Supplementing these activities is an ongoing email conversation in which members throughout the country participate. These discussions cover a wide range of topics from reactions to social policies (for example, standards, high stakes testing); to the sharing of protocols and other strategies used to facilitate meaningful CFG discussions; to problems that coaches are having with either their CFG, their school or school district; and/or to the sharing of books, articles, films or other resources that individuals have found useful in their roles as parents, teachers, administrators, counsellors and/or members of a CFG.

Although the basic purpose of the NSRF is to provide educators with social locations in which to participate in thoughtful, progressive conversations regarding the education of children in our imperfect democracy, recently Harmony merged its Office for Outreach Services with NSRF for the purpose of responding to more specific projects. While space does not allow for a comprehensive discussion, a brief presentation of several representative projects provides an illustration of the potential educational activities that can be generated by a committed network of progressive thinking educators during a conservative era.

Small schools initiative

As will be discussed in the conclusion of this chapter, HEC recognizes the ways in which the 'politics of size' influences democratic living and efforts to authentically reform the education of our children. The larger the institution, the more complex and difficult it is to generate the type of discourse we believe will transform a school from a production-of-test-scores facility into a more authentic learning community. In response, NSRF, the Coalition of Essential Schools, the University of Washington and the Gates Foundation have collaborated to create over 200 high schools each with no more than 400 students. Although the number of students and faculty in a given school is crucial, it is only one aspect of this experimental effort. In addition to reconstructing the organizational size, this project also calls for establishing several CFGs in every school so that all members of the community will have opportunities to discuss regularly substantive issues of educating their students with their colleagues. In particular, NSRF provided initial coaches for these CFGs as well as beginning coaches seminars for those individuals in participating schools who expressed a desire to become a leader of their CFG.

Every student a citizen project

This effort represents a collaboration between the Education Commission of the States (ECS) and the NSRF. As the name suggests, this project is designed to revitalize the civic (as opposed to strictly economic) purpose of public education. This project has three guiding goals:

1 to develop within participating schools a democratic ethos within which to discuss issues of education
2 to explore the uses of service learning (for example Goodman *et al.* 1994) and its role in citizenship education
3 to examine ways in which students can have an authentic voice in matters that directly effect them in school.

Although service learning often gives students a sense of accomplishment, the focus of this project was to place these activities within a historical context that emphasizes our social responsibility to each other, as citizens of a common polity. Towards this end, ECS and NSRF helped teachers create curricula in ways that are more meaningfully connected to service learning and democracy, as well as form stronger and more reciprocal relationships with participating community organizations.

VISTA in schools project

Volunteers in Service to America (VISTA) is the 'Peace Corps' that operates within the borders of the United States. The purpose of this project is to explore the nexus between school reform and anti-poverty work. A VISTA volunteer and a faculty member from each of the 25 participating schools (located in low income neighbourhoods) enrolled in specially designed coaches seminars and then established joint community/school CFGs throughout the two participating states, Indiana and Vermont. In addition, school coaches work with their colleagues while VISTA volunteers work with local community members to develop meaningful and authentic ways to involve students in local anti-poverty work.

The lucent peer collaboration project

This project selected four school districts (Albuquerque, NM; Seattle, WA; Broward County, FL; and Lancaster, PA) from a pool of applicants to participate in a multi-year staff development initiative. At first, 25 percent of the faculty from each school in these districts participated in year long CFGs expedited by NSRF coaches. During this same time, selected members from these CFGs participated in coaches seminars. During the second year, more than 50 percent of the faculty in each of these schools were participating in CFGs. Most of the coaches for these CFGs are now district employees. Eventually, the goal is to have all faculty, administrators and support staff participating in one or more CFGs within schools and among faculty across elementary, middle and high schools in a given neighbourhood. As we have discussed elsewhere (Goodman 1994), rather than relying on 'experts' to provide staff development, this project emphasizes working with one's colleagues to raise and resolve issues that they, themselves, deem as necessary and worthwhile.

The progressive education summit

Organized by HEC/NSRF and the John Dewey Center for Democracy at the University of Vermont, several progressive educational organizations (for example, the Rouge Forum, Educators for Social Responsibility, the Virginia Parents Coalition, Coalition for Collaborative Education, Bay Area

Coalition for Equitable Schools) came together in May 2001 to explore potential responses and share plans/activities in light of the previously mentioned conservative restoration that has taken place in the United States. Although the 25 individuals who attended this summit represented organizations with different foci, at this meeting there was concerted effort to find 'common ground' and to support each other in our desires to keep progressive educational ideas and ideals alive during these difficult times. A commitment was made at the end of the summit to seek more collaboration, communication and solidarity and to explore ways to foster a more unified challenge to the conservative educational agenda in the nation. The representatives from NSRF, for example, expressed the hope that within the next decade, these organizations would be in a position to have a more public voice in the mass media. Another suggestion was to hold 'teach-ins' on high stakes testing around the country during a particular month of the year. Unfortunately, due to 9/11, these plans have been difficult to act upon.

These projects represent a sample of the numerous projects in which NSRF (as an extension of Harmony's Office for Outreach Services) is currently involved. As the popularity of these efforts have grown, HEC has had to face many difficulties as our capacity is limited by both financial and human resources. As a result, this chapter concludes with a few comments related to the politics of size brought about by the rapid growth of the NSRF.

Conclusion: politics of size

This chapter has described the efforts of Harmony Education Center and a nationwide network of educators (NSRF) committed to keeping a progressive pedagogical discourse alive in the United States during what is turning out to be a prolonged conservative domination over the culture. In addition, and perhaps more important, it has situated this centre, and by extension, this network within a non-Marxist, reformist tradition of leftist political activism. From the response we have received from around the country, it seems clear to us that there is a deep thirst and hunger for this type of socio-educational discourse. As a result, the biggest challenge facing this network concerns the problem of capacity building and the organizational politics of size.

As previously mentioned and described (Goodman 1992), throughout its more than 20 years of existence, Harmony has been kept purposefully small to facilitate a democratic ethos within an 'organization of intimates'. The challenge to create the same ethos and atmosphere within an organization of tens of thousands of people spread across the country has indeed been daunting. As Diamond (1999) illuminates, the population density of a polity (or organization) is the single most important factor that influences the type of governance apparatus needed. The larger the polity, the greater the need for centralized authority. The greater the central authority, the greater chance there is of power becoming overly concentrated into the hands of an unresponsive elite; leading to eventual hegemony and abuse of that power.

Given HEC/NSRF's commitment to democracy, we are continually experimenting with a decentralized organizational structure for NSRF. Initially, NSRF was 'controlled' by the founders associated with the Annenberg Institute for School Reform. Within the first year of its transfer to the Harmony Education Center, we began a discussion around issues of organizational governance. These discussions resulted in the establishment of a self-selective, volunteer 'Governing Council' with representatives from around the country. Council meetings are open to all NSRF members, and anyone who comes has a voice in discussions and decision making; however, the council always has representatives from HEC and at least one individual from each of its standing committees (referred to as 'Clusters of Interest') and each of its Centers of Activity (see below). Decisions are made by consensus, and when consensus is not achieved, a proposal can be accepted only when affirmed by 75 per cent of those attending a given council meeting.

As previously mentioned, NSRF recently established Clusters of Interest which explore issues as they emerge around a particular 'topic' and offer proposals to the council in light of their ongoing deliberations. Currently, there are seven Clusters of Interest: Governance, Finance, Diversity, Communication, Learning From Each Other, Research and Leadership. Members volunteer for two-year terms on a Cluster of Interest, and there is a strong effort made to ensure volunteers reflect the diversity (for example, gender, ethnic, class, geographic, type of school and grade level/subject area, age, years in NSRF) of the membership at large. Finally, and perhaps most crucial in our effort to balance the needs for centralized governance and coordination with the need to promote as much decentralized power as possible, NSRF recently established 25 regional Centers of Activity. These centres are located in schools or other organizations that are engaged in the work of NSRF. These centres help establish CFGs in their region, offer seminars for members who want to be coaches, communicate with other regional centres and between their centre and the national office (located at HEC), participate in the previously mentioned annual coaches conference, and have at least one representative on the NSRF Governing Council.

However, as this manuscript is being written, a new governance proposal has emerged. Many members felt that the previously described organization was too cumbersome, and decisions needed to be made more timely and effectively than is possible with the current structure. This proposal calls upon the creation of a three-person Executive Council, which would be empowered to make decisions by consensus. These decisions would remain in place until a report is made at the bi-annual meetings of the Governing Council, which would, at that time, affirm or question a given decision.

Developing a relatively large organization while maintaining our commitment to a democratic ethos is, indeed, challenging, and as one might expect, there have been concerns expressed by some members about the role of HEC and its influence within NSRF as a whole. The need and benefits (i.e., potential to participate in and thus influence the education of our nation's children) that come from having a coordinated, national network should always cause tension with the need to create an organization that recognizes the danger of this centralization. Without grassroots, decentralized governance and participation, NSRF will likely fail in its efforts to build a progressive, effective network of educators committed to the authentic intellectual, emotional and communal growth of our children. Creating a governance structure that allows a large and diverse organization to make decisions quickly in light of emerging circumstances and, at the same time, provide its members with authentic opportunities to have their voices heard is perhaps our most difficult challenge to date. Although we are still very much in the early and experimental stages of developing such an organization, HEC and NSRF are acutely aware that the politics of size needs to be constantly addressed.

In spite of the most recent swing to the right brought about by the first 'election' of G.W. Bush and 9/11, HEC and NSRF are determined to bring together, support and expand, wherever possible, people who are interested in the progressive education of our nation's children. The NSRF network is more resolved than ever to foster Dewey's (1940) notion that the primary purpose of education is to help young people live more meaningful lives and assume the responsibilities for exploring and enriching our democratic polity.

We are living in dangerous times. The rise of Islamic fascism (Webman 1994; Dennis 1996; Kepel 2002) and its direct attacks against our country has made it even more difficult to engage people in our schools and society regarding the substantive education of our children. One does not need to be a sociologist to recognize that the impact these attacks (especially the 9/11 bombings of the World Trade Center and Pentagon) has been a sharp movement of the country 'to the right'. Nevertheless, the NSRF network will persevere even during these most difficult times, and will continue to provide a social location for the thoughtful exploration of education as long as fiscally possible.

References

Apple, M. (2001) *Educating the 'right' way: Markets, standards, God, and inequality.* New York: Routledge/Falmer Press.

Barber, B. (1998) *A place for us: How to make society civil and democracy strong.* New York: Hill & Wang Press.

Bellah, R., Madsen, R., Sullivan, W. and Tipton, S. (1985) *Habits of the heart: Individualism and commitment in American life.* Berkeley, CA: University of California Press.

Bintz, W. (1995) *Curriculum and curriculum development as inquiry.* Bloomington, IN: Indiana University Dissertation.

Blau, J. (1999) *Illusions of prosperity: America's working families in an age of economic insecurity.* New York: Oxford University Press.

Brock, D. (2001) *Blinded by the right: The conscience of an ex-conservative.* New York: Crown Press.

Cummings, S. (1998) *The dixification of America: The American odyssey into the conservative economic trap.* Westport, CT: Praeger Press.

Dennis, A. (1996) *The rise of the Islamic empire and the threat to the west.* Bristol, IN: Wyndham Hall Press.

Dewey, J. (1920) *Reconstruction in philosophy.* New York: Holt and Co.

Dewey, J. (1927) *The public and its problems.* New York: Henry Holt.

Dewey, J. (1940) *Education today.* New York: Putnam's Sons.

Dewey, J. (1946 [1929]) *The problems of men.* New York: Philosophical Library.

Dewey, J. (1966) *Democracy and education: An introduction to the philosophy of education.* New York: Free Press.

Diamond, J. (1999) *Guns, germs, and steel: The fates of human societies.* New York: Norton & Co.

Fraser, N. (1997) *Justice interruptus: Critical reflections on the 'postsocialist' condition.* New York: Routledge Press.

Fromm, E. (1956) *The art of loving.* New York: Harper & Row.

Goodman, J. (1991) 'Redirecting sexuality education for young adolescents' *Curriculum and Teaching*, 6 (1): 12–22.

Goodman, J. (1992) *Elementary schooling for critical democracy.* Albany, NY: State University of New York Press.

Goodman, J. (1994) 'External change agents and grassroots school reform: Reflections from the field' *Journal of Curriculum and Supervision*, 9 (2): 113–35.

Goodman, J., Baron, D., Belcher, M., Hastings-Heinz, U. and James, J. (1994) 'Towards a comprehensive understanding of service education: Reflections from an exploratory action research project' *Research in Middle Level Education*, 18 (1): 39–63.

Goodman, J., Baron, B. and Myers, C. (1999) 'The local politics of school reform: Issues of school autonomy' *Research for Educational Reform*, 4 (2): 22–49.

Goodman, J., Baron, B. and Myers, C. (2001a) 'Bringing democracy to the occupational life of educators in the United States: Constructing a foundation for school-based reform' *International Journal of Leadership in Education: Theory and Practice*, 4 (1): 67–86.

Goodman, J., Baron, D. and Myers, C. (2001b) 'Talking back to the neo-liberal agenda from the ground floor: School-based reform discourses in difficult times' *International Journal of Educology*, 12 (1): 1–38.

Goodman, J. and Holloway, L. (2000) *Dewey or Marx: Which way for leftist educators and scholars?* Paper presented at the annual Curriculum and Pedagogy conference, Austin, November.

Goodman, J. and Kuzmic, J. (1997) 'Bringing a progressive pedagogy to conventional schools: Theoretical and practical implications from Harmony' *Theory into Practice*, 36 (2): 79–86.

Heilman, E. and Goodman, J. (1996) 'Teaching gender identity in high school' *The High School Journal*, 79 (3): 249–61.

Habermas, J. (1994) 'Struggles for recognition in the democratic constitutional state' in C. Taylor (ed.) *Multiculturalism: Examining the politics of recognition.* Princeton, NJ: Princeton University Press.

Kepel, G. (2002) *Jihad: The trail of political Islam.* Cambridge, MA: Harvard University Press.

Kuzmic, J. (1990) *Toward a practice informed theory of critical pedagogy: individualism, community, and democratic schooling.* Bloomington, IN: Indiana University Dissertation.

Kozol, J. (1991) *Savage Inequalities.* New York: Crown Publishing Group.

MacEwan, A. (1999) *Neo-liberalism or democracy: Economic strategy, markets, and alternatives for the 21st century.* New York: St. Martin's Press.

Maslow, A. (1976) *The farther reaches of human nature.* New York: Penguin Books.

McDonald, J., Morh, N., Dichter, A. and McDonald, E. (2003) *The power of protocols: An educator's guide to better practice.* New York: Teachers College Press.

Miller, R. (1995) *Educational freedom for a democratic society: A critique of national educational goals, standards, and curriculum.* Brandon, VT: Great Ideas in Education Press.

Nisbet, R. (1990) *The quest for community: A study in the ethics of order and freedom.* San Francisco: Institute for Contemporary Studies.

Nussbaum, M.C. (1997) *Cultivating Humanity.* Cambridge, MA: Harvard University Press.

Rawls, J. (2001) *Justice as fairness: A restatement.* Cambridge, MA: Harvard University Press.

Rorty, R. (1989) *Contingency, irony, and solidarity.* New York: Cambridge University Press.

Rorty, R. (1998) *Achieving our country.* Cambridge, MA: Harvard University Press.

Sen, A. (1992) *Inequality reexamined.* Cambridge, MA: Harvard University Press.

Skulnick, R. (forthcoming) *What's your sign: A study of adolescent image making and interpretation.* Bloomington, IN: Indiana University Dissertation.

Wallerstein, I. (1995) *After liberalism.* New York: The New Press.

Webman, E. (1994) *Anti-Semitism motifs in the ideology of Hizballah and Hamas.* Tel Aviv: Tel Aviv University Press.

Conclusion

twelve

Networking for learning and change

Wiel Veugelers and Mary John O'Hair

Based on an analysis of the chapters, in this final chapter we draw a number of conclusions on networking as a strategy for educational change.

We focus on the following issues:

- learning in networks
- networks as communities of practice
- shared leadership
- professional development and school development
- keeping networks fluid
- network philosophy
- school–university partnerships
- networks and educational policy
- the effects of networking on educational change
- starting a network.

Learning in networks

The most important characteristic of networks involves the learning of colleagues within and across schools. In networks, teachers and principals learn from colleagues in other schools, which helps them to deepen the learning in their own school. It is a collegial, horizontal way of learning. Teachers and principals reflect on their experiences, construct new knowledge, and develop skills and attitudes that enhance student achievement. Networking helps to develop trust among the members, which allows an open forum for collective enquiry to emerge. It creates a structure within which new meaning can be explored and difficult questions asked. Learning in networks, as supported by the examples in the book, is a social-constructivist practice.

Networks use different methods to create learning environments. What is typical of network learning is the common reflection on experiences and practices and the understanding of each educational practice in connection with student achievement. Some networks work with one particular method, for example an autobiographical approach (Autio and Ropo, Chapter 8) or action research (Day and Hadfield, Chapter 4).

In network learning, participants 'own' their practice, with the learner's experiences serving as the starting point for the learning process. Network learning re-articulates the Deweyan notion of learning by experience. Like all learning by experience, network learning balances knowledge from within (professional judgement) with knowledge from outside (scientific-based knowledge). The examples in the book demonstrate how in networks university professors, in particular, try to present knowledge as conceptual tools for helping teachers and principals in analysing their own practices. A second way of introducing knowledge is by paying attention to alternative practices and theories for the existing educational practices of the network participants; here it is a broadening of the scope of possibilities. A third activity of university professionals is to assist network participants in developing new skills and attitudes. Learning from each other is then complemented by an explicit broadening of competences. It is interesting to see that these connecting initiatives of university professors are particularly visible in larger networks (O'Hair *et al.*, Chapter 5; Wu *et al.*, Chapter 9). The methods are more mixed in these larger networks than in the smaller networks.

The learning of colleagues remains central to network learning. The teachers' collaborative learning interaction shapes their practices, and creates purpose, relationships and opportunities for leadership acts (Wenger 1998). This way of learning is fostered by a network's distinctive organization and structures for learning. In networks that have a long tradition, the emphasis on the collegial learning process becomes even stronger (see, for example, Veugelers and Zijlstra, Chapter 3). What is interesting is the observation that networks return continuously to more collegial learning, as we can see in the League of Professional Schools (Allen and Hensley, Chapter 2). This permanent emphasis on learning from each other encourages all network participants, but in particular network directors and university staff, to extend the learning process above the level of pure experience. By reflection, dialogue and action research, one deepens the learning process without losing the personal experiential process of the participants themselves. Barber (2002) describes the process through his knowledge poor/rich, prescription/judgement matrix. Network learning can be a model for developing knowledge-rich, informed professional judgement. Fullan (2003: 5) believes that we might portray what informed professional judgement might look like, but the pathways for getting there will be enormously complex and different depending on the starting point. For example, if morally purposeful policy, coherence, capacity, knowledge management and continuous innovation are conditions for collectively informed professional judgement, how do you establish these 'facilitative system conditions'? We believe one particularly promising pathway is through networks and through the networking of networks.

In network learning the personal meeting of participants is very important. Despite the use of email, websites and video-conferences, all networks continue to meet in person to promote trust, collegiality and community. The most powerful learning for the improvement of already skilled teachers, is the fine-tuning of practices that can only occur in collegial settings (Darling-Hammond 1997: 3). After firmly establishing collegial settings for informal learning processes to occur, most networks encourage forms of distance learning to keep the learning process alive.

Networks as communities of practice

In networks, teachers and principals from other schools become part of communities of practice. Communities of practice are created by groups who share common concerns and issues and who, through their passion, deepen their understanding and knowledge in areas of concern through interaction and learning together (Wenger 1998). From being strangers or even competitors they become 'critical friends', partners in a joint exploration of experiences and new opportunities. School networking links institutions that maintain their own autonomy while seeking collaboration and cooperation. In this cooperation we see processes of both accommodation and profiling. In the joint reflection of experiences and in the exploration of opportunities, schools can make their own choices. Schools often develop in an unconscious way; networking makes this process more explicit and open to reflection and change.

It is the first attempt for many network participants at collaborating with colleagues from other schools. Networks break down, to some extent, the walls between schools and eventually, within schools. Networks give teachers and principals the opportunity to be part of a broader educational community. This creates horizontal links between schools on the level of the educational practitioners themselves.

These links create productive communities of practice that have an impact on student achievement. Results indicate that the greater the participation by teachers and administrators in communities of practice, the greater the collective capacity of the faculty to adjust and adapt their instructional practices (Printy 2004), bringing value to both the community members and to the organization (Wenger *et al.* 2002).

Student achievement is linked to schools that operate collaboratively rather than conventionally (Lee and Smith 1994) and that develop shared purposes for student learning, work collaboratively towards purpose, and take collective responsibility for *all* student learning (Newmann and Wehlage 1995; Newmann 1996).

The social-constructivist way of network learning and communities of practice (Wenger 1998) is aimed at a transformation of educational practice itself. This requires a learning environment in which each voice can be heard, in which everyone has a feeling of empowerment, a feeling of belonging, of mutual care. All the networks in the book describe how they try to develop such communities of practice, and how they permanently need to maintain the common feeling of communities of practice (see, for example, Veugelers and Zijlstra, Chapter 3). In particular, while starting up a network, it is important to work on these affective and supportive elements of a learning community (see, for example, the Catalan experience by Rué, Chapter 6 and the example from the Middle East by Jarchow *et al.*, Chapter 7).

In the book we only find descriptions of successful networks, of networks that have succeeded in creating communities of practice. However, most of us know of initiatives to start networks that were unsuccessful. Important factors in this failure were participants who did not want to regulate their own learning process, did not believe that they could learn from colleagues and, on a more institutional level, schools that did not regard each other as learner facilitators. The combination of schools and the combination of people is important in creating and maintaining a network.

Shared leadership

All networks develop structures to give the participants a voice in the network. Most networks have regular meetings with a group of formal representatives from member schools, and larger networks in particular ask participants to elect representatives and develop smaller cluster groups within the network that facilitate greater opportunities for leadership acts among its members. In addition to the formal governance and structures of the network, leadership of the network itself is shared. Most networks require school participants to chair project groups, serve as members of the leadership team (O'Hair *et al.*, Chapter 5) or as co-directors of the network (Veugelers and Zijlstra, Chapter 3).

In particular, at the level of the daily practice of the networks, shared leadership is the norm. The participants often develop the agenda collaboratively, prioritize initiatives and organize activities. Each member experiences ownership of the network and ultimately develops ownership in the daily practice in their own schools.

In the third part of the book, we have chapters authored by networks that work together at the national level in which the networking of networks is the goal. For these meta-networks the same networking processes and network learning is realized. It becomes not only the linking of schools but the linking of networks. As in the school networks, the question of shared leadership is important here. The networks in this book are members of the International Networks for Democratic Education (INDE) founded in 1999 and function as a network of networks by promoting enquiry and dialogue through annual meetings, web contacts, visits to each other's networks, and through presentations and the publication of experiences. In writing this book we share experiences, help each other to constitute networks and serve as 'critical friends' for each other.

Professional development and school development

Most networks in this book involve 'whole-school change' and seek to involve all stakeholders in networks rather than only the teachers. The argument for having schools in the network and not individuals, is that the network seeks to stimulate educational change through whole-school development. An individual's development may create a change in the classroom, but the organization must also change in a coordinated and focused effort (Newmann *et al.* 2000; Fullan 2001). 'The collective power of the full staff to improve student achievement school-wide can be summarized as school capacity' (Newmann *et al.* 2000: 261). Network schools seek to develop school capacity and avoid the danger of working with a few people who themselves stimulate top-down developments in their own school. Lieberman and Grolnick (1996) speak of the insider/outsider dilemma of networks. Networks seek to develop leadership capacity (Lambert 1998) in all members by building broad-based, skillful involvement on the part of their participants.

Networks are communities of practitioners who together construct the educational change process, assume internal responsibility for learning, and sustain a momentum for self-renewal. In particular, Day and Hadfield write in Chapter 4 about developing the capacity in the school and the way their network supports this process of capacity building. Professional development and school development that builds capacity also helps to sustain initiatives worth sustaining and to build long-term capacity for improvements, such as the development of teachers' skills, which will stay with them for ever, long after the funding has disappeared (Hargreaves and Fink 2003). Networks in the book describe building and sustaining initiatives through action plan feedback, peer coaching, book studies, site visits, conferences and small cluster meetings. See, for example, the Oklahoma network (O'Hair *et al.*, Chapter 5) and the Hong Kong network (Wu *et al.*, Chapter 9).

The professional development of the participants in the network consists of the following:

- sharing and gaining first-hand experience
- sharing and gaining new knowledge and insights
- creating new knowledge
- developing a variety of research in their school
- reflecting on personal educational experiences and discussing personal and others' experiences and reflections
- creating communities of practice in their schools
- feeling of belonging to a larger professional educational community
- empowering self and others – believing that every voice matters
- creating meaningful learning experiences for students and adults.

Keeping networks fluid

Network organizations are flexible and their members organize themselves in ways that constantly change the organizational structures, goals and methods to better meet the needs of the organization (Castells 1996). The danger in creating networks is that they may become a new formal organization. The networks in the book are aware of this danger of 'freezing' growth patterns in networking. All the networks are changing constantly as evidenced by their organizational structures, activities, methods and participants. They try to stay fluid, to maintain the strengths of a networked organization. They let the participants shape the network, with the goals, methods, activities and 'network rules' subject to ongoing dialogue. Even ten-year-plus networks like the League of Professional Schools (Allen and Hensley, Chapter 2), the Amsterdam School network (Veugelers and Zijlstra, Chapter 3) and the Oklahoma K20 network (O'Hair *et al.*, Chapter 5) are constantly changing the way they function to better meet the needs of their members. Fullan (2001: 44) suggests change is not about adopting the latest innovation, but is about creating a culture for change that involves 'the capacity to seek, critically assess, and selectively incorporate new ideas and practices – all the time, inside the organization as well as outside it'. The networks in this book are developing a culture for change by ongoing enquiry and discourse involving purpose, structures and actions.

Network philosophy

Networks develop trust among members which facilitates an open forum for collective enquiry to emerge, a place to explore new meaning and ask difficult questions. Some networks have a clear philosophy. Their philosophy attracts certain schools and distinguishes the network and its schools from other networks and other schools. A philosophy binds them internally and differentiates them from the outside world. The educational philosophy can, for example, be aimed at stimulating creative and critical thinking (Wu *et al.*, Chapter 9), at social justice and democracy (Goodman, Chapter 11) or at stimulating a critical-democratic citizenship (Veugelers and Zijlstra, Chapter 3; Allen and Hensley, Chapter 2). Some networks, for example, the League of Professional Schools (Allen and Hensley, Chapter 2), struggle with the question of being small with a specific philosophy, or large with a more broadly formulated educational philosophy and greater diversity.

Networks that work with a whole district (Day and Hadfield, Chapter 4), a whole state (O'Hair *et al.*, Chapter 5), a considerable part of civic society (Jarchow *et al.*, Chapter 7) or even a whole nation (Hadfield, Chapter 10) cannot articulate a vision that attracts certain schools and deter others; they have to include most schools. The educational philosophy of this kind of network has to concentrate not so much on a specific educational philosophy but on a more generally accepted educational philosophy such as professional learning communities (O'Hair *et al.*, Chapter 5; Day and Hadfield, Chapter 4; Rué, Chapter 6). These networks are not wed to a particular philosophy, but tend to focus on empowering teachers and principals to develop their own philosophies through informed professional judgement (Fullan 2003), clear common objectives for teaching and learning (Glickman 1993) and empowerment of participants to actualize their vision and assume responsibility for *all* student learning.

An interesting case is the linking of the Harmony Education Center and the National School Reform Faculty (Goodman, Chapter 11). It is a large coalition of schools, groups and individuals with a strong orientation towards progressive education and towards functioning nationally as a political force.

All networks in the book celebrate equity and diversity in their educational philosophy. The argument is that equity and diversity stimulate the learning process by challenging the foundations of choice, of practices, of a presupposed normality. Equity and diversity stimulate enquiry and dialogue in networks.

School–university partnerships

All the networks presented include universities. As networks strive for a strong influence of both universities and schools, the relationship between schools and a university can be different. The US networks, in particular, are themselves centres or organizations within the university and interact collaboratively with faculties, schools and communities. The European networks tend to be more related to teacher education (Autio and Ropo, Chapter 8) and centres for further education. Networks of networks are non-university based centres that ask university centres and university staff to become involved in their work. The United Arab Emirates (Jarchow *et al.*, Chapter 7) is a good example of the different types of collaboration between schools and universities in a network organization.

University staff are included in networks because of their knowledge about education, their capacity for conducting research and for leadership in educational change. The university partners seek to understand educational change processes and to incorporate pre-service educational programmes for teachers and administrators as well as university outreach programmes for local schools and communities.

Networks and educational policy

In our view, networks are bottom-up movements that give a voice to teachers and principals and that provide them with the opportunities to express their ideas about education. Of course, networks can be used in educational policy, but a necessary condition for their use is that the policy is aimed at empowering schools, at building capacity in schools, at giving them more autonomy in decision making, impacting on their students and communities see, for example, Rué, Chapter 6.

Most of the networks in the book have developed formal and informal communication channels with educational policy makers and try to influence educational policy. Some networks, such as the National School Reform Faculty (Goodman, Chapter 11) and the Amsterdam School network, attempt to counterbalance the more traditional educational policy (Veugelers 2004). The Hong Kong case (Wu *et al.*, Chapter 9) is interesting because it gives examples of using networking as a policy-related way of implementing change and examples that build on the capacities and interests of teachers. In all the countries represented in this book, there is political support for school networks. The authors in this book see networks as a powerful tool for empowering schools and teachers, for giving them the opportunity to determine more of the educational agenda and their own educational practice. Educational policies that promote top-down control and manipulation often run counter to networks described in the book that concentrate on enquiry, shared leadership, collaboration and collective responsibility. All the networks struggle with the dilemma of being in the system, safe and secure, and with being outside the system, fighting to sustain the creative and powerful forces led by the participants.

The effects of networking on educational change

Despite the growing number of publications about school networking, no systematic and well-organized research has yet been undertaken into the effects of networks on educational change in schools. The authors in this book and authors on educational change, such as Fullan (2003) and Lieberman and Wood (2003), strongly believe in the effects of networking, in the possibility that networks can bring about change in educational practice. They also believe that active participation on the part of teachers and principals, the focus on their own practices, experiences, reflections and theories; and the cooperation with 'critical friends' and colleagues, can all bring about significant changes in educational practice rather than the more traditional top-down implementation of educational change.

The authors in this book suggest that networking works and they provide an abundance of examples. More research is, however, needed to determine the effects and crucial elements in networks that impact educational change.

Starting a network

We conclude by presenting a few suggestions and ideas about starting a network. The list is not long and detailed, it simply sets out a few important remarks. A long list would only suggest that there are well-defined strategies for starting a network. The networks described in this book began in a variety of different ways – by learning from earlier networks, using their community resources, and engaging in reflective enquiry and discourse around embedded networking learning and implications for daily school and classroom practices. Networking is a creative situated-bounded process.

1. In the cases described, the initiative to start a network always came from university staff, but from the outset they worked *together* with people from schools. We cannot overemphasize the importance of including both teachers and school principals in the initiating phase of networking. Examples of failing to build a network are often the result

of people using the network metaphor to just continue with the old top-down way of trying to implement educational change. Networks cannot emerge without the active participation of schools and their leaders.

2. A second remark about starting a network is that a network must develop a clear goal, its own *educational philosophy*. In developing goals and a philosophy, a network can create coherence and shared values that binds people within a common framework. A framework they construct themselves.

3. *Network learning* is both formal and informal. Each way of learning enforces the other, however, both types of learning do have to be organized. In network learning the personal concerns, interests and concepts of all participants are the constituent elements of the learning process.

4. For network learning aimed at challenging practice and producing educational change, many *different methods* are desirable, for example school visits, book studies, critical friends, presentations, action research, reflection, explorations of new opportunities, and so on.

5. *Using theory to reflect on practice* raises network learning above merely exchanging experiences. Understanding theory, in particular 'change' theory, helps participants understand and analyse practices, challenges and results. Network learning uses theoretical concepts as tools instead of guidelines.

6. *Shared leadership on all levels* is necessary to give ownership to the participants. Networks should be dynamic and horizontal organizations.

7. The organization of a network should be characterized by *structuring the fluid*. It is necessary to build some structures, however, these structures should be as flexible and as temporary as possible.

8. *Capacity building* in schools is necessary to bridge the personal development of the participants with the school development.

Conclusion

Learning in networks occurs as professionals come together as a result of their shared values, engage in social activity and produce shared resources in the process. Networks seek to develop what is in our hearts, pursuing what matters most to us rather than settling for what we already know how to do, or can learn to do, and requires living with the adventure and anxiety that this pursuit requires (Block 2002: 1). *Network Learning for Educational Change* represents the lessons from a network of networks that live everyday with the adventure and anxiety necessary to develop sustainable, self-renewing schools.

References

Barber, M. (2002) *From Good to Great: Large-scale Reform in England*. Paper presented at Futures of Education conference, 23 April, Universität Zurich, Zurich.

Block, P. (2002) *The Answer to How is Yes*. San Francisco, CA: Berrett-Koehler.

Castells, M. (1996) *The Rise of the Network Society*. Oxford: Blackwell Publishers.

Darling-Hammond, L. (1997) *The Right to Learn: A Blueprint for Creating Schools that Work*. San Francisco: Jossey-Bass.

Fullan, M. (2001) *Leading in a Culture of Change*. San Francisco: Jossey-Bass.

Fullan, M. (2003) *Change Forces with a Vengeance*. London: Routledge Falmer.

Glickman, C.D. (1993) *Renewing America's Schools*. San Francisco: Jossey-Bass.

Hargreaves, A. and Fink, D. (2003) 'Sustaining Leadership'. *Phi Delta Kappan*, 693–700.

Lambert, L. (1998) *Building Leadership Capacity in Schools*. Alexandria, VA: Association for Supervision and Curriculum Development.

Lee, V.E. and Smith, J.B. (1994) 'High school restructuring and student achievement: A new study finds strong links' *Issues in Restructuring Schools*. University of Wisconsin: Center on Organization and Restructuring of Schools.

Lieberman, A. and Grolnick, M. (1996) 'Networks and Reform in American Education' in *Teachers College Record*, 98 (1): 7–45.

Lieberman, A. and Wood, D.R. (2003) *Inside the National Writing Project*. New York: Teachers College Press.

Newmann, F.M. (1996) *Authentic Achievement*. San Francisco: Jossey-Bass.

Newmann, F.M., King, M.B. and Youngs, P. (2000) 'Professional development that addresses school capacity: Lessons from urban elementary schools' *American Journal of Education*, 108 (4): 259–99.

Newmann, F.M. and Wehlage, G.G. (1995) *Successful School Restructuring*. Madison, WI: Center on Organization and Restructuring of Schools.

Printy, S.M. (2004) 'The professional impact of communities of practice' *UCEA Review*, XLVI (1), 20–3.

Veugelers, W. (2004) 'Between control and autonomy: Restructuring secondary education in the Netherlands' *Journal of Educational Change*, 5 (2): 141–60.

Wenger, E. (1998) *Communities of Practice: Learning, Meaning and Identity*. New York: Cambridge University Press.

Wenger, E., McDermott, R. and Snyder, W.M. (2002) *Cultivating Communities of Practice: A Guide to Managing Knowledge*. Boston: Harvard Business School Press.

Index